# HARRY POTTER AND INTERNATIONAL RELATIONS

EDITED BY DANIEL H. NEXON AND
IVER B. NEUMANN

ROWMAN & LITTLEFIELD PUBLISHERS, INC.
Lanham • Boulder • New York • Toronto • Oxford

ROWMAN & LITTLEFIELD PUBLISHERS, INC.

Published in the United States of America
by Rowman & Littlefield Publishers, Inc.
A wholly owned subsidary of The Rowman & Littlefield Publishing Group, Inc.
4501 Forbes Boulevard, Suite 200, Lanham, Maryland 20706
www.rowmanlittlefield.com

P.O. Box 317, Oxford OX2 9RU, UK

British Library Cataloguing in Publication Information Available

**Library of Congress Cataloging-in-Publication Data**
Harry Potter and international relations / edited by Daniel H. Nexon and
Iver B. Neumann.
    p.   cm.
   Includes bibliographical references and index.
   ISBN-13: 978-0-7425-3958-7 (cloth : alk. paper)
   ISBN-10: 0-7425-3958-X (cloth : alk. paper)
   ISBN-13: 978-0-7425-3959-4 (pbk. : alk. paper)
   ISBN-10: 0-7425-3959-8 (pbk. : alk. paper)
   1. Rowling, J. K.—Influence. 2. Rowling, J. K.—Criticism and interpretation. 3.
Rowling, J. K.—Characters  Harry Potter. 4. Potter, Harry (Fictitious character) 5.
Children's stories, English—History and criticism. 6. Fantasy fiction, English—History
and criticism. 7. Literature and society. I. Nexon, Daniel H., 1973– II. Neumann, Iver B.
PR6068.O93Z688 2006
823'.914—dc22                                                                   2005035250

Printed in the United States of America

&#8734;™ The paper used in this publication meets the minimum requirements of American
National Standard for Information Sciences—Permanence of Paper for Printed Library
Materials, ANSI/NISO Z39.48-1992.

# HARRY POTTER AND INTERNATIONAL RELATIONS

# CONTENTS

# Acknowledgments

WE WOULD LIKE TO THANK Patrick Jackson for crucial help in the initial stages of the project. Steve Burt, Ronny Lipschutz, Jutta Weldes, and Rowman & Littlefield's anonymous reviewers provided invaluable comments on various stages of this project. We would also like to thank Ashley Thomas for the significant research assistance and Jonathan Monten for his editorial work. We are particularly grateful to our editors at Rowman & Littlefield, Renée Legatt and Jenn Nemec, for all their help, encouragement, and patience. We apologize to Jane McGarry, for the state of the manuscript she so diligently copyedited. Our many thanks to her as well.

# Introduction
## Harry Potter and the Study of World Politics

IVER B. NEUMANN AND DANIEL H. NEXON

THIS VOLUME IS ABOUT HARRY POTTER and world politics. This may seem like an odd topic. What, one might ask, can works of children's fantasy possibly teach us about war, peace, intervention, international trade, transnational movements, and other core concerns in study of international politics? The answer is that the Harry Potter books, films, and merchandise provide insights into an increasingly important issue in international-relations theory: the relationship between popular culture and world politics. J. K. Rowling's stories of young witches and wizards enjoy extraordinary global popularity. They are, therefore, an excellent vehicle for exploring the variety of ways in which popular culture intersects with the study, teaching, and practice of international relations.

In this sense, the chapters in this volume serve two purposes. On the one hand, they are reflections by international-relations scholars on aspects of the Harry Potter phenomenon, ones that we hope will interest fans and others who care for Harry Potter in print and in film. On the other hand, the chapters also explore the nexus between popular culture and world politics. In doing so, they illustrate the variety of ways that the study of popular cultural artifacts, such as Harry Potter, can inform our understandings of international politics and of the discipline of international relations.

This introductory essay has three sections. We begin by discussing in more detail why we selected Harry Potter as a focus for this volume. We next discuss the organization and contents of the volume. In the last section, we reflect on the relationship between popular culture and international politics.

The last section is oriented toward scholars and theorists of international relations; hence, those who are primarily interested in the analysis of Harry Potter may want to skim it or skip it altogether.

## Why Harry Potter?

Many artifacts of popular culture, as well as genres of film and literature, are important to world politics. A number of scholars have written on the relationship between science fiction and international politics;[1] an ever-expanding literature studies the interaction between popular culture and specific aspects of American foreign policy.[2] What does a volume on Harry Potter, then, bring to such discussions?

We decided that a systematic treatment of the engagement between international relations and popular culture is best served through a focus on a single franchise. Having only one subject allows the contributors to illustrate different ways of apprehending the relationship between world politics and popular culture while giving the volume an overall coherence. The fact that they all share a deep interest in Harry Potter was also a major consideration, as was the continuing popularity of the franchise. When we first began to discuss the idea for this volume at academic conferences, we quickly learned that many of our peers already noticed that the books speak to issues in international politics. The fact that almost all academics and students within the English-speaking world have at least some familiarity with Harry Potter means that the volume should be readily accessible to our intended audience. Furthermore, the success of Harry Potter has already produced a significant body of critical commentary.[3] By engaging with, and contributing to, this commentary the authors not only participate in an emerging field of inquiry within cultural, film, and literary studies, but they also demonstrate what international-relations scholars can contribute to debates about popular culture.

The most important reasons for choosing Harry Potter, however, are substantive. The extraordinary *international* success of the Harry Potter books, films, and merchandise makes the franchise a ripe subject for scholars of world politics. The royalties it generates made the books' author, J. K. Rowling, the wealthiest woman in England. Over 250 million copies of the series have been sold worldwide. *Harry Potter and the Half-Blood Prince* had the largest printing of a first-run hardcover book in the history of the United States; it broke all previous records for copies sold in its first twenty-four hours after release in the United States and the United Kingdom.[4] In the People's Republic of China, "the first three Harry Potter books" were "released as a box set with a first run of 600,000—the largest first printing ever for a commercial release in China."[5] The books have been translated into at least fifty-four languages and proven popular in such diverse places as Thailand and Iceland.[6] Together, the first three film adaptations grossed over three billion dollars and were themselves released in over forty dubbed or subtitled versions.[7] Commercial success has also had its downsides. For example, the diminished profitability of Harry Potter merchandise contributed to a recent shakeup at the Danish toy company, Lego.[8]

Harry Potter's commercial success has brought it into the realm of cultural politics. In Russia, accusations that the film visage of one character— the house elf "Dobby"—was a caricature of President Vladimir Putin created a minor uproar.[9] Many compare the incoming Dutch prime minister, Jan Peter Balkenende, to Harry Potter. According to one report, "he was even photographed during elections in 2002 holding a picture of himself and Potter film actor Daniel Radcliffe." But when the Belgian prime minister, Guy Verhofstadt, described Balkenende as "a mix between Harry Potter and a brave rigid bourgeois," it strained relations between the two governments.[10]

In the United States, the Harry Potter series has drawn the ire of some fundamentalist Christians, who complain that the books promote Satanism and witchcraft. The books have become one of the most challenged works in school and public libraries, and one of the most frequent subjects of book burnings. People have raised similar objections to Harry Potter in countries such as England, Australia, Russia, and Thailand.[11]

The fact that Harry Potter has emerged as an important cultural force not simply on a national level, but also on a global level, gives its analysis particular resonance for those interested in how popular culture relates to international politics. The study of Harry Potter interfaces, for example, with a number of ongoing themes in the study of international political economy. According to Patricia Goff, there are close, if underexplored, connections between national identity, the circulation of cultural "goods," and efforts to resist foreign cultural products. Cultural protectionism has not directly affected Harry Potter, but the franchise implicates a number of more traditional concerns in international political economy.[12] Conglomerates, such as Time Warner, play an important role in the marketing of Harry Potter, while the distribution and licensing of Harry Potter to local media outlets sheds light on international economic relations between firms. Copyright infringement, black market sales, and the distribution of copies licensed in one market to other markets have been recurring issues in the business of selling Harry Potter in a global market.[13]

Cultural historians and theorists also place Harry Potter in the context of globalization. Some scholars link Harry Potter to the "commercialization" of childhood at the global level, the formation of "corporate" cultural hegemony, and to more general processes associated with late capitalism.[14] Whatever one thinks of such arguments, analysis of Harry Potter *should* shed light on how a variety of processes associated with globalization work in practice. Harry Potter is a British novel that has been marketed, with varying degrees of success, to consumers in a wide variety of cultural and linguistic communities. Differences in its reception, in the political and cultural concerns of translators, and in its relative popularity among various ethnic, religious, and national groups elucidate on the intersection between global and local forces in the current era.[15]

Thus, Harry Potter provides particularly fertile ground for evaluating and illuminating the engagement between popular culture and international politics. The international and political dimensions of the Harry Potter phenomenon, we believe, make it uniquely suitable for analysis by scholars of international relations.

## Plan of the Volume

From its inception this volume has had two agendas, one methodological, the other substantive. On the one hand, the volume seeks to survey different ways that international-relations scholars can engage with popular culture. On the other hand, this is also a collection of essays about the relationship between Harry Potter and world politics. As such, we seek to address both scholarly and nonscholarly fans of Harry Potter. We decided that, in the final analysis, it would be best to organize the volume thematically, with different sections covering different aspects of Harry Potter and international affairs.

Thus, the volume is organized into four sections. The first part focuses on the relationship between Harry Potter and globalization. In chapter 1, "Producing Harry Potter: Why the Medium Is Still the Message," Patricia Goff situates the marketing of Harry Potter within broader changes in global media production and distribution. In chapter 2, "Glocal Hero: Harry Potter Abroad," Patrick T. Jackson and Peter Mandaville focus on how the localization of Harry Potter has contributed to its success. In doing so, they argue that cultural globalization is as much about local adaptation and translation as about the spread, whole cloth, of American and "Western" culture.

In chapter 3, "Foreign Yet Familiar: International Politics and the Reception of Potter in Turkey and Sweden," Ann Towns and Bahar Rumelili compare the reception of Harry Potter in Sweden and Turkey. They argue that commentary on Harry Potter in both countries reflects differing conceptions of national identity vis-à-vis, on the one hand, the Anglo-Saxon world and, on the other, the West. Chapter 4, "Children's Crusade: The Religious Politics of Harry Potter," by Maia A. Gemmill and Daniel H. Nexon, situates the religious backlash against Harry Potter in the broader context of traditionalist responses to global modernity. Gemmill and Nexon trace traditions within Christianity about witchcraft in order to show that opposition to Harry Potter draws on long-standing representations of the malevolence of magic within Christianity—representations directly appropriated by Rowling in her creation of Harry Potter's fictional world. They argue, however, that the dynamics of the backlash complicate simplistic assessments of "modernity against tradition," "secularism against religion," and "globalization against localism."

The second part of this book, "Conflict and Warfare," examines the relationship between Harry Potter and political conflict. In chapter 5, "Conflict and the Nation-State: Magical Mirrors of Muggles and Refracted Images," Jennifer Sterling-Folker and Brian Folker examine the relationship between group identity and conflict in Harry Potter. They argue that Harry Potter teaches us important lessons about the inevitability of *realpolitik* in world politics, even in the absence of powerful nation-states. The next chapter in this section, David Long's "Quidditch, Imperialism and the Sport-War Intertext," reflects on the complicated interaction between international relations, conflict, and games and sports.

The third part, entitled "Geography and Myth," contains two chapters that locate Harry Potter within broader mytho-religious structures relevant to world politics. In "Naturalizing Geography: Harry Potter and the Realms of Muggles, Magic Folks, and Giants," Iver B. Neumann analyzes the geographical landscape of Harry Potter, which draws on long-standing folkloric traditions in western Europe, and draws parallels with the emerging landscape that undergirds American and European foreign relations. Martin Hall's "The Fantasy of Realism, or Mythology as Methodology," in contrast, explores the moral space of the fantasy genre in which Harry Potter is located in relation to major Christian traditions about the nature of evil, on the one hand, and realist understandings of international politics, on the other.

The final part of the volume, "Pedagogy," contains one chapter: "Dumbledore's Pedagogy: Knowledge and Virtue at Hogwarts," by Torbjørn Knutsen. Knutsen provides us with a detailed analysis of the pedagogy of Hogwarts in relation to the English boarding school genre from which Harry Potter is, in part, derived. He finds important lessons for the pedagogy of international relations, particularly with respect to the problem of making moral choices in a world often inhospitable to students' ideals.

## Popular Culture and International Relations: Four Approaches

Over the last decade, the discipline of international relations has shown an increasing interest in the relationship between popular culture and various aspects of international politics. Scholars influenced by constructivism and post-structuralism now recognize that any attempt to understand the influence of cultural forces—such as ideas, identities, language, discourses, and symbols—requires moving beyond the statements of political elites and inquiring into the broader cultural resources that shape political processes. If culture profoundly affects politics, then we cannot neglect popular culture, since it is within popular culture that morality is shaped, identities are produced and transformed, and effective analogies and narratives are constructed and altered.[16]

Popular culture is a crucial domain in which social and political life are *represented*. For example, NBC's drama *The West Wing* was a fictional representation of political and personal struggles in the White House. Family situation comedies aim for humorous representations of daily life in a nuclear or extended family. Popular music, for its part, packages and represents a host of themes, including lost love, sexual desire, material success, personal feuds, and moral values.

Such representations are not merely passive mirrors; they also play a crucial role in constituting the social and political world. In their pioneering work, *The Social Construction of Reality*, Peter Berger and Thomas Luckmann argue that most human knowledge consists of typifications: generalizations, or stereotypes, about other people, the world, political life, and so forth. Most of these typifications do not derive from direct experience. We learn them from the testimony of others: parents, peers, teachers, and a variety of scientific, religious, and political authorities. Many of us, for example, do not have direct proof that the world is round. We "know" the world is round because people whom we trust tell us so: those, for example, who have circumnavigated it or have seen it from orbit. Similarly, most of us gain our knowledge of foreign countries from journalists, scholars, and other people who have been to those places, who testify to the fact that those countries do exist, and who tell us about the politics, beliefs, and customs of the people who inhabit them.[17] As C. Wight Mills argues,

> The first rule for understanding the human condition is that men live in second-hand worlds. They are aware of much more than they have personally experienced; and their own experience is always indirect. . . . Their images of the world, and of themselves, are given to them by crowds of witnesses they have never met and never shall meet.[18]

A great deal of politics relies upon, operates through, and produces representations. President George Bush's famous address after al Qaeda's attacks on New York and Washington, D.C., was itself a *representation* of the events. It drew on representations from the media and intelligence communities about the attacks themselves, relied on representations of America and the world deeply ingrained in American political culture, and presented a representation of the meaning and significance of the attacks that it then tied to specific courses of action, such as the imminent invasion of Afghanistan.

There are many differences between the kind of representation involved in a politician's speech and that of a fictional television program, but many of these differences are ones of degree. The former might be thought of as a *first-order representation*.[19] It seeks to directly re-present political events. In this terminology, television and print journalism are also examples of first-order representation. Although a speech by a politician is often a re-presentation of facts and narratives reported in the media, both claim to be direct representations of the "real world."

Popular entertainment usually takes the form of *second-order representations*, in that its narratives re-present elements of social and political life through a layer of fictional representation. If a politician is always a kind of actor, attempting to convince us with her speeches, "act presidential," or "feel our pain," then a professional actor playing a politician is an actor portraying an actor.[20] Consider the extensive literature on *Star Trek*, which examines how it describes and represents the Cold War, humanitarian interventions, and so forth. *Star Trek*, in this sense, represents representations.

International-relations theorists often neglect second-order representations. They also view first-order representations as relatively unproblematic expressions of the "facts" of international politics. The speeches and debates of political elites are often the "stuff" of our investigations, whereas we usu-ally treat books, films, and television as afterthoughts or indirect commen-tary on political events. For many purposes, there is nothing wrong with this mode of analyzing the social world. At the same time, both speeches and television dramas are *representations* of social life, and they interact with one another in a variety of important ways. We need to keep in mind that, for many people, second-order representations are often more significant sources of knowledge about politics and society. Popular entertainment not only commands a larger audience than the news or political events, but it frequently has a more powerful impact on the way audiences come to their basic assumptions about the world.

The distinction between first-order and second-order representations is not always easy to draw. As we suggest, first-order and second-order representations interact in a variety of ways. Moreover, sometimes one person's second-order representation is another person's first-order repre-sentation. In the philosophy of the social sciences, a famous debate turned on exactly these issues. The topic happened to be witchcraft, and the issue was whether witches existed or not. The key question was how to study societies where representations of witches and their purported actions played a key role in constituting the social matrix. Peter Winch, who opened the debate, held that the way to go about it was to forget about the question of whether witches existed or not. If representations of witches played a key role in constituting social life, then those repre-sentations should be among the starting points of any inquiry into this particular social world. It is no coincidence that this debate fastened on a religious theme. One can study religion as a set of beliefs—rather than as theological truths—but, from that perspective, religion is definitely a second-order representational system, one with a profound influence on world politics.[21]

A better understanding of world politics, we believe, requires an inves-tigation of a broad array of second-order representations. Popular enter-tainment is but one form of second-order representation in which individuals invest an enormous amount of time and energy. Such phe-nomena play an important role in creating our social reality; just as much as first-order representations, they are part of what the French philosopher Michel Foucault refers to as the "archive," that is, the broad stock of social knowledge, forms, analogies, symbols, and techniques through which ac-tors are able to communicate and otherwise influence their environment.

# Hudson News

LOGAN INT'L AIRPORT
300 TERMINAL C
EAST BOSTON, MA 02128
STORE: 00003   REG: 002   CASHIER: ASMAE
CUSTOMER RECEIPT COPY

GIRL W  THE DRAGON TATTO
9780307454546  1 @ 14.95          14.95
SUBTOTAL                           14.95
SALES TAX (6.25000%)                 .94
## TOTAL                           15.89
AMOUNT TENDERED
MasterCard                         15.89
  ACCT: *************374
  EXP: ******
  APPROVAL: 025148

TOTAL PAYMENT                      15.89
Transaction: 174993        1/13/2011 1:50 PM

174993000030020113201

174993000300201132011

Such forms include ritual recitals, festivals, public performances, and "entertainment."[22]

International-relations theory's engagement with popular culture is not only driven by the need to better understand processes and outcomes in world politics. Pedagogical considerations also play an important role. Courses on "politics and film" or "politics and literature" have long been popular among undergraduates. As teachers, we frequently find that popular culture provides an important medium for the communication of ideas, concepts, and theories of politics. Some scholars argue that changes in the way that our students process information will force us to make even wider use of novels, films, and music in our classes if we wish to remain effective teachers. If we are to do this well, we need to be more reflective about the uses and abuses, as well as the power and limits, of popular culture as a means of teaching international relations. Indeed, in their attempts to study and utilize popular culture, international-relations scholars are beginning to tread on territory already occupied by cultural studies, communications, anthropology, literature, and cultural sociology. This raises two important questions. First, what new insights and approaches can international-relations scholars bring to the table in the analysis of popular culture? Second, how can engagements with popular culture truly inform the study of international politics? If international-relations scholars cannot give good answers to these questions, then we should restrict ourselves to borrowing from the insights of others.

What do those trained in international relations bring to the analysis of popular culture? One answer is our comparative expertise in political processes: how world politics and international-political economy function, how actors legitimate foreign and economic policy, what constraints and opportunities cultural resources create for political action, the dynamics of transnational and national movements, and so on. This answer suggests a number of different ways in which popular cultural artifacts—such as Harry Potter—intersect with international relations. We argue that there are four ways through which international-relations scholars can engage popular culture, which we call *popular culture and politics, popular culture as mirror, popular culture as data,* and *popular culture as constitutive.* The distinctions between these categories are imperfect, but they have served us well as a starting point for thinking and writing. These approaches, their underlying assumptions, and the kinds of analysis they give rise to, are summarized in table I.1. We introduce them in turn.

**Table I.1. International-Relations Approaches to Popular Culture**

| | Approaches | | | |
|---|---|---|---|---|
| | *Popular Culture and Politics* | *Popular Culture as Mirror* | *Popular Culture as Data* | *Popular Culture as Constitutive* |
| Status of Popular Culture | As a cause or outcome in world politics<br><br>As an element of political processes in world politics | As a medium of inspiration for exploring themes/processes in international relations and international-relations theory | As evidence of the norms, beliefs, identities, etc. | As interactive with other representations of political life |
| Typical Mode of Analysis | Mainstream international-relations approaches | Pedagogical and analogical | Ethnographic, content analysis, etc. | Structural, post-structural, and other forms found in cultural studies |
| Key Questions | *Significance:* Are elements of popular culture a significant cause or outcome for international relations? | *Communicative:* Does the use of popular culture help to explain or elucidate issues in world politics? | *Quality:* Is the interpretation of the data correct; is it a good indicator of the existence of the norms, beliefs, identity, etc.? | *Relevance:* Are the interactions between popular culture and other representational system important to understanding international political process? |

## Politics and Popular Culture

In May 2005, *Newsweek*, a U.S. news magazine, wrote that a Defense Department report was about to confirm accusations that American interrogators had flushed a copy of the Koran down a toilet as part of an attempt to "break" a detainee suspected of being a terrorist. The report "set off the most virulent, widespread anti-American protests in Afghanistan since the fall of the Taliban government." *Newsweek* later retracted the story, claiming it was inadequately sourced and probably inaccurate.[23] In this case, a representation, now reportedly fictional, was the proximate cause of death, property destruction, and a setback for U.S. foreign relations.

In fact, one of the most straightforward ways to study the intersection between popular culture and world politics is to treat popular culture (and its artifacts) as causes and effects of the kinds of political processes familiar to any student of international relations. Popular culture itself, as well as the books, films, music, and merchandise produced for popular consumption, have a variety of relationships to concerns in international political economy. Examples include issues of copyright infringement, international marketing and licensing, cultural protectionism, and the integration and regulation of national and multinational media corporations. Similarly, works of popular culture shape the broader terms of political discourse, influence debates about specific policies, and galvanize movements. At the same time, popular culture itself is influenced by events central to the discipline of international relations, such as wars, terrorist attacks, political movements, and the like. Anti-Tutsi propaganda in Rwanda, D. W. Griffith's *Birth of a Nation*, American protest music of the 1960s, Errol Morris's *The Fog of War*, and Tom Clancy's technothrillers can all be analyzed as causes and effects of political phenomena.

The first substantive chapters in this volume reflect the politics and popular culture approach. Patricia M. Goff (chapter 1) argues that the worldwide popularity of the Harry Potter franchise cannot, ultimately, be divorced from the marketing power of an increasingly conglomerated global media. Maia A. Gemmill and Daniel Nexon (chapter 4) explore why Harry Potter provoked a highly mobilized backlash among members of the Christian Right. In both instances, the object of analysis is how a popular cultural artifact is causally influenced, or itself becomes a cause, of political processes.

## Popular Culture as Mirror

This is how popular culture is often used in teaching: to illuminate various concepts and processes from IR. Whenever a professor shows a sequence from *Monty Python's Life of Brian* to illustrate factional politics among revolutionary movements or has her class watch *Doctor Strangelove* to gain an appreciation of theories of nuclear deterrence, she uses popular culture in this way. The mirror approach is broader than simply deploying popular cultural artifacts as a teaching aid. IR scholars can examine popular culture as a medium for exploring theoretical concepts, dilemmas of foreign policy, and the like. Popular culture can also serve as inspiration, leading IR theorists to adopt terms or even develop theories as a result of engagement with books and films. One example would be "the Rashomon effect." Drawn from the title of an Akira Kurosawa film, the term refers to a situation in which people see the same event in entirely different ways. Uses of popular cultural texts and images as mirrors can force us to reflect on our theoretical and pedagogical assumptions.[24] Popular culture thus serves as a medium for what critical analysts of science fiction call "ontological displacement." Such works invite us to step back from our ingrained suppositions about a certain phenomenon and our vested interests in ongoing debates to gain a different perspective upon our social world.

We restrict the category of "popular culture as mirror" to the use of popular culture as a pedagogical or analogical tool. Nevertheless, important aspects of the mirror-quality of popular culture are at work in other categories of analysis. Sometimes, seeing historical events reflected in the mirror of popular culture gives plausibility to a particular interpretation of those events.[25] The same can be said of fictional accounts that appear to be analogies for current events, such as the debate over whether the film *Star Wars: Revenge of the Sith* betrays conservative fans by suggesting an analogy between George H. W. Bush's "War on Terrorism" and the transformation of the Galactic Republic into a Galactic Empire.[26]

Indeed, the effects of politics as mirror become perhaps clearest when the mirror fails to reflect the desired image. For example, when works of popular culture tell stories that a group sees as undermining their own stories about sacred realms, how to find them, and what to find there, trouble ensues. The case of Salman Rushdie's *Satanic Verses* turned on this issue. As Peter Beyer explains,

> The Rushdie affairs does more than demonstrate the link between religious faith and particularistic identity. On the whole, outraged Muslims are, in fact, not concerned that Rushdie's book will undermine their faith—all the less so since few devout Muslims will ever read it. What troubles them much more is the notion that they are being asked to surrender the core of that faith—the *immutable sacredness* of the Qur'ran—as the price

for full inclusion in a global system currently dominated by non-Muslims. Khomeini and many other Muslims equate the relativization of Islam declared by *The Satanic Verses* with the marginalization of Muslims in the overall society. Khomeini's condemnation of Rushdie is therefore part of a much larger Muslim effort to counter inequalities within the global system, through the revitalization of Islamic particularity.[27]

A number of chapters in this volume explore popular culture as a mirror for international-relations theory and scholarship. Jennifer Sterling-Folker and Brian Folker (chapter 5) argue that Harry Potter illustrates how realist accounts of international politics apply even in the absence of strong states. Harry Potter itself is treated as a kind of "case" to examine the naturalness of human in-group identification, and the reciprocal inevitability of intergroup conflict. Thus, they contend that realist theory will remain highly relevant even if the world becomes increasingly globalized. An important narrative in popular culture, in this chapter, is a vehicle for elucidating a particular approach to world politics. Torbjørn Knutsen (chapter 9) uses a similar form of analysis when he argues that Harry Potter is an important mirror for considering the pedagogical task of international-relations theory.

David Long's essay (chapter 6) does not fall neatly into any of our categories. He uses the relationship between Rowling's invented sport of Quidditch and the broader struggle between good and evil in the Harry Potter novels as a way of discussing the complicated relationship among sports, games, and international relations. Like the other two essays mentioned here, Long's chapter demonstrates how the mirror of popular culture and international relations can work in both directions; not only does the role of Quidditch in Harry Potter allow us to interrogate the use of sports and games metaphors in the theory and practice of international relations, but understandings of sports and games also illuminate tensions within the Harry Potter narrative.

## Popular Culture as Data

Popular culture can be treated as evidence about dominant norms, ideas, identities, or beliefs in a particular state, society, or region. This approach draws on insights from hermeneutics, forms of content analysis, and ethnography, in which cultural texts and images are seen as storage places for meaning in a particular society. Popular culture is particularly useful in this context, in that it may reflect general cultural themes and assumptions better than elite discourse.

For example, in *Social Construction of International Politics: Identities and Foreign Policies, Moscow 1955 and 1999*, Ted Hopf argues that scholars can predict a state's foreign-policy behavior by understanding its domestic identity. Rather than simply reading speeches by political officials, Hopf looks closely at the Soviet and Russian press, popular novels, and a variety of other "textual sources of identity" that are part of the popular culture of the Soviet Union and Russia in 1955 and 1999.[28]

Ann Towns and Bahar Rumelili (chapter 3) demonstrate how Harry Potter can be used as an important source of data about attitudes in Sweden and Turkey. They argue that the reception of Harry Potter confirms broader claims about key aspects of national identity in both countries. Many other chapters in this volume also deploy Harry Potter as data about cultural values, norms, and beliefs that are relevant to international politics. This should not be surprising, since treating popular culture as data is often a precondition for other forms of exploration into the relationship between popular cultural artifacts, such as Harry Potter, and international relations. One of the important things about the approach taken by Towns and Rumelili, as well as a number of other contributors to this volume, is that they study the interplay between the content of Harry Potter and its reception by various audiences. How a broader audience interprets and responds to a text or film, particularly one as popular as Harry Potter, should provide very good evidence about collective beliefs in a state, society, or political movement.

Popular culture does not only provide evidence about cultural values, however. It can also be used as a source of data about ongoing political processes. Patrick T. Jackson and Peter Mandaville (chapter 2) call our attention to the importance of localization in the overall process of globalization. By studying the translation (in multiple senses) of Harry Potter they find evidence for the ways in which localization works in the production of "global" popular culture. In doing so, they use popular culture to provide interesting insights into broader processes of significance to the study of international change.

## Popular Culture as Constitutive

There is often a subtle, but important, difference between treating popular culture as "data" and looking at the ways in which popular culture may itself constitute beliefs about international politics. When popular culture is treated as data, we generally maintain a clear distinction between the different orders of representation. Popular culture is treated as a second-order representation that, nonetheless, reveals important facts about collective beliefs. Thus, we use popular culture to give us good evidence about dominant norms, values, identities, and ideas. When we claim that, for example, a state's foreign policy is driven by its national identity, we can look to popular culture to get a better handle on the content of that national identity.

When we turn to the role of popular culture in *constituting* norms, values, identities, and ideas, however, we relax the distinction between first-order and second-order representations. This is because we want to understand how popular culture actively shapes first-order representations and thus plays a far more important role in the actual conduct of world politics. In international-relations theory, both constructivists and poststructuralists are most interested in this kind of approach. For instance, Michael Shapiro writes that:

> Part of what must be rejected is that aspect of the terrain predicated on a radical distinction between what is thought of as fictional and scientific genres of writing. In the history of thought the distinction has been supported by the notion that the fictional text, e.g., the story, play, or novel, manufactures its own objects and events in acts of imagination, while the epistemologically respectable genres, such as the scientific text, have "real" objects and events, which provide a warrant for the knowledge-value of those of the text's statements purporting to be about the objects and events.[29]

As we argue when we introduce the distinction between first- and second-order representations, scholars interested in the ways that second-order representations shape social and political life have often focused on religion and mythology. Myth, understood as founding stories that create and sustain a community, is at the center of *both* religion *and* popular culture.[30] Both give rise to beliefs and values that are, for individuals, "taken for granted" in the conduct of everyday life. Both, from a social-scientific standpoint, mix belief and make-belief. Indeed, Emile Durkheim famously argued that nationalism is, in essence, society worshipping itself,[31] and what is popular culture but the medium societies use to shape themselves a community through fact and fiction?

This is precisely the kind of approach taken by Michael Jindra in his studies of fandom in the United States and Europe. Jindra examined the fan cultures surrounding *Star Trek* and found a number of similarities between them and religious communities. As he argues, *Star Trek* fandom "is an example of play and ritual coming back together, back to their 'natural' condition of coexistence and ambiguity."[32]

Similarly, the social anthropologist Daniel Miller documents how the TV show *The Young and the Restless* meshed into the fabric of Trinidadian life.[33] Specifically, tailors, goldsmiths, and other craftsmen changed their products to reflect shifting popular tastes generated by the show. Miller also stresses that *The Young and the Restless*, which highlights flamboyant and carnivalistic consumption, reflected already existing preferences among Trinidadians.[34] Another American show, *Sex in the City*, has inspired—and been the explicit theme of—large-scale singles parties for the young and the restless in Oslo, Norway.[35] Here too, the popularity of the series both reflects previously existing cultural patterns—the mating activities of young, urban Norwegians—and alters them in demonstrable ways. In both cases, fictional second-order representations integrate into the actual practices of communities and, in the process, redefine those communities. Both cases also demonstrate the ways in which popular culture is an integral part of globalization, a theme taken up in many of the chapters of this volume.

Because Miller studies the impact of *The Young and the Restless* through the prism of consumption studies, he focuses on how acts of consumptions are strung together through the stories and narratives that lend meaning to the direction of social activity.[36] Miller pinpoints one of the effects of a particular kind of television show, and relates it to the overall patterns of everyday Trinidadian life. Many of the chapters in this book also seek to understand how one particular second-order representation, namely Harry Potter, intertwines with different first-order phenomenon. But this raises a problem faced by all international-relations scholars who seek to account for the constitutive influence of popular culture on international politics. Since Miller studies everything about Trinidadian life, he finds its effects everywhere. Indeed, many studies of popular culture tend to have a rather free-floating character precisely because they lack an obvious site to study. One way of managing this issue is to focus on three different aspects of popular culture: production, content, and reception. For serials such as *Star Trek*, this is particularly appropriate, inasmuch as they

> are distinguished as a narrative form by the discourse they trace between the producing industry and the readers/spectators/listeners who consume them. [Of particular importance is] the production and distribution of fragmented narrative in a mass medium that is consumed at regular intervals. Historically, for this to occur, one needs a social context characterized by three essential elements: a market economy, a communications technology sufficiently developed to be commercially exploited, and, as Barthes suggests, the recognition of narrative as commodity.[37]

International-relations scholars deal largely with the domain of "high politics." They study war, peace, trade disputes, diplomacy, international law, and so forth. It is much more difficult to establish the impact of popular culture on these kinds of issues—to establish the relationship between first-order and second-order phenomena. Some structuralists and post-structuralists assert a fundamental equality between orders of representation. For them, there is no difference between an episode of *Dallas* and a speech by Ronald Reagan.[38] While this position, or one like it, is acceptable for some in the discipline of cultural studies, many international-relations scholars and political scientists are rightly uncomfortable with collapsing different forms of representation into one another.

These conceptual problems should not stop us from trying. There are, as we have already argued, good reasons to believe that interactions between orders of representation play an important role in international politics. For instance, the growing attention to the role of stories and narratives in politics, even among scholars who once placed little emphasis upon them,[39] implies that international-relations scholars need to better understand why certain narratives are effective or ineffective in legitimating political action. There are undoubtedly a number of relationships between popular cultural and political narratives. Political narratives draw from and inform popular cultural stories, while the effectiveness of both kinds of narratives may derive from similar features; both politicians and entertainers need to tell "good stories" if they want to "sell" a product or a policy.[40]

We argue that there are roughly four different ways in which popular culture has constitutive effects on international politics. It can be *determining*, *informing*, *enabling*, and *naturalizing*.

## *Determining Effects*

In political science, one way of accounting for political action is to argue that actors relate to a given situation by following a "logic of appropriateness." People ask themselves: what kind of situation is this? Who am I, and what is my role in this situation? How can I act so that what I do is appropriate to that role?[41] In rare cases, however, decision makers lack the knowledge or experience to appropriately frame an issue. Under those circumstances, popular cultural representations—fictional or nonfictional—may fill the void and exercise a determining effect on policy making. For example, Kevin Dunn argues that, during the 1960 Congo crisis, U.S. policymakers acted on what they held to be knowledge of the local historical and social context of the crisis. However, Dunn argues, closer scrutiny makes clear that this "knowledge" came largely from *Tarzan* films, texts such as Joseph Conrad's *Heart of Darkness*, Graham Greene's *A Burnt Out Case*, and the comic book *Tintin in Congo*.[42] The Congo case is a reminder that popular culture sometimes does supply the "knowledge" upon which even political elites base their decisions. The U.S. policymakers wanted to do what was appropriate, and in order to do that, they drew on the only sources of knowledge that were readily available to them. This is an extreme example, and such *determining importance* must be rare—if it may be found in pure form at all.

## Informing Effects

Post-structuralists, such as Michael Shapiro, argue that the frames and narratives offered by popular culture mix inextricably with other aspects of political and social practice. The upshot is that, because "power often hides itself" by working through advertisements, fiction, and other apparently nonpolitical forms of communication and representation, one has to explore those social sites in order to understand the true contours of political power.[43] Indeed, the argument goes, both political and apparently nonpolitical representations must be studied if we want to understand world politics. In this view, popular culture can *inform* world politics without determining international political outcomes; popular culture provides diffuse knowledge that people bring to bear on political issues.

The *informing effects* of popular culture are thus more widespread than its determining effects, but they are also more difficult to assess. Harry Potter, we believe, is probably too new to have strong informing effects. In contrast, the informing effects of *Star Trek* on, for example, American space policy is well documented.[44]

## Enabling Effects

Popular culture may lend metaphorical strength to the appeal of a certain policy and so take on *enabling importance* for political action. Political speeches are full of allusions to narratives already known to the public. By relying on familiar narratives, politicians draw analogies that make their positions intuitively plausible to their audiences. Because these narratives, and their significance, are widely accepted in a particular culture, the very act of linking them to the policy is sometimes sufficient to build support for a political movement's goals.

If one thinks of religion and politics as two separate systems of meaning, then in most historical cases the political function of religion seems to have been to enable politicians to perform in a given set of ways: "Religions can become the source of collective obligation, such that deviation from specific religious norms will bring in its wake negative consequences for adherents and non-adherents alike; and collective action in the name of these norms becomes legitimate."[45]

Popular culture often has this kind of importance. Ronald Reagan, for example, used popular culture to great effect in order to make his audiences more receptive to his positions. One of Reagan's speeches argued the case against trade protectionism by comparing it to a pie fight, a stock-in-trade of a certain kind of popular culture. When Reagan ended a speech delivered to NASA, he lifted the roof by tapping the potential of *Star Wars* in wishing them all well: "May the Force be with you." After 11 September 2001, a swathe of U.S. newspaper cartoons drew Bush as Harry Potter, with captions suggesting that producing a Voldemort-like enemy for his "war on terror" would be a smart move. However, we have not found any significant examples of the use of Harry Potter in speeches by Western officials to date. Thus, just as Harry Potter has not had demonstrable determining or informing effects, it also has probably not had much of an enabling effect on world politics either.

## Naturalizing Effects

If there are similarities between the politics of an artifact of popular culture and other political representations, then popular culture may be said to "clear the ground" for the reception of political representations. For example, the more popular culture and political representations display a Manichean way of thinking about politics (in which good and evil are absolutes that always clash in any particular political moment), the easier it should be for a public to accept a Manichean message in a speech by a state official. Popular culture may thus have *naturalizing importance*: it makes a particular way of looking at the world appear to be part of the natural order, "just the way things are," and hence difficult to argue against.

The naturalizing effects of popular culture are not limited to domestic politics, but also may operate transnationally. Audiences not used to Manichean views of political conflict, for example, will have an easier time grasping Manichean politics generally if they are already familiar with the Manichean aspects of the Harry Potter series. If an American TV show may shape mating practices in Oslo, Norway, then it stands to reason that a global blockbuster like Potter may shape thinking about the political.

Iver B. Neumann's essay (chapter 7) explicitly takes up the issue of naturalizing effects. He argues that the spatial geography of the Potter universe represents as natural a world in which savagery and barbarity emanate from the north and from the east. Martin Hall (chapter 8) "explores structural similarities and differences between the mythmaking prevalent in the fantasy genre, Christian monodemonologicalism (the view that evil stems from a single figure, Satan) and that deployed in realist theory." In doing so, Hall explicitly studies the interaction between different kinds of representations of political conflict, with an eye toward how the assumptions of all three frameworks do and do not naturalize one another.

It follows that, when we try to make sense of a certain phenomenon, we will draw on representations whose origins are uncertain. We contend that a number of these representations emanate from the realm of popular culture. If this is so, then it should be a scholarly task to assess how popular culture impinges on global politics. In this introduction, we suggest some general ways to think about this. The rest of the book substantiates these speculations by looking at some of the enjoyable evidence.

## Abbreviations

Throughout this book the following abbreviations of Harry Potter titles are used in parenthetical citations:

| | |
|---|---|
| Harry Potter and the Philosopher's Stone | PS |
| Harry Potter and the Chamber of Secrets | CS |
| Harry Potter and the Prisoner of Azkaban | PA |
| Harry Potter and the Goblet of Fire | GF |
| Harry Potter and the Order of the Phoenix | OP |
| Harry Potter and the Half-Blood Prince | HBP |

## Notes

1. Weldes 2001; 2003a; 2003b.
2. See, for example, Lipschutz 2001; McAlister 2001.
3. Anatol 2003; Heilman 2003; Whited 2003.
4. Associated Press 2005a; Associated Press 2005b.
5. *The Nation* 2000.
6. *Straits Times* 2003.
7. Data from www.thenumbers.com.
8. MacCarthy 2004.

9. Nathan 2003; Wines 2003.

10. Reuters 2005.

11. Lawrence 2001; Morrison 2002; Osnos 2003.

12. Goff 2000, 2002.

13. See the chapters in this volume by Goff and by Jackson and Mandaville.

14. Turner-Vorbeck 2003.

15. Jentsch 2003; Nel 2002. Many of the chapters in this volume take up these themes.

16. Shapiro 1992a, 1992b; Enloe 1996; Hopf 2002.

17. Berger and Luckmann 1966.

18. Mills 1959, 45. See also Luhmann 2000.

19. Barthes 1972; Hoenisch 1996.

20. As Erving Goffman 1990 [1959] famously argues, social and political life can be likened to a series of performances, in which individuals, like professional actors, act out roles such as "doctor," "wife," "child," and "firefighter."

21. Winch 1988.

22. Foucault 1994 [1968].

23. Hauser and Seelye 2005.

24. Weber 1999.

25. Weldes 2003a.

26. Burr 2005.

27. Beyer 1994, 3.

28. Hopf 2002.

29. Shapiro 1988, 7.

30. Kottak 1990; 106; Laustsen and Wæver 2000, 717: Hall in this volume.

31. Durkheim 1965.

32. Jindra 1994, 47. Jenkins 1992, 45, 41, documents that fandom is a multi-media phenomenon both in its expressive dimension "friends and letters and crafts and fanzines and trivia and costumes and artwork and filksongs [fan music-making] and buttons and film clips and conventions" and where the object of desire is concerned. Thus, "To focus on any one media product—be that Star Trek or [the pop song] 'Material Girl'—is to miss the larger cultural context within which that material gets embedded as it is integrated back into the life of the individual fan." These are, however, not problems for a symptomatic reading such as this one. Jenkins's and Ang's attacks on traditional audience research follow Michel de Certeau's work on how readers and listeners "poach" texts, i.e., edit and rework them for their own purposes. Inasmuch as de Certeau pinpoints Lévy-Strauss's "bricoleur" approach, where actors are seen simply to pick pieces and rearrange them without really adding or subtracting anything, Jenkins's and Ang's moves are part of a broader move from structuralism to post-structuralism.

33. It is instructive to compare Miller's work to that of the one scholar of literature who has made his name during the final decades of the last century by grappling with the circulation between text and public. Steven Greenblatt 1988, 5 refers

to the "study of the collective making of distinct cultural practices and inquiry into the relations among these practices" as a poetics of culture, and uses the concept of "social energies" to investigate this. Greenblatt's investigations often focus on Shakespeare. He asks what it was and is in his plays that fascinates the audience—which energies circulated between the play and the public and gave the text the force to come alive. His answer is that there are parallels between the form and subject matter of the dramas, and the form and subject matter of political life at the time. Tensions of everyday life are played out, and he does not deny an element of mimesis and a possible effect of catharsis, and Shakespeare makes this happen in such a way that the lines between the stage and everyday life are blurred. The social energies of everyday life circulate to the production of reality on stage. The play in turn fascinates and animates the public. For Greenblatt, as a literary scholar, the main point is to demonstrate how this circulation may account for the power of the plays. For an anthropologist, in contrast, the main point will be how the representations offered in plays, novels, television series, etc. contribute to the constitution of the social.

34. Miller 1995.

35. *Aftenposten*, 11 February 2002.

36. He gives as one reason for studying the narratives offered by television that, whereas narrative is ubiquitous in social life, the ones he has singled out for study approach an ideal type: "Ricoeur provides a substantial argument for the centrality of narrative to modernity. . . . Ricoeur's study is largely based in 'high' rather than popular traditions; the conflict over the place of narrative is first posed as a conflict between St. Augustine and Aristotle. The sense of the event and recapitulation are evoked with Proust not soap-opera. In many ways this is a pity. It is precisely in the semi-industrialized massive production field of soap opera and its multiple readings that perhaps a better sense of the actual place of narrative in human relations could be revealed" (Miller 1995, 229).

37. Hagedorn 1995, 27, 29.

38. It seems to us that these post-structuralists have not really taken to heart the gist of the break with structuralism, which was exactly a dissatisfaction with the view held by Lévi-Strauss and others that any observable structure was simply a manifestation of a latent or deep structure. Since any manifest structure—be that a novel or a political debate on a specific question—was ultimately a configuration of the same latent structure, the same code was on display in all loci of social life. The post-structuralist project was to discard the very idea of a latent structure, not to reinscribe it by arguing in favor of identity between different kinds of cultural artifacts.

39. Tilly 2002.

40. Jackson and Nexon 2003; Weldes 2003a.

41. March and Olsen 1989.

42. Dunn 2003, especially chapter 3.

43. Shapiro 1988, 29.

44. One extant study that aims to demonstrate this kind of connection is Constance Penley's 1997 *NASA/Trek*, which aims to tease out the interdiscursivity between American space travel and *Star Trek*: "NASA first began its *Star Trek* makeover in the mid-seventies when the space agency yielded to President Gerald Ford's demand prompted by a *Star Trek* fan letter-writing campaign to change the name of the first shuttle from Constitution to Enterprise. Many of the show's cast members were there as the Enterprise—an experimental model used only to practice takeoff and landing—was rolled out onto the tarmac at Edwards Air Force Base to the stirring sounds of Alexander Courage's theme from *Star Trek*. After *Star Trek* creator Gene Roddenberry dies in 1991, NASA let an unnamed shuttle astronaut carry his ashes—classified as 'personal effects'—into space. And NASA actually hired Nichelle Nicols at one point in the late seventies to help recruit women and minorities into the astronaut corps. Mae Jemison [a female astronaut] later invited Nicols to her launch and began every shift of her shuttle mission with Lt. Uhura's famous line, 'hailing frequencies open.' Even the Smithsonian's national Air and Space Museum, which produces and houses the historical record of U.S. space flight, has made a point of including *Star Trek*. In March 1992 the museum mounted *Star Trek: The Exhibition*, a show that turned out to be wildly popular (much to the surprise of many): in response to the question of what a pop-culture phenomenon like *Star Trek* was doing in a place which honors real-life conquests of air and space, the curator said, simply 'There is no other fantasy more pervasive in the conceptualization of space flight than *Star Trek*.' One might conclude from these examples that *Star Trek* is the theory, NASA the practice." Penley 1997, 51.

45. Beyer 1994, 71. See Beyer 1994 for a Luhmannian discussion of the degree in which we now see a return of this state of affairs.

# GLOBALIZATION

I

# Producing Harry Potter

1

## Why the Medium Is Still the Message

PATRICIA M. GOFF

> *To understand popular culture is to understand the conditions of its production. It is not enough to look only at the text or its audience; we need also to look at the way popular culture is organized and made available.*
>
> JOHN STREET, *POLITICS AND POPULAR CULTURE*

IN THE CASE OF HARRY POTTER, investigating production is especially illuminating. The boy wizard is working commercial magic as part of a broader effort by transnational media conglomerates to navigate a shifting technology and business landscape. These media conglomerates are key agents of cultural globalization. They are instrumental in the global spread of internationally recognizable consumer brands, like Harry Potter. As publicly traded, for-profit corporations, their preference for lucrative properties is not surprising, but their ability to privilege this business strategy is greatly enhanced by a favorable regulatory climate. Lying behind the phenomenon of cultural globalization, therefore, we find not only large media enterprises, but also national governments that are willing to put into place laws that allow them to grow larger and to emphasize their commercial agendas.

This observation suggests two things about the globalization of culture: first, it is not solely the result of impersonal market forces or technological advances, which governments cannot control. Rather, government action can influence the pace and direction of some key aspects of cultural globalization. This, in turn, suggests that globalization is not irreversible. If we are uncomfortable with the pervasive presence across a range of media outlets of brands like Harry Potter, we may be in a position to influence this through national political processes.

We can only engage in these sorts of debates about globalization if we look at the production of cultural products. Our conversations about globalization and culture often appropriately focus on the reception of cultural products, as Towns and Rumelili do in the present volume. To be sure, it is important to reflect on the implications of not just the penetration of foreign values, ideas, and images, but their prominence. This prominence carries the potential to affect local identities and practices. Equally important, however, is an awareness of how "cultural globalization is transforming the *context* in which and *means* through which national cultures are produced and reproduced,"[1] as well as attention to the infrastructures of cultural production and transmission. Attention to the production side shifts the debate away from the apparent consumer demand for certain types of products to a discussion of the constricted supply available to those consumers because of a particular production infrastructure that gives content producers power over distribution networks.

Contemporary transformations and developments in the media industries are technological, commercial, and regulatory. Together, they have catalyzed the emergence of a media landscape peopled by a handful of large conglomerates with arguably unrivalled influence across the range of traditional and new media. That these media industries bring to life beloved characters like Harry Potter is good for many. That they do so efficiently and profitably is good for some. Nonetheless, as the media landscape continues to evolve (for example, it may not be long before our access to television and internet is bundled into one device, possibly handheld and wireless), it is worth noting that this evolution has consequences for core sociopolitical values. In particular, media power concentrated in the hands of a few commercial conglomerates has implications for our access to the media, as well as the diversity of output. As a consequence, it is unlikely that the regulatory frameworks put in place to govern the media outlets of the past will continue to serve us in the integrated, digital media environment of the future.

## The Changing Media Landscape

It is by now a cliché to say that many aspects of culture have become commercialized. Contemporary cultural artifacts, like films and books, emerge from an entertainment *industry*. As media scholar Nicholas Garnham pointed out over two decades ago, culture industries are increasingly a global, market-based activity, rather than a national public service. We have seen the emergence of a "a two-tier market divided between the information rich, provided with high-cost specialized information and cultural services, and the information poor, provided with increasingly homogenized entertainment services on a mass scale." The result has been "to shift the dominant definition of public information from that of a public good to that of a privately appropriable commodity."[2] Other media scholars[3] make similar observations but date the commercialization of media back even further, suggesting that the seeds of this trend were planted at the beginning of the twentieth century.

The increasing commercial importance of cultural products has led to a more recent development: cultural policy is now crosscut with trade policy. National governments no longer think solely (or even primarily) about the sociopolitical contributions that a vibrant local book publishing or television production industry can make. They think about the possibilities for export, barriers to market access, and the various economic and noneconomic costs of imports. Such concerns stalled major multilateral trade talks twice in the 1990s—North American Free Trade Agreement (NAFTA) and Uruguay Round General Agreement on Tariffs and Trade (GATT) negotiations. In addition, in 1997 the World Trade Organization (WTO) adjudicated a trade dispute over magazine subsidies.[4]

This transnational or global dimension is arguably an outgrowth of the recognition on the part of culture industry leaders, in such sectors as film, book publishing, and sound recording, that national markets no longer suffice. It is now necessary to expand markets beyond national borders, often to cover costs and to reduce risk. In sectors like television and film, production costs have been steadily rising in recent decades as consumers show a preference for expensive special effects and highly paid stars. In addition, unique to all cultural products is the fact that there is no way to know if a product is going to be a success. The majority of the production costs go into creating the first copy of the book or film or TV program. Yet many never recover those costs. Instead, the occasional blockbuster brings in enough both to cover costs and make a significant profit. Since the blockbusters need to cover not only their own costs, but also those of their parent companies' failures, they need to succeed in a large market, ideally a global one.

Given this imperative, it makes sense for media companies to favor properties that are likely to resonate across national cultures. As Lynn Hirschberg observes, "This change in perspective has, naturally, resulted in a change in content: nuances of language or the subtleties of comedy do not translate easily between cultures, but action or fantasy or animation is immediately comprehensible, even if you live in, say, Japan, which is the country that most big studios long to reach."[5]

It is not surprising that Harry Potter would do well in this new climate wherein media companies seek to make "event films" that can appeal to a wide, global audience. Fantasy fiction, pitting good against evil and set in an imagined world, travels across cultural boundaries. Hirschberg quotes Sherry Lansing, outgoing head of Paramount Pictures: "It's hard, for instance, to pick a villain with a global audience in mind. If we're in a global market, it's going to be a challenge to find credible villains." Hirschberg goes on to comment that, "generally the studio heads agreed: countries (with the possible exception of North Korea, which is not a big movie market) can no longer be demonized."[6] Voldemort, on the other hand, offends no one.

If the commercialization of culture industries is not new, nor is its global reach, then what has changed? At least three things: media conglomerates are bigger; the number of media conglomerates is smaller; and perhaps most importantly, contemporary media conglomerates increasingly subsume under one umbrella the full range of content production, distribution, and exhibition. Time Warner, Harry Potter's parent company, is among the first to experiment with this new model and perhaps the most fully realized example of a comprehensive effort in this direction.

Corporate ownership can usefully be subdivided along three axes: concentrated ownership; public versus private ownership; and foreign versus domestic ownership. Along the axis showing varying degrees of concentrated ownership, we find horizontal integration (a television broadcaster acquires several other television broadcasters); vertical integration (a television broadcaster acquires a company that produces television serials); and cross-media integration (a radio station acquires a newspaper and a television station, typically in the same market). When earlier media scholars commented on the increasing commercialization of media, they were primarily focusing on movement along the public versus private ownership axis. Time Warner's growth and its latest merger with America Online certainly cement this earlier trend toward private ownership. However, it also shifts our attention to the concentrated ownership axis. The merger is especially noteworthy for the new heights in vertical and cross-media integration that it represents, which Harry Potter has navigated with great commercial success.

# Time Warner

Time Warner is the "world's largest media company." Industry insiders and media analysts, aware of the commercialization of culture, commonly describe the company as a premier "content provider" working across "multiple platforms" to sell its "brands." Grant and Wood call Time Warner "by a substantial margin the most powerful single player in the marketplace of consumer culture."[7] The current composition of Time Warner is the result of a series of mergers, including the purchase of HBO in 1975, the merger of Time Inc. and Warner Communications in 1989, the acquisition of Turner Broadcasting in 1996, culminating in 2001 with the acquisition of Time Warner by America Online.

At the time of the Time Warner–America Online merger, CNN reported that the move "created a digital media powerhouse with the potential to reach every American in one form or another" boasting "unrivaled assets among other media and online companies." CNN quoted one media analyst as saying, "If their mantra is content, this alliance is unbeatable. Now they have this great platform they can cross-fertilize with content and redistribute." Then-AOL CEO Steve Case called it a "historic merger," noting that "AOL–Time Warner will offer an incomparable portfolio of global brands that encompass the full spectrum of media and content."[8] The merger between Time Warner and America Online was heralded as such a historic event in media marriages because it created one of the first possibilities to experiment fully with what many media industry watchers believed—and many still believe—would be the key to future success— synergies, or "consumption webs,"[9] that allow diverse media outlets within the same corporate family constantly to advertise each others' products.

Synergies go beyond the pursuit of ever-larger markets in the quest to reduce risk. The synergy strategy seeks to layer multiple global markets on top of each other so that a cultural property can be exploited repeatedly in several forms. As Grant and Wood explain, few films actually pay off at the box office. "Cinema exhibition represents only the warm-up round of a much larger game. Payoffs—and they are many—come elsewhere. The objective of play is to wring the greatest profit possible from products whose appeal, animated by the imagination, is easily transferred from one medium to another. . . . The game then is to play out a property across as many windows and territories as possible, extracting maximum return from each. To do this, it is helpful if you happen to own or control a significant number of windows or territories."[10] Of course, synergies flow not only from films, but from books and other cultural products. The logic is the same.

"When most single plays fail, the only winning strategy is to enter often. But that strategy is available only to players of significant size."[11]

The synergy strategy is not entirely unfamiliar to media companies. "Content companies currently rely on being able to repackage and resell prime content in a number of ways in order to recover investment and production costs. . . . These include syndication and VHS and DVD repackaging for retail sale. These revenue streams currently are a major subsidy of new content production in the movie and TV worlds."[12] Nonetheless, the current synergy strategy is distinguished by the fact that "multiple product lines in numerous corporate divisions are promoted simultaneously."[13] In the past, synergistic promotion was sequential—once a product proved its bankability in one division, only then would it be transferred to another division. And, of course, the number and type of divisions was much more limited. Vertical and cross-media integration allows Time Warner to reach new heights in the "streaming of content across parallel media formats (what were once discrete media operating platforms)"[14] and across geographical space.

Time Warner is better positioned than most to pursue such a strategy. Their 2001 merger with AOL unites AOL, CNN, HBO, Warner Bros. studios, Time Inc.'s over 140 magazines, Time Warner Cable, the WB television station, and more. These entities offer "multiple platforms" across old and new media, including cable, internet, instant messaging, magazines, television, and film, allowing "cross-purposing"—airing its movies on its cable network; promoting its book publishing on its internet service portal, and so on. Time Warner is arguably the quintessential marriage of content and delivery, making it possible to mine its own content and make it available on its own delivery mechanisms. Acquiring a wider variety of delivery outlets, especially an internet portal, reputed to be the content delivery vehicle of the future, opens up a raft of new possibilities. As Time Warner reports on its website, "Warner Bros. Entertainment stands at the forefront of every aspect of the entertainment industry, from feature films to television, home video/DVD, animation, comic books, interactive entertainment and games, product and brand licensing, international cinemas and broadcasting." This is the first time we have seen this breadth, although it is likely not the last, given that mergers of this nature are reputed to be the model of the future.

The Time Warner website goes on to note that, "with distribution to 89 international territories—more than any other studio—Warner Home Video commands the largest distribution infrastructure in the global video marketplace." Not only is it true that, "through the first half of 2004,

Warner Home Video held 20.2% of the home video overall market (consumer spending on DVD and VHS sales and rentals)—the most of any studio"; but also, "with Toshiba, WHV spearheaded the development of DVD and holds several enabling patents."

From this standpoint, Time Warner has added yet another dimension to the synergies it is creating by wading into hardware production in response to recent technological shifts. Film studio executives used to pour over box office numbers and many North American news shows persist in reporting these numbers to the public, perhaps to create a buzz around a new release. Hollywood executives are more interested now in DVD sales.

> From about 2002 on, the larger stakes in Hollywood—the revenue that enables studios to finance blockbusters and to pay Brad Pitt and to keep the lights on—have come to ride mostly on those little silver discs that go on sale four or five months after a theatrical release. This year, for instance, 63 percent of studio feature-film revenues in the United States will come from movies sold to retail stores; actual box office will generate only 21 percent.[15]

This "shift from a rental-model business to the far more lucrative sell-through model"[16] has been accompanied by an interesting alliance. The studios producing the films and the major outlets for DVD sales—Best Buy and Walmart, for example, in North America—are increasingly tying their fortunes to one another. Not only do studios study the demographics of the retail shoppers that favor certain outlets, which influences which films get made and which do not; they also have computer links so that companies like Time Warner or Fox can "know what sells on an hourly basis."[17] Interestingly, "the *Lord of the Rings* and *Harry Potter* helped sales of DVDs increase by 75% in 2003 compared with the previous year. An average of 380,000 DVDs were sold every day" during 2003, bringing the total to 140 million. "Consumer spending on DVDs and videos was more than double the $9.2 billion taken at the U.S. box office, according to the Digital Entertainment Group, the DVD industry association, in its annual sales report."[18]

For Time Warner, this interest in DVDs is not solely about mining their extensive library to serve this new home entertainment market. The nearly dozen patents that Time Warner holds on DVD technology guarantee royalties on DVDs sold with content from *any* library. Benghozi argues that "the convergence of cultural enterprises and products and the growing integration of markets are also reflected by the increasingly important role of technology providers in the cultural sector. Today, telecommunications and

network operators, software designers (Microsoft) and hardware manufac-
turers (Sony) have considerably greater means than the majors in the cultural field and are even able to directly influence the direction and
development of cultural branches."[19] In the case of Time Warner, they
have seen the wisdom of joining the technology provider.[20]

## Time Warner and Harry Potter

> *Harry Potter is much more than a book and much more than a*
> *movie. The boy wizard is the centerpiece of a global corporate*
> *strategy.*

ABC NIGHTLY NEWS REPORT, 2004

It is a lucrative brand, an entertainment franchise, with potential for sequels
and marketing of licensed merchandise. In November 2001, *The Economist*
called Harry Potter "the biggest test yet of claims made by AOL Time
Warner, formed in a much-hyped merger at the start of 2001, that an integrated media conglomerate can conjure up spellbinding cross-promotion
synergies."[21] As the magazine reported, AOL–Time Warner does not own
the publishing rights to the book, "but it does own everything else to do
with Harry Potter: the rights to the films (seven are planned) and all licensing and merchandising deals."

Grant and Wood articulate the ways in which Harry Potter has been
spread across the Time Warner family in what Ken Auletta has called the
"Potter offensive."[22]

> Consider the many ways in which AOL Time Warner brought Harry to
> U.S. audiences in the autumn of 2001. At the centre of the marketing of-
> fensive was a movie that AOL Warner Brothers studio produced, *Harry
> Potter and the Philosopher's Stone* (*Harry Potter and the Sorcerer's Stone* in the
> United States). AOL's Moviefone promoted and sold tickets to the 3,672
> theatres unspooling the movie on 8,200 screens (roughly one quarter of all
> the screens in America on the film's opening weekend). AOL's online por-
> tal, which serves one in two American internet subscribers, peppered its
> pages with Potter promotions and links to related sites; AOL's 137 million
> members were also directed to sites selling Harry merchandise. Time
> Warner magazines like *People, Time, Entertainment Weekly* and *Sports Illus-
> trated* carried ads, contests and editorial content about the film. More ads
> appeared on Time Warner's cable system, which serves about one in five
> American homes, and on those four top-ten cable channels that its Turner
> Broadcasting subsidiary owns. Warner Music Group produced and sold

CDs of the film's soundtrack. With Harry's ubiquity assured, AOL turned exclusive worldwide rights to promote the film and its sequel into yet another asset, selling those to Coca-Cola for US$150 million.[23]

Of course, Time Warner has also developed a long list of Harry Potter merchandise, including predictable items like bed sheets, towels, wall calendars, scarves, key chains, dolls, action figures, plush toys, watches, posters, and trading cards. On the more creative end of the merchandising spectrum, for both children and adults, are leather wallets, briefcases, Lego sets, a Gryffindor necktie, a levitating wand pen, a sterling silver flying Hedwig brooch, Harry's Quidditch goggles, and a variety of hats. In the latter category, Warner Brothers offers the money-saving three-hat set—a sorting hat, Harry's student hat, and McGonagall's hat—for a bulk price. The extensive list of licensed merchandise that has been mined from the Potter books and films has led one commentator to suggest that the films "resemble a series of home shopping advertisements with unusually high production values."[24]

It is worth noting that not all Harry Potter merchandise is sold for commercial purposes. J. K. Rowling published two short stories in 2001 that she penned under pseudonyms, marketed as replicas of Harry's school books—*Fantastic Beasts and Where to Find Them* and *Quidditch through the Ages*. They have, to date, earned over thirty million dollars (U.S.) for the British poverty relief charity, Comic Relief, which uses the money for global projects targeting the poorest children. Nonetheless, this is the exception where licensing and merchandising of Potter products are concerned.

"Harry Potter, argues Richard Parsons, AOL–Time Warner's co-chief operating officer, is a prime example of an asset 'driving synergy both ways.' He explains that 'we use the different platforms to drive the movie, and the movie to drive business across the platforms.' So, in America, AOL.com has offered subscribers the chance to win tickets to an advance screening; while in Britain, AOL has attracted new subscribers with the promise of tickets."[25]

Grant and Wood even go so far as to equate this strategy with Harry Potter. "In deference to a particularly dazzling display of its effectiveness in late 2001, this might be thought of as the 'All *Harry Potter*, all the time' strategy. Its essence is to leverage the emotional appeal of a core property (in this case, the engaging boy hero of a series of fantasy novels by British writer J. K. Rowling) across as many different forms of exploitation as possible."[26] Author J. K. Rowling reportedly made certain demands that limited the commercial exploitation of Harry Potter. "Even so, the Potter franchise (including books) could bring in $1 billion."[27] AOL–Time Warner leadership insists that such profits would not have been possible without the synergies provided by the merger with AOL.

Warner Brothers' commercial performance in the last two years is at least partially due to the success of the Harry Potter franchise. As the Time Warner website indicates, in June 2004, *Harry Potter and the Prisoner of Azkaban* opened, "surpassing $200 million in worldwide box office in less than a week of its release." Not coincidentally, "also in June, Warner Bros. Pictures International crossed the billion-dollar mark—for the fourth year in a row and the seventh time overall—in record time for the Studio." The Time Warner website indicates that the company is expecting a similarly stellar performance from the next installment in the Harry Potter film series in 2005. Interestingly, elsewhere in their highlights report for 2004, Time Warner notes that the WB television network is doing particularly well, in part because it can boast "network television's lowest median age (33.3) and a core demographic of 12–34 year olds." "The WB has the audience that is the hardest to reach and most desired by advertisers— first-time buyers (just starting to build brand loyalty) and prime moviegoers," giving further insight into the great promise that Harry Potter holds for the company.

At this writing, it is questionable whether the AOL–Time Warner merger, and its synergy strategy, will pay off as significantly as was anticipated in 2000. AOL's fortunes suffered with the bursting of the dot-com bubble and the announcement of questionable accounting practices at America Online. Both of these events had serious consequences for Time Warner's stock prices, making Harry Potter's future performance even more important for its parent company. As Murray reminds us, "AOL-TW needs the Harry Potter brand as much as the global commercialisation of Harry Potter requires AOL-TW."[28] Time Warner relies not only on the commercial success of current film releases and merchandising campaigns, but also on the repeated deployment of the entire range of Harry Potter products for future generations of adolescents.

Some commentators remain skeptical about the synergy strategy. Others suggest that it is too early for such a sweeping change to take hold.[29] In addition, as Towns and Rumelili report elsewhere in this volume, the strategy could backfire if the target consumers come to resent the fact that Harry Potter emanates from a consumerist marketing machine. Nonetheless, despite the fact that the synergies strategy is unproven, Time Warner continues to use it to promote Harry Potter and other properties—for example, the Warner Bros. film, *Interview with the Vampire*, based on Anne Rice's Time Warner paperback of the same name (and distributed on DVD by Warner Home Videos) provides the inspiration for a Warner Bros. Theatre Ventures musical to appear in 2005. Tentatively titled *The Vampire Lestat*, the musical also draws on the other *Vampire Chronicles* novels, whose television, movie, and theater rights belong to Warner Bros. Time Warner's website explains that "Theatre Ventures mines the myriad Warner Bros. Entertainment library titles and iconic characters that might lend themselves to theatrical presentation and instead of just licensing them to others, serves as the developer and producer." Perhaps it is only a matter of time before we see a stage version of Harry Potter to complete what Murray has called the "cross-promotion of the Harry Potter brand in an endless web of corporate self-referentiality."[30]

This strategy is not the sole preserve of Time Warner, although the company possesses an unparalleled collection of "delivery mechanisms." Working with synergies is arguably becoming the standard operating procedure for media concerns of all shapes, nationalities, and sizes, although the largest are likeliest to be best-positioned to benefit from it. Viacom, Disney, and News Corporation all have holdings to rival Time Warner. Increasingly, too, media conglomerates outside of the United States have adopted this strategy. Bertelsmann in Europe and CanWest Global in Canada are two examples of large media conglomerates that are also pursuing a "cross-purposing" strategy, suggesting that size and vertical integration in one country beget more of the same in other countries.

## Does It Matter?

Harry Potter is well on its way to becoming one of the most beloved stories of this generation. The series is, for the most part, viewed as a positive development in the life of the contemporary adolescent, firing her imagination and awakening the reader within. So does it matter if Time Warner also benefits? Does it matter if Harry Potter emerges from a media landscape increasingly characterized by fewer, bigger conglomerates, the marriage of content and delivery, and the exploitation of the most popular brand properties across multiple media outlets? The short answer is, "it might."

Civil society groups caution against the growing influence of a small number of media conglomerates. Perhaps more surprisingly, many of the flags that are being raised come from people working within the industry. Many individuals who stand to benefit from these trends recognize that it may be difficult to achieve certain political and sociocultural goals in such a media landscape, including guaranteeing a diversity of output and fair and equitable access to media outlets (both for the artist/entrepreneur and the consumer). For example, Barry Diller has been at the helm of several of the largest players in the entertainment industry. Nevertheless, the former head of Paramount studios, Twentieth Century Fox, and most recently, Vivendi Universal, bemoans the evolution of the media conglomerates. In a speech to the National Association of Broadcasters, Diller said

> The oligopoly has been restored—the barrier to entry is now so incredi-bly high that the ability of a new entrant to actually go out and get voice is practically nil. . . . The possibilities today of somebody launching a new Fox network, a truly independent new network, are non-existent. Where do new, fresh-thinking young people go today? Once upon a time there were hundreds of places they could go to try their imaginations, to get their wings. Now, they are up against a few vertically integrated monoliths, acting with each other in their own horizontal keiretsu, everything inter-related—they only have to do favors for each other—they only have to ac-commodate each other—no one else matters.[31]

Diller goes on to note that big is not necessarily bad. Consolidation may make good business sense. Nonetheless, he argues that "there must be fierce focus and vigor for the appropriate safeguards. . . . The old paradigm is gone. Now, we are in a new universe and the question is—what to do? There are real dangers in complete concentration. The conventional wis-dom is wrong—we need more regulation—not less."[32]

Auletta explains opposition to the AOL–Time Warner merger:

> Corporations, such as Disney, and consumer groups worried that AOL Time Warner could try to trap consumers in what is called a "walled gar-den" of its own content, shutting out competitors and nonprofit commu-nity groups. "AOL Time Warner would be like an air-traffic controller, deciding who gets landing rights and who gets gates," said Jeffrey Chester, the executive director of the nonprofit Center for Digital Democracy, one of the consumer groups questioning the merger. "They can make sure that their services and content get preferential treatment."[33]

Shister expresses similar concerns, noting that "what is left in the aftermath of the 1990s media megamergers is an emerging communication 'network of networks' in which, critics point out, there are fewer and fewer gatekeepers deciding who gains entry."[34] Many people may be producing high-quality content, but without access to distribution and delivery mechanisms, it may be difficult to make it available to the public now that those who control these mechanisms increasingly rely on their own repertoire of content.[35]

This is especially worrying for groups who place great hope in the Internet as a fundamentally democratic communication space. Their concerns may be justified. In 2001, Warner Brothers sent a letter to a fifteen-year-old Potter fan who had created a website in honor of Harry and his pals. The letter reportedly indicated that her site infringed on the parent company's intellectual property rights and asked that she transfer her domain name to Warner Brothers.[36] The fan did not roll over. Rather, she contacted the press and turned the incident—apparently not an isolated one—into a public kerfuffle, eventually forcing Warner Brothers to back down.

Many of the concerns about the evolution of media are not new. They have been applied to the news media for decades. It is widely acknowledged that concentrated ownership of news media threatens to limit the variety of views expressed. Citizens who rely on the media, both as a source of information and as an outlet for ideas, will consequently have an impoverished experience of their democratic society. As a result, a variety of regulations have been put in place over the years to provide "the free flow of substantive information deemed critical to keeping democracy's inner workings lubricated."[37] What may be new, however, is that the same sorts of questions that to date have most often been raised with regard to the news media are now being raised with regard to the entertainment media. Whether this is appropriate is still under debate. For example, former Federal Communications Commission (FCC) Chairman Michael Powell acknowledges that he does not have a clear answer to this question. In a PBS interview, Powell said, "I think that when you get to the arguments about democracy and citizenship, you tend to get down to the focus on news—critical information, political information, to which we make informed choices (sic). But it's also important to remember that the vast majority of programming that's on television in a given moment, in a given day, is entertainment. I don't know what the effect is on democracy if *Friends* gets on versus *The Sopranos* at a given hour."[38] What is the effect on society if Harry Potter is on the bookshelves, on theater screens, on DVD, and in the toy stores, rather than a diversity of characters emanating from a variety of corporate and independent sources?

Formulating an answer to the question requires inquiring into what the public interest responsibility of the entertainment industries may be. In addition to assured, equitable access—the flip side of the "walled garden" discussed above—many focus on concerns about diversity of output, which the synergy strategy does not guarantee. According to the synergy model, "an idealised modern consumer avidly samples the diversified product range of the parent conglomerate, but does so specifically by consuming multiple products derived from essentially the same content reservoir."[39] There is little incentive for the conglomerates that control the major media outlets to admit other sources of content, thus limiting the range of ideas and images that will circulate. Effective regulatory frameworks could create the conditions under which a diversity of ideas might flourish. Current regulatory arrangements make efforts in this direction, although in many instances, they rely on market competition to provide this outcome.

The challenge of updating regulations to reflect the new media environment must be met alongside an effort to figure out exactly what producing diversity might mean. Diversity in the news media has meant both ideological variety and localism. It may mean other things with respect to entertainment. For example, DeFrancia identifies "source diversity, outlet diversity, and viewpoint diversity"[40] as among the goals we want to consider. Nongovernmental organizations seeking to enshrine a right to cultural diversity at UNESCO highlight national cultural diversity and a concern over too many foreign voices drowning out local ones in national contexts.

Tyler Cowen argues that the market can provide for diversity; however, it is diversity of a certain kind. Cowen distinguishes between "diversity within society" and "diversity across societies."[41] He explains that the first concept captures "the richness of the menu of choice in a given society," while the second concept portrays "whether each society offers the same menu."[42] The market—and the synergy strategy—is arguably very good at providing the second kind of diversity in the current circumstances, but less effective at providing the first. Children across the world have access to Harry Potter products. However, a smaller number of alternatives to Harry may be available in any given market.

To be sure, Time Warner does not operate in a free market environment. It functions within an extensive regulatory framework. Nonetheless, it is a regulatory framework designed for the broadcasting environment of the past rather than the digital environment of the future. In addition, the regulatory framework that approved Time Warner's merger with America Online relies on a belief that market liberalization, and the competition it is designed to facilitate, will deliver sociopolitical and economic benefits. The centerpiece of the FCC model is antitrust regulation. The FCC chairman who oversaw the Time Warner–AOL merger, William Kennard, explains some of the key concerns to which his agency responded:

> Their burden was to come to the FCC and demonstrate that this merger would serve the public interest. We took a hard look at it and we determined that it could only serve the public if it would not jeopardize what we cherish about the Internet, which is being an open, robust place where competitors can come and offer their services to consumers. So we imposed some very important conditions on our approval to make sure that consumers are protected.[43]

Indeed, this approach does address concerns over the creation of "walled gardens." As former chairman Kennard explains, the FCC was particularly concerned with ensuring that Internet and broadband cable services remain open.

> It is all about competitive choice for consumers. . . . We don't want to create a situation where one company becomes so dominant that no other competitors have a chance. . . . We've worked too hard to create competition in this space. So we are ensuring that consumers will be able to have a competitive environment for instant messaging. . . . When you can marry a company like Time Warner that has lots of content and libraries with a company like AOL, we don't want to deprive consumers of these new products but nor do we want to allow one company to become too dominant.[44]

Such an approach may lead to lower prices for consumers and may solve some of the access concerns. Nonetheless, it is unlikely to ensure the sorts of sociopolitical outcomes associated with diversity that many may favor.

> Antitrust law as a tool was not designed to promote the democratic value of diverse discourse, and it would be difficult to develop appropriate standards to gauge desirable levels of competition in a business that is unlike virtually any other in terms of the unique importance it plays in the political life of the society. Classic criteria of competition employ economic measures, not subjective considerations such as "the people's need to know."[45]

Former FCC chairman, Reed Hundt, confirms the inapplicability of antitrust law in this context:

> Antitrust law is concerned solely with the goal of efficiency. Its purpose is to make sure that markets are competitive, so that they maximize output from productive capability. There are at least two reasons why antitrust law

alone is an inadequate paradigm for determining how many broadcasters or newspapers or any media outlet we might wish in order to perpetuate our democracy, entertain ourselves, grow our economy, or provide outlets for creative energy. . . . antitrust law will almost always conclude that markets with five competitors are competitive, provided that no one has price-setting market share. Yet from the perspective of forming an inclusive, diverse democracy, we might well conclude that we need at least six, or seven, or some such higher number of outlets. An example is the persistent if intermittent effort by government to create outlets for different language, or for media owned by women or minorities or small businesses. Such outlets might be sixth, or seventh, or eighth entrants in media markets; antitrust law might not regard them as necessary to create competition, but for other reasons we might value them very highly.[46]

An inquiry into the implications of evolving media structures or the continuing usefulness of our regulatory frameworks often emerges from a crisis. For example, groups in the United States were moved to action in 2003 when a number of American radio stations removed the Dixie Chicks from their playlists after a band member made unflattering public remarks about George W. Bush. Many of the stations belonged to the Clear Channel Entertainment empire known to have links to the Republican Party, prompting an outcry over concentrated ownership, bias in the media, and free expression.

The same sorts of concerns are not in play when we examine Harry Potter as the most fully realized example of Time Warner's synergy strategy. The fact that Harry and his gang have enchanted so many leads us to conclude that the production structures that create and disseminate him are working just fine. And this may be true. Nonetheless, the sweeping changes to the media landscape, of which Harry Potter's ubiquitous presence is evidence, at a minimum should not go unnoticed and, at a maximum, might provoke a comprehensive assessment of the degree to which public interest goals are being served by contemporary media regulations. In addition, this perspective calls into question the tendency to equate cultural globalization with Americanization. It is true that most powerful culture industry conglomerates are American. However, it is not their "American-ness" that produces the sorts of outcomes that we associate with cultural globalization—it is their size and their reach, structural qualities that are increasingly being embraced around the world.

# Notes

1. Held, McGrew, Goldblatt, and Perraton 1999, 328. Emphasis in original.
2. Garnham 1986, 38.
3. McChesney 1993; Pike and Winseck 2004.
4. Goff 2000, 2002.
5. Hirschberg 2004. Harry Potter has, incidentally, been "phenomenally popular" in Japan.
6. Hirschberg 2004.
7. Grant and Wood 2004, 87.
8. Johnson 2000.
9. Kapur 2003.
10. Grant and Wood 2004, 85.
11. Grant and Wood 2004, 84.
12. Godwin 2003.
13. Murray 2002.
14. Murray 2002.
15. Gertner 2004.
16. Gertner 2004.
17. Gertner 2004.
18. "Blockbusters Boost UK DVD Sales" 2004.
19. Benghozi 2003.
20. Time Warner has divested itself of its own CD/DVD manufacturing concern, but retains lucrative and influential ties to this world through its hardware patents.
21. "Harry Potter and the Synergy Test" 2001.
22. Auletta 2001.
23. Grant and Wood 2004, 96.
24. Murray 2002.
25. Quoted in "Harry Potter and the Synergy Test" 2001.
26. Grant and Wood 2004, 95.
27. "Harry Potter and the Synergy Test" 2001.
28. Murray 2002.
29. Shister 2003.
30. Murray 2002.
31. Diller 2003.
32. Diller 2003.
33. Auletta 2001.
34. Shister 2003, 28.
35. Shister 2003, 25.
36. Ingram 2001.
37. Shister 2003, 1.
38. Quoted in Rick Karr 2003.

39. Murray 2002.
40. Defrancia 2002, 4.
41. Cowen 2002, 14.
42. Cowen 2002, 14–15.
43. Suarez 2001.
44. Suarez 2001.
45. Shister 2003, 20.
46. Quoted in Shister 2003, 20.

# Glocal Hero
## Harry Potter Abroad

2

PATRICK THADDEUS JACKSON AND PETER MANDAVILLE

NO ONE COULD DENY that the Harry Potter books are a worldwide phenomenon. Over 260 million copies of the books have been sold to date, and the books have been translated into sixty languages.[1] Intense anticipation greets the announcement of each new book in the series, with regular press runs selling out in record time in multiple countries; the fifth book in the series broke all sales records in India within a few weeks of its release,[2] and reports from other countries are broadly similar. It may be a slight exaggeration to compare the success of the Harry Potter books to the Bible,[3] but the extent of the books' reach cannot be doubted.

This worldwide distribution network, however, should not be taken to mean more than it does. From sales figures and reports of lines outside of bookstores we can conclude only that people worldwide have been *exposed* to Harry Potter and his fantastic cosmos. The widespread sales of the Harry Potter novels, and the equally widespread marketing and merchandising avenues that follow those sales, are thus an illustration of the integration of the market for cultural goods to form something like a world-system. Empirically, we can trace the flow of such goods from place to place, determining the effective boundaries of the modern world-system by looking for areas where such flows cease.[4] But such an analysis, while clearly demonstrating that cultural products are more mobile now than they used to be, tells us nothing about the *meanings* that attach to the cultural goods thus produced and consumed. Just because Harry Potter is a worldwide phenomenon does not mean that it is a *global* one.

Indeed, we would posit that part of the reason for the worldwide success of Harry Potter, like the worldwide success of other cultural products, such as American-produced television programs like *Dallas*,[5] is due to quite the opposite process. Rather than worldwide distribution promoting and sustaining something like a "global village" within which everyone shares a consensus on basic meanings, we submit that worldwide distribution is sustained and enhanced by a process of *localization* whereby a cultural product from one context is translated into different local contexts. We refer to this conjunction of worldwide distribution and local translation as *glocalization*, since the result is something that only appears to be "global" when it is better understood as an amalgam of local engagements.

## Translation

We approach glocalization by thematizing the process of *translation*. Translation might be thought of as the effort to take something that is meaningful in one context and reproduce it so that it is meaningful in another context. The most obvious example of this involves a work of literature written in one language that is then rendered into another language, but translation as an activity is broader than this. Anthropologists translate customs and ceremonies from one cultural context to another; scientists addressing popular audiences translate their technical knowledge into a more widely accessible form; art and drama critics translate from the arcane customs and conventions of their particular empirical focus in order to apprise others of the significance of a particular work. Indeed, translation is a ubiquitous feature of social life and can be found wherever people endeavor to communicate across significant boundaries.

Two options present themselves to every translator: should she try to stick as closely to the contours of the original product as she can, or should she depart from that original product in order to achieve an effect in the new context that will be similar to the effect that the original product generated in its original context? Rigorously followed, these two pathways produce two different kinds of translations: the first pathway produces more or less *literal* translations, whereas the second produces more *free* translations. Literal translations have the advantage of preserving more of the original author's intent, as expressed in such things as word order and other specific nuances of creative choice, but they often appear awkward in the new context. Conversely, free translations have the advantage of being easier to read and understand, but at the cost of obscuring many of the details of the original product.

As an example, consider this famous passage from the conclusion of Max Weber's *The Protestant Ethic and the Spirit of Capitalism*:[6]

The Puritan wanted to work in a calling; we are forced to do so. For when asceticism was carried out of monastic cells into everyday life, and began to dominate worldly morality, it did its part in building the tremendous cosmos of the modern economic order. . . . In Baxter's view the care for external goods should only lie on the shoulders of the "saint like a light cloak, which can be thrown aside at any moment." But fate decreed that the cloak should become an iron cage.

At issue is the phrase "iron cage," which the translator has chosen to render the German *Stahlhartes Gehäuse* into English. As a literal translation, this rendering is quite ridiculous, since the German phrase refers to steel rather than iron and a shell rather than a cage: "a shell hard as steel" would be a more strictly accurate version. At issue here is more than mere semantics or quality of tone, inasmuch as there is quite a bit of *conceptual* difference between the two images: the "iron cage" stands as something within which modern humans are entrapped, whereas a "shell hard as steel" signals a more fundamental alteration in the very constitution of modern human beings.[7] Understood as a free translation, however, "iron cage" succeeds inasmuch as it captures the bleak and pessimistic *spirit* of Weber's conclusion, and in fact does so in terms that the readers of the translation might find very familiar indeed—the "iron cage" image derives from Bunyan's *Pilgrim's Progress*, a book with which American readers at the time would most likely have been familiar.

It is important to bear in mind that no *actual* translation is either completely free or completely literal. A translation that takes great liberties with a text is still, in the end, at least marginally constrained by the overall shape of the original work of which it is a translation; conversely, even a translation that traces the subtleties of the original work meticulously cannot avoid making a few judgment calls about ambiguous words or phrases. "Literal translation" and "free translation" are *ideal-types*, artificially pure conceptual constructs that allow us to make sense of the activity of translation by observing how these two pure constructs are combined in practice.[8] Some actual translations will veer closer to one of these poles than they will to the other, but all will have traces of both approaches embodied within them.

Taking these two ideal-types as the limiting cases of translation, we can specify a number of mixtures of the two approaches that will flesh out the middle part of the scale. Each of these categories of translation poses specific challenges and engenders specific discussions about the fidelity of the translation thus produced. And each produces a particular glocalization, fraught with its own tensions and exemplifying its own way of processing the transactions between the worldwide and the local. Products with distribution networks as widespread as the Harry Potter novels should feature opportunities to observe all of these categories.

- Close to the "literal translation" end we have those translations that try to reproduce the original product as faithfully as possible. Such translations pose questions about word choice and specific phrasing, especially when it comes to puns, evocative proper names, and the like. The Harry Potter books are full of words and phrases that present such problems, and have thus produced a number of discussions and controversies about these nuances.
- Further toward the middle of the scale we have those translations that seek to *explain* the original product to a new audience, or to place the work in a novel context. Such translations operate largely at the level of summary, seeking local parallels for themes and situations invoked in the original work. The Harry Potter books have generated a number of conversations about their thematic significance, all of which balance the literal and the free aspects of translation in an effort to assess the meaning of Harry Potter in contexts more or less far removed from the English boarding school environment where much of the action of the novels takes place.
- Closest to the "free translation" end of the scale we find more radical departures: stories and accounts that are tangentially related to the original, but which make little or no effort to be limited by the contours of that work. Although we might tend to think of these as "based on" or "inspired by" the original rather than as translations of it, such a distinction implies a certainty of knowledge about the original that is very difficult to sustain when dealing with an original work of any complexity. When dealing with the Harry Potter novels, the most obvious examples of such a radical departure are the fake stories and novels that periodically circulate, claiming to be the next chapter in the saga.

## Translating Harry Potter

In what follows we examine how all three categories of translation play out as the Harry Potter phenomenon continues its worldwide trek. Each of these categories lends itself to specific challenges and tensions and provides an illustration of the complexities involved in attempting to communicate meaningfully across cultural boundaries. Harry Potter provides an ideal lab-

oratory for exploring how efforts to make cultural products "travel" produce, simultaneously, a variety of localized versions of the product *and* an
overarching, if vague, set of characters and situations that command virtually worldwide recognition.

## Faithful Translations

Translators working primarily in the vein of "literal translation" have en-
countered significant difficulties in dealing with the Harry Potter novels.
Some of this stems from the fact that the books are characterized by interplay between at least two distinct but overlapping worlds: a domain of the
magical (inhabited by wizards), and a domain of the mundane (inhabited
by "muggles"). The range of characters and objects found in the latter cor-
respond closely to a sort of generic contemporary England, and hence pose
fewer translation challenges for a readership accustomed to the inventories
of late capitalist society.[9] The magic—and exoticism—of the wizard world
in Harry Potter, however, is partially embodied in the very language and
lexicon that constitute its holdings. Names are frequently alliterative
("Moaning Myrtle") and possessed of multiple layers of meaning, such as
the case of the lycanthropic Remus Lupin in *Prisoner of Azkaban*. The magical qualities inherent in objects both familiar and arcane add another layer
of complexity when it comes to rendering them in languages culturally
and linguistically distant from English. For example, the idea of a broom
that flies sits comfortably with children already familiar with the iconic images of European witchcraft. How does such a concept, however, play in a
context, such as India, without a preexisting chain of meaning in which to
situate aeronautic custodial gear?

Translators of the Harry Potter books have frequently alluded to such
difficulties, and often in terms that tacitly echo the analytic distinctions we
have drawn above. Many non-English editions of the novels, for example,
alternate between the transliteration of certain names, in which English
phonemes are rendered as cognates in the second language, and more extreme modifications, where the names of characters are changed in order to
preserve specific literary and tonal qualities. Chinese translations often opt
for the former course, so that Dobby the house elf becomes Duo-bi, while
Uncle Vernon and Aunt Petunia become Fu-nong and Pei-ni De-si-li.[10]
Leaning toward more extreme modifications, Moaning Myrtle becomes
Jammerende Jennie in Dutch and Gemma Gemec in Catalan.[11]

Relatively faithful translators also sometimes take advantage of local
meanings and references to communicate the basic idea encapsulated in a
given place or character name. Hebrew translators, for example, rendered

The Leaky Cauldron—the popular meeting-spot in Hogsmeade Village—as "HaKalakhat HaRotakhat," which literally means "The Boiling Kettle" but is also an idiomatic expression for a community bubbling with gossip. Along similar lines, the N.E.W.T. exams taken by advanced wizarding students become the "Habkhinot HaKshifometriyyot" in Hebrew: the "sorceometric exams," a title that invokes the psychometric exams required for admission to Israeli universities.[12]

The books' Hindi translator also struggled to communicate aspects of the Hogwarts School of Wizardry and Witchcraft, much of which derives from the culturally specific world of the English boarding school. Similarly stumping were certain Rowling neologisms deemed wholly unmanageable in Hindi, such as the "Remembrall" from the first book of the series.[13] Faced with such dilemmas, many translators have chosen simply to leave such terms in the original English. It is not uncommon to find online Harry Potter discussions jumping back and forth between two languages, with magical objects and character names generally appearing in English.[14]

These relatively minor verbal modifications made as the text of each Harry Potter novel moves from one linguistic and cultural context to another might seem relatively unobjectionable. After all, no important changes to plot or overall thematics are introduced if Blast-Ended Skrewts become "Explosivins" as they do in Brazilian Portuguese. And those translation ambiguities that do introduce important alterations into the plot of the books—such as when Dumbledore's comment about Sybil Trelawney having made a total of two correct predictions becomes, in Mainland Chinese, a comment about Trelawney being a second-level (or second-rate) seer[15]—can be plausibly explained as simple mistakes rather than as efforts to localize the novels.

But even the most minor change can apparently become a cause for controversy. This is especially the case when those changes involve the "Americanization" of the novels, perhaps most clearly expressed in the alteration of the title of the first novel from *Harry Potter and the Philosopher's Stone* in the original British edition to *Harry Potter and the Sorcerer's Stone* for the American edition. Philip Nel provides an exhaustive catalogue of places in the first four novels where British terms have been altered in the American editions, including a transmutation of the British "bogies" to the American "boogers" and the British praise term "cracking" to "spanking good."[16] But Nel draws a sinister conclusion from these seemingly minor modifications: "The cumulative effect is a pervasive if subtle dulling of Rowling's original language. Losing puns, poetry, onomatopoeia, and some of the very 'British-ness' of the author's style is a form of transfiguration . . . something of the original disappears in the process."[17]

It is worth noting that in the sixth book, *Harry Potter and the Half-Blood Prince*—with teenage hormones running full tilt at Hogwarts—the U.S. edition retains the distinctly British English idiom of "snogging" in favor of American-style "making out." Interestingly, however, Rowling writes about students "hooking up" with each other, an Americanism that has entered the British youth lexicon only during the past decade. Nel's lament underscores an important point about even the most faithful of translations: moving from one linguistic and cultural context to another necessarily involves modifications from the original text. Any such modifications, however trivial, can become an opportunity for contestation, even as they simultaneously exemplify efforts to render a cultural product comprehensible in a new context. Such are the promises and perils of glocalization.

## Explanatory Translations

The shift from the faithful to the "explanatory" mode of translation has produced its own distinct engagement with the Harry Potter texts. As detailed above, this approach focuses more on the idea of imparting a general sense of the author's meaning and worries less about the linguistic idiosyncrasies in which such hermeneutics are embedded. In other words, authorial intent is "explained" in terms that make more sense in the second language, even at the expense of a certain literary fidelity. And when it comes to the Harry Potter novels, world politics and globalization intervene quite interestingly in this process.

In Harry's world, the sport with the mass appeal of soccer is Quidditch, a broom-mounted activity combining elements of rugby, shinty, basketball, and capture-the-flag. The definitive sport at Hogwarts, Quidditch also has its own World Cup in the wider magical world (which Harry attends in the opening of *Goblet of Fire*). In the Chinese translation, however, Quidditch becomes baseball, a noteworthy reproduction insofar as baseball is not, obviously, an indigenously Chinese pastime, but rather a post–World War II import most popular—largely due to American influence—in Taiwan rather than mainland China.[18] So here is the idea of popular sport, ordinarily understood as a soccer—and therefore truly global—surrogate, rendered through a neocolonial lens as baseball, with its decidedly more limited appeal, for the benefit of Taiwanese readers.

Another ambiguity relates to the ability of an increasingly bi- or multi-lingual readership to appreciate and monitor the very act of translation itself. Harry's Hebrew interlocutor, for example, speaks of her readers almost as *activist* recipients of the text, hypersensitive to any instance in which she departs from the "major original."[19] This is not a readership that requires translation in order to engage with the Potter text, but rather one that can insert itself between distinct language worlds, moving comfortably and critically across both. The growth of English as a global medium, particularly among the current generation of African and Asian youth, has meant that Harry's sojourns abroad often occur in his native language—but not always, as is made clear below, to the same effect. That is to say, even if the books are read in English, they nonetheless interact with and become enmeshed within other cultural lifeworlds.

Translation and glocalization are hence not always such seamless processes, particularly when these encounters with other cultural lifeworlds seem to produce friction. A case in point relates to the reception of the Harry Potter books in certain parts of the Muslim world, where they have raised concerns echoed, interestingly enough, by the Christian Right in the United States. On this reading the wizardry and magic of the Potter world represent a slippery slope to the occult and satanic practice in the Christian variation, and toward paganism—or *shirk*—in the Muslim account. Writing on the conservative Muslim website *Albalagh*, Khalid Baig decries the behavior of the main characters in the Potter books, noting that it is hardly surprising that their obsession with magical themes has led them away from social morality. "[T]hey lie with impunity," he points out, "use profanity, don't respect their elders, break rules regularly, and are unrepentant." His critique goes on to gesture toward parallels between magic in the book and magic performed in the world at large:

> Welcome to the world of capitalism and paganism, where superstitions and the occult reign supreme in the hearts and minds of people, and where the twin forces have forged an "alliance of the willing" that is doing its "magic" on a global scale.

Muslims are then castigated for their failure to condemn the dangerous distractions of Harry Potter and accused of colluding in bolstering the regime of global capital and commodification that lies behind the Potter "empire." Latent in his text are allusions to the socioeconomic environment surrounding the Prophet Muhammad in early Islamic history. Rampant commerce and commodity fetishism are seen to seep the spiritual and moral strength of society, trapping Muslims today in a similar state of *jahiliyya* ("ignorance") about the higher calling of their religion. In response to the common claim that, at the very least, the Harry Potter books have reacquainted a sound bite and multimedia-obsessed generation with the joys of reading, Khalid Baig asks "Reading what? It doesn't occur to [Muslims] to ask that."[20]

Commentator Dan Drezner argues that what worries Muslim and Christian fundamentalists alike about the Harry Potter books is not necessarily the Satanist/paganism issue—although those particular codes constitute a useful vocabulary of fear in which to express concern—but rather the rise of texts beyond their control, or where they feel powerless to intervene in the chain of meaning making.[21] Worry about specific issues expressed in the text is thus part of a more subtle strategy of glocalized resistance: the Harry Potter books and films are made meaningful as threats in a local context, so that they can then be opposed in the name of a more or less pure and unsullied traditional past.

Religious authorities in conservative Arab Gulf states (even the relatively liberal United Arab Emirates) have gone so far as to ban the Harry Potter books, citing their depiction of magic and witchcraft as incompatible with Islam.[22] The modern revivalist movement in eighteenth-century Arabia, led by Muhammad ibn Abdul Wahhab (hence "Wahhabism") was strongly opposed to various esoteric and mystical practices that had entered popular Islamic practice, often condemning such adherents as magicians and witches. The religious establishment in contemporary Saudi Arabia is still beholden to such views, and one will often see reports today of followers of "heterodox" (i.e., non-Wahhabi or, more accurately, non-Salafi) sects being prosecuted as "magicians" and "warlocks." The Saudi "General Presidency for the Promotion of Virtue and the Prevention of Vice," connected with the country's religious police, operates a website encouraging citizens to report incidents of neighbors practicing witchcraft.[23] But despite the activism of certain elements within the religious sector, the Potter books have been phenomenally successful in the Gulf, where the movies of the books have also played widely.

The official response in other Muslim majority countries has varied. The Iranian government has had relatively little to say on the matter, with four of the books now translated into Farsi, and the Harry Potter films playing on limited release. An active and thriving Persian-language Harry Potter blog has also been established.[24] Malaysia has expressed concern—although not in specifically religious terms—about books with ghostly and mystical themes, but the "benign" Harry Potter apparently does not warrant the intervention of the state censor.[25] As we might expect, responses to the Harry Potter phenomenon vary with different local conditions.

In countries such as Malaysia, Turkey, and India where authorities push various models of the rational developmental state, Harry Potter becomes an interesting space in which to read a global politics commonly framed in terms of "modernization" versus "traditionalism."[26] The threat here is perhaps perceived less as one to indigenous culture, but rather conversely, as something that endangers instead the modernizing developmental regime (itself often highly glocalized) to which the state is committed. According to the stewards of modernization, texts replete with spells and superstition risk reminding a local population of its all-too-recent premodern past and hence disrupting more "progressive" (i.e., rational) projects. Such sentiments are echoed in comments by Alaka Shankar of the Children's Book Trust in India: "It's ironic that sometimes the West criticizes India for its magic and witchcraft. But what is Harry Potter? It also talks about the same magical things."[27]

When it comes to glocalization, explanatory translation would hence seem to create the closest thing to a "zone of encounter" between texts—and often, as we have seen, with some ensuing politics. Themes resonate, yet still remain distinctly "other." If the faithful translation seeks to preserve as much as possible the cultural specificity of the original and the radical translation to dissolve it, explanatory translation represents a middle space of interchange. This is a mode of glocalization that lays bare as many cultural tensions as it resolves.

## Radical Translations

In some cases, the glocalization of Harry Potter has entailed far more than the isolated transmutation of an occasional name or concept. In several instances we have seen wholesale attempts to read the wider Potter cosmos into disparate cultural life worlds. The Chinese edition, for example, incorporates various elements of classical Chinese mythology into the series' backstory and iconography.[28] Calcutta in India has seen the publication of an unauthorized sequel to the first book in which Harry befriends a young Indian boy named Junto and embarks on a series of subcontinental escapades. "The way the stories have been lifted out of Bengali literature and incorporated into Harry's adventures makes it very real for Bengali children," suggests a leading Indian publisher.[29]

A more ambiguous case is provided by Russian author Dimitri Yemetz, who speaks of his character Tanja Grotter—a round-spectacled wizard school student with distinct facial marks—as a "cultural reply" rather than as a direct copy of Harry.[30] J. K. Rowling has sued in a Dutch court to prevent the publication of a translation of the Grotter books, arguing that Yemetz violated copyright law in producing his novels. Legal issues aside, the notion of a retelling of a story in a different cultural context is certainly not a novel one, and it represents nothing so much as a particularly radical form of translation—akin to producing a local version of a myth that originated abroad.

Indeed, the line of demarcation separating retellings from fakes is a very tenuous one. Before *Harry Potter and the Order of the Phoenix* was released, a bogus fifth novel—*Harry Potter and Leopard-Walk-Up-To Dragon*—was released in China; it sold briskly, even though it was rather shoddily put together and featured a plot in which Harry was transmogrified into a fat hairy dwarf by a rain of hot-and-sour soup.[31] Here we have an example of an extremely radical localization, whereby traditional Chinese images and myths are tapped to produce an original story that would resonate in a particular local context—one in which the anticipation for the next installment in the Harry Potter series could be tapped easily, even with an obvious fake.

What separates these localizations from official translations *conceptually*, except for their legal status? Both are local retellings and could easily be considered "fabrications" or "distortions" if a critic was so inclined. Indeed, both the Grotter books and the fake Chinese novels seem quite similar to the recent announcement by Marvel Comics that an authorized Indian version of *Spider-Man* would be produced. This Indian Spider-Man would be named Pavitr Prabhakar (a close transliteration of "Peter Parker") but would obtain his powers from a Hindu holy man rather than from the bite of a radioactive spider.[32] This kind of blurring of edges between cultural contexts requires something like the power of the state and its legal apparatus in order to temporarily arrest it, and to distinguish between acceptable and unacceptable efforts to retell a popular story in a novel context.

Egyptian poet Ahmed Shablool goes even further, citing a distinct "eastern influence" in J. K. Rowling's formulation of the philosopher's stone in book one of the series.[33] His essay seeks to draw lines of continuity between the world of Harry Potter and the evolution of science in Islamic history. For Shablool, readers would do well to recognize the Philosopher's Stone as the bequest of numerous Arab chemists dating back to the eighth century. Shablool also wants to naturalize wizardry in a Qur'anic worldview, suggesting that the Muslim holy book makes numerous references to wizardry. Rowling's treatment of the Philosopher's Stone is depicted as closely mirroring that of the classical Arab alchemists, as a potentially powerful and divisive force that must be kept hidden from common knowledge and use; hence Dumbledore's destruction of the relic at the end of the volume. In Shablool's radical translation, then, the Harry Potter cosmos becomes an intrinsic extension of Arab scientific history—and the Abrahamaic saga more broadly—a wholly familiar world of tinker chemists, magicians, and enchanted wands.

In focusing on particular aspects of the novels and then setting those features in different contexts, Shablool's exercise in radical translation seems virtually indistinguishable from the widespread practice of "fanfic," or fan fiction, whereby individual readers undertake to create their own tales that depart from the text of books by envisioning novel situations or even novel characters. A number of these stories are available online, and they take the basic storyline of the Harry Potter books in some unexpected directions—including developing female characters such as Hermione in a more explicitly heroic direction.[34] In contrast to her reaction to the "Tanja Grotter" novels, J. K. Rowling recently expressed her *support* for these activities, as long as the stories were not obscene and were clearly identified as not having been written by her.[35] While legal issues surrounding the use of domain names featuring the name "Harry Potter" continue, the practice of fans writing their own Harry Potter stories is flourishing.

The controversies over radical translations underscore a fundamental point about cultural products that travel over significant boundaries: preserving a homogenous central meaning to those products demands deliberate social and political action. Even though the original Harry Potter novels were quite rooted in a specific cultural context, they can be and have been rewritten in numerous ways. While posing thorny questions about intellectual property, this rewriting also appears to be a not insignificant part of the process that gave the novels their worldwide appeal in the first place. It makes little sense to enquire into whether the Harry Potter who makes his way into India or China is "the same" as the Harry Potter known to British or American readers, because the answer will always be both yes and no. Glocalization simultaneously presents us with worldwide distribution *and* with innumerable local variations. Radical translations, and struggles over the acceptability of those translations, are only the most extreme examples of this process.

## Conclusion

An emphasis on glocalization allows us to understand the emergence of globality as a process of cultural differentiation rather than as an effect of cultural homogenization.[36] Through their multiple and diverse renderings—

linguistic and cultural—the Harry Potter books serve as a prime example of how a cultural object with worldwide distribution and exhaustive marketing can nonetheless come to lead a polysemic and fractured existence. The examples rehearsed above suggest that it would be inaccurate to view Rowling's books as culturally invasive emblems of neo-imperial capital, or as agents of Westernization *qua* Potterization. Rather, there is something far more nuanced going on here, and its significance lies in the various idioms of translation we detail above.

Translation, we argue, goes both ways. Far more than simply the reproduction of a text in a language other than its original, translation is also a space in which meanings are mediated and adapted—or, very often, wholly new meanings created. Translation sets a text in motion, rendering it malleable and open to recontextualization in disparate cultural worlds. Translation occurs in various forms, each with significant qualitative differences. These we have outlined above, namely the literal, explanatory, and radical modes of translation. To thematize translation in such terms helps to unpack and reveal the multifaceted nature of glocalization—itself, like globalization, an aggregate concept too often and too easily rendered in lowest common denominator terms. As a cultural phenomenon truly transnational in scope, the Harry Potter books offer a useful space in which to explore the interplay between "worldwide" as a descriptor of geographic reach and "global" as an indicator of cultural universalism. As we have demonstrated through numerous examples, the worlding of Harry Potter has not been the same as the globalization of Harry Potter. Throughout his travels, Harry has been actively embraced by other languages and cultures —but certainly not verbatim (except in rare cases of literal translation), often critically, and usually with a considerable degree of interpretation and local adaptation. Put simply, Harry Potter abroad transcends the cultural specificity of his initial (British) English articulation and comes to mean different things to different people.

Yet lest our argument be understood as a claim that this glocalization serves to disrupt and subvert the dominance of the global, we should point out that the corporate world has practiced "localization" for decades, and that "postmodern" insights about the importance of local conditions animate the literature on marketing and business management.[37] An appreciation for the subtle ways that cultural products are translated into different contexts demonstrates neither that the local is able to liberate itself from the forces of global capitalism, nor that we have nothing to fear from the worldwide marketing of books, films, and other such products to create something like a single worldwide culture. Instead, our analysis suggests that we need to be cautious in defining the challenges posed by the increasing unification of world markets and the enhanced interchange between world societies. Homogenization, we suggest, is not likely, as widely circulated products like the Harry Potter novels undergo a number of processes of translation as they interact with and are inserted into local cultural contexts. Whether the glocalization that sustains this worldwide circulation represents the triumph of hybridity or the dominance of a more subtle form of capitalist hegemony is an entirely different question. But the prelude to answering that question is asking the question clearly, and the careful empirical analysis of worldwide phenomena—like the Harry Potter novels and films—gives us the resources to do just this.

## Notes

1. Free Press Staff 2004.
2. Bhushan 2003.
3. Sreekumaran 2004.
4. Chase-Dunn and Hall 1997, 52–55.
5. Ang 1985.
6. Weber 1930 [1992], 123.
7. Baehr 2001, 164.
8. Weber 1949, 92–94.
9. It is interesting to note, however, that the Chinese edition includes a footnote to explain cornflakes (Goldstein 2005).
10. Remí 2004.
11. Press 2003.
12. Remí 2004.
13. Wang 2003.
14. See, for example, www.myglobe.com.ph/portal/forum/topic.asp?TOPIC_ID=2983&whichpage=15.
15. Pringle 2004.
16. Nel 2002, 275–77.
17. Nel 2002, 282.
18. University of Surrey 2001.
19. Press 2003.
20. Baig 2003.
21. Drezner 2003.
22. BBC 2002a.
23. See www.hesbah.com [in Arabic]. The *hesbah* is a state institution charged with ensuring and encouraging social conduct within the boundaries of religious law.
24. See www.harrypotter2003.persianblog.com/.

25. IOL Staff 2003.
26. See, inter alia, Lerner 1958 and Nandy 1987.
27. Bhushan 2003.
28. BBC 2002b.
29. BBC 2003.
30. Schofield 2002.
31. On the Media 2002.
32. Srinivasan 2005.
33. Shablool 2003.
34. Bond and Michelson 2003, 117–18.
35. Waters 2004.
36. Robertson 1992.
37. Hardt and Negri 2000, 150–53.

# Foreign Yet Familiar

**3**

## International Politics and the Reception of Potter in Turkey and Sweden

ANN TOWNS AND BAHAR RUMELILI

ORE THAN FIVE YEARS HAVE NOW PASSED since the first Harry Potter book was released in Swedish in 1999 and four years since it was released in Turkish. The five books have made an enormous splash in both countries. The first three books alone sold over one million copies and saw large lending rates at the public libraries in Sweden, a country of barely nine million. In Turkey, where book sales rarely exceed one hundred thousand, the first four books had sold over seven hundred thousand copies in September 2003. What is more, the Turkish publisher of the Potter books was the first in the world to translate the fifth book. With so many children (and adults) reading these books, it is not surprising that they have generated a great deal of discussion that asks what these books really mean to Turkish and Swedish children. What kinds of values and worldviews do the books relay? ask reviewers, culture critics, and others.

Although Harry Potter's story itself takes place in the magical world of Hogwarts, the reviews and discussions on Potter in Turkey and Sweden are inevitably mired in questions of real world politics in at least two ways. First, the critical discussions draw upon and reimagine national identity. Swedish and Turkish reviewers and critics must contend with the fact that Harry Potter is a foreign piece of literature—its foreignness specifically identified as "British" in Sweden, and more generally construed as "Western" in Turkey. This directs the discussions at least partially toward identifying that which is interpreted as foreign about the world of Potter, and situating it in relation to phenomena seen as familiar to the national self. Critical studies of foreign policy as well as the recent literature on nationalism have underscored that national/state identities do not exist as given and have to be reproduced through practices of differentiation.[1] Therefore, these discussions around what is familiar versus foreign in a global cultural product like Harry Potter provide excellent data to analyze the construction of Swedish and Turkish national identities in relation to Others.

More specifically, and as we see below, the division of the world into the West and its various Others is foundational in the reading of Potter in both countries. However, with Sweden and Turkey situated rather differently in relation to this West, the West serves dissimilar functions in the reviews. This point thereby draws upon and validates the insights of postcolonial theories of international relations that emphasize the importance of imaginations of the West in nation-building.[2] Whereas the Swedish debates operate with the West as a constitutive background condition and foreground the differences between Sweden and Britain, the Turkish discussions put the West at the center and agonize over how to read Turkey, the West, and the East in Potter.

Second, discussions on particular themes, characters, and events in the Harry Potter books reveal the predominant understandings about international life and difference. We have selected two broad themes through which we analyze the international politics of the books' reception: economics and gender. The dimension of economic relations (including the class themes prevalent in Harry Potter, and commercialism and globalization as conditions of its production) appears to have triggered the most critical debate about the books in both countries and it therefore serves as a first-rate entry-point of analysis of how the nationally familiar is constructed.[3] We are interested in analyzing how the economic dimension of Harry Potter books is perceived in the diverse socioeconomic settings of Sweden and Turkey, and the extent to which these perceptions function as markers of national identity.

Similarly, the status of women, or their relation to men, has been a crucial component in the construction of nationhood since the early nineteenth century.[4] Although women have been understood as productive of the nation in several different ways—for example, as biological producers of soldiers and as transmitters of national culture to children—we investigate the symbolic importance of the status of women in drawing the line between the foreign and the familiar. The perceived situation of women is often used as a shortcut to assess the nature and familiarity of an entire society and thus whether that society is similar to or different from one's own.[5] This, we presume, might also be the case in the Turkish and Swedish interpretations of Harry Potter.

Along the lines of treating popular culture as data—the third approach to studying popular culture presented in the introduction—we regard the media's treatment of Potter as one arena where national identities and understandings about the international are negotiated and defended. As our empirical material, we therefore use the 1998–2004 reviews and articles in the main Swedish and Turkish daily papers, focusing specifically on the reviews that treat the economic or gender dimensions of the Potter book. As interesting additional material, we add some comments from Internet fan site discussions of the books.

It is important to keep in mind that our analysis is selective and focused. We do not purport to carry out a comprehensive analysis that tells the whole story of how Harry Potter was received in Turkey and Sweden. We ask the following two questions of the reviews and discussions: (1) What phenomena are constituted as foreign or nationally familiar, and on what basis? And (2) What international stratifications appear in the reviews, and how is the national self represented in relation to these international divisions?

## Sweden

Since Harry Potter first arrived on the Swedish literary scene in 1999, the discussions of the books share a presumption of their Western origin and nature, a West within which Sweden is firmly located. All the treatments and analyses of the books take for granted that they come from an environment that is fundamentally familiar to a Swedish reader. Despite the "totally different environment," as one critic states of the books, "most of the students and teachers [in the Potter books] think in a way that we can understand and identify with."[6] These are Western and European books, and as such, they get treated as artifacts of a cultural framework that encompasses Sweden.

At the same time, the Potter books are regarded as foreign and the "different environment" does not simply refer to the books' magical life world. Indeed, while certainly seen as a Western artifact and thereby something shared and familiar, Potter is also construed as an Anglo-Saxon phenomenon in contrast with the Nordic world. In the most general genre discussions, for instance, the books are identified as stemming from "the fantasy genre, which is very influential in Anglo-Saxon parts of the world."[7] As such, they are commonly compared with other Anglo-Saxon works, such as the British fantasy books of Tolkien and C. S. Lewis.

There is a long and lively history of differentiating Sweden as a Nordic or Germanic society distinct from the Anglo-Saxon tradition. It is noteworthy that the Potter discussions see a particularly stark distancing of Sweden from the Anglo-Saxon world around the question of the books' treatment of class and gender. Class and gender hierarchies are held forth as exceptionally problematic and *foreign* aspects of what is otherwise largely hailed as worthwhile children's books. More specifically, the questionable gender relations are read as symptomatic of two characteristics held to be typical of the Anglo-Saxon world: conservatism and, to a lesser extent, commercialism. Indeed, the allegedly warped and unequal gender relations of the Potter books are understood as reflective of a society that is thoroughly saturated by conservatism and commercialized social life, presumably unlike Sweden. To delve deeper into how class and gender in Potter are construed—and these are virtually always treated as problems of the books—we turn to each of these characteristics.

## British Conservatism and
## Swedish Progressive Egalitarianism

To understand how the alleged gender inequality of the Harry Potter series becomes interpreted as a foreign problem, we must first look into the Swedish reading of the books as relics of Anglo conservatism. Throughout most of the post–World War II period, Swedes seldom discussed themselves as a people with a national culture.[8] Instead, economic production and class antagonism were seen as the primary driving forces and shapers of the world, domestic and international alike. Although this social democratic lens was weakened during the 1990s, when conceptions of culture and cultural difference made headway together with more liberal conceptualizations of the world, the attentiveness to class inequalities and Left-Right ideological divides remains pervasive. As we will see, it is also through this lens that gender emerges as a problem to the Swedish reviewers of Harry Potter.

The conservatism of the Potter books seems to have become taken-for-granted knowledge about Rowling's authorship in Sweden. One aspect of this conservatism concerns the books' acceptance and normalization of class inequality. Swedish university students can be overheard joking about the four houses of Hogwarts representing class society: Slytherin as the privileged upper class, Ravenclaw as the intelligentsia, Hufflepuff as the industrious bourgeoisie, and Gryffindor as the brave working class. The young magicians "become alienated from their own essence" at Hogwarts, an *Aftonbladet* review similarly claims, thereby alluding to Marx's work on the alienation of man under capitalism.[9]

The conservatism is primarily traced to the alleged elitism and authoritarianism of Hogwarts as a boarding school. There is widespread concern among reviewers that the Potter books romanticize the hierarchical authority relations of boarding schools among Swedish children. Even the conservative daily *Svenska Dagbladet* prints that "the books contain an alarming celebration of a conservative and oppressive school form."[10] "Under the surface, the story is not particularly generous but rather whiningly moralistic, slyly authoritarian and punitive," a *Göteborgs-Posten* critic similarly contends.[11] As is typical in authoritarian settings, weakness is despised at Hogwarts, where students becomes "afraid to show weakness (which is Harry Potter's greatest fear. Nobody has told him that weakness is OK)."[12]

The authoritarian world at Hogwarts is understood to be sustained by conformism, which is encouraged by the rules and values of the school. No creatively or democratically insubordinate children who seek ways to challenge hierarchy and bring about an alternative order are formed by reading Harry Potter, in other words. There is no promotion of civic disobedience or imaginative solutions to the problems generated by rigidity and order. No need for authoritarian regimes to censor these books, if one were to adopt the Swedish interpretations. Puzzling over what makes the books so popular, a review in *Aftonbladet* notes that

> the children at Hogwarts are involved in some sort of grade frenzy, they harass one another, and they compete in a brutal sport named Quidditch. Harry Potter's highest wish is not to resist evil or find the way to bliss but to win the Quidditch goblet. That is also the only wish of his coach.[13]

Indeed, despite appearances, there is virtually nothing rebellious or defiant about the Potter books in the eyes of Swedish reviewers. "The book transmits a conformist dream of transformation, from a failed to a successful citizen. Is there really nothing more wonderful to dream about than to scrape together as many points as possible in your world's version of order and behavior?"[14] Similar thoughts lead another reviewer to state that, in essence, "there are no ethics and morality in Rowling's world of magicians."[15]

Swedish children seem to be of a somewhat different opinion. Rather than authoritarian conformism, their discussions point out and celebrate instances of upheaval in the Potter books. As one "Pansy-lover" explains, Pansy Parkinson is "the best! She is so cool, because she goes up against

Harry!" Another child states: "I like Hedwig because she is charming, cool and cute and she shows that Harry can't do whatever he wants to her by snapping at his hand." Like the discussions in the daily papers, the children seem to value a defiant attitude toward authority. In contrast with the book critics, they actually find cases of such behavior. The class inequalities do not go unnoticed by the children either, however. One girl explains that Gyllenroy Lockman (the Swedish Gilderoy Lockhart) is her least favorite character because "he is a cheesy upper class sissy."[16]

In the daily papers, the normalization of elitism, authoritarianism, and conformism are identified as three of the components of the conservatism of the Potter series. This conservatism, as we see below, is presented as typical of British society, in contrast with the more egalitarian Swedish life. Here, it is worth pointing to a fourth and related aspect of conservatism identified by Swedish reviewers: the denigrating imagery of common people. In a review titled "The Hatred of Normality" in *Aftonbladet*, we read that

> Rowling teaches children the wrong things. The really evil beings in the Potter books are regular people, "muggles." The normal ones. There are no limits to Rowling's contempt for these evil mediocre folks, especially Harry's spoiled cousin Dudley. He is described as fat and porky, a pig and a gorilla. This is particularly strange since the books are presumably targeted to (and about) people like Dudley—normal, high-consuming children.[17]

A *Svenska Dagbladet* review agrees. "Rowling wallows in scurrilous portraits of the middle class family. Their TV-watching and disgusting gluttony seems to make up their essence, in addition to their fear of the unknown."[18] This defense of regular people, of ordinariness and of mediocrity, can be read as yet another anti-elitist statement, along with the others discussed above. However, it can also be read as a defense rooted in Swedish national identity as average and regular. Swedish nationhood is prevalently constructed around notions of Swedes as ordinary and even mediocre, as a fairly bland bunch of folks who struggle with life's dull chores and who take pleasure in rather mundane events such as TV-watching. Rowling's contempt for the common people may thus strike doubly at a Swedish audience, displaying at once an elitist disdain for regular people and a foreign dislike of Swedish blandness.

In sum, what is of particular importance for our purposes is that the conservative nature of Hogwarts is understood as characteristic of Britain, in contrast with the egalitarian and nonauthoritarian ideals of Swedish schools. Whereas this rejection of Potter conservatism as foreign is often implicit, many of the reviews state so explicitly. "These boarding school portrayals are of the typical English genre," as one critic contends.[19] An article in *Expressen* elaborates:

> For a Swedish reader, the boarding school is hopefully just an exotic element. Many British children unfortunately recognize this hard world filled with accomplishment anxieties, competition and bullying. Sure, the good people of the school get Rowling's sympathies, but she herself adopts the conservative environment with its antiquated class and gender structures.[20]

## Gender and British Puritanism

The Swedish interpretations of gender in Potter develop out of the broader ideas about British class society. And if the general conservatism of Potter is rebuffed as British and thus foreign, the books' gender norms are subjected to particularly forceful disapproval and rejection. An *Expressen* review states that 2001 was a year of "encouraging fairytales about insecure boys who gain self-confidence and grow to become proud heroes in the most magical ways."[21] The critic goes on to ask "where are the chics?" and laments that these stories are about "men, men, men or rather boys, boys, boys. Hermione may be important to Harry Potter, but she is still a sidekick" and concludes with a call for action: "more female fairytale heroes for the people."

Time and again, Rowling is charged with reproducing conservative British gender structures that subordinate women and stereotypically female characteristics to male ideals of courage and competition. Because of the British heritage,

> it is of course Harry's female friend that is the tiring good girl and orderly one in the gang. Sure, she gets to demonstrate how important theoretical knowledge is in adventurous situations, and she does develop somewhat along the way to become a little bit tougher, but this is still the boys' world and particularly the world of Harry Potter.[22]

A *Svenska Dagbladet* reviewer similarly contends:

> what irritates me is Rowling's portrayal of female characters, particularly Harry's friend Hermione. She is the most diligent, well-read and understanding one and she follows all the rules. Her stereotypically female ambitions are depicted from a condescending male perspective.[23]

The reviewer then draws parallels with two British children's authors—Enid Blyton and C. S. Lewis—who have become representative of sexist and British children's literature:

> The portrayal of the best friend Ron's mother, Mrs. Weasley, who comes with gifts, self-knitted sweaters and consoling hugs is in full parity with Blyton's or C. S. Lewis's view of women. Rowling's female magicians are accordingly scatterbrained, overprotective or responsible for care and healing. Well, if you want a vision of gender relations that is more modern than the 1950s, then keep on searching.[24]

In other words, the gender relations of Potter are seen as antiquated and something of the past. The identification of Potter and the British values represented therein as old-fashioned is a consistent theme and one that draws meaning from the widespread view of Sweden as the most advanced and modern society in terms of the status of women.[25] A review in *Dagens Nyheter*, Sweden's largest daily paper, states that "Harry's friends Ron Weasley and Hermione Granger are given a lot of room, which is naturally right given that he largely owes his successes to them. J. K. Rowling knows that single heroes are hopelessly out-of-date."[26] On the note of modern qualities, the author then states that

> Rowling has ended up in the customary gender clichés, however. Sure, Hogwarts is mixed and the sex distribution among the students is relatively equal. But this is still the world of and for men and boys. And despite the fact that Harry owes Hermione a lot, she is portrayed as a pedantic study animal, who loves to cite the school rules and teach her friends about proper behaviour. At least in the first two books.
>
> J. K. Rowling lets go a little in *Harry Potter and the Prisoner from Azkaban*. That is a good sign for the future and it is of course necessary to successfully defeat Voldemort. But so far the relationship male-female is like 1 to 10.[27]

If the validation of male over female is presented as characteristic of British society and thus alien to Swedish values, so is the lack of more explicit sexual contents in the Potter books. Concepts of "nature" as the absence of artificial and thus inhibiting cultural constructs have long been prevalent in Sweden. Narratives of Swedes as a people that has largely been sexually liberated from cultural norms and of Sweden as a place where sex and nudity is considered "natural" are tremendously common. Victorian society and British (and American) Puritanism have served as crucial points of contrast in the construal of Sweden as the place of a natural and healthy attitude toward sexuality and the body. Such views are reproduced in the reviews of Harry Potter, as we can see in one critic's contention that

> Harry Potter is a brand that follows its readership—when the readers get older, he gets older. So the new thing in the *Phoenix*-book is teenage frustration and sexism. Harry now falls in love for real with Cho Chang and is allowed to kiss her, even if that, in true Anglo-Puritan spirit, is not depicted. All the Harry Potter books deny carnality and you wonder where in the castle—or even *if*—the little magicians masturbate, but that will probably never be a sellable theme for Rowling.[28]

# Turkey

Like their Swedish counterparts, the Turkish discussions of Harry Potter share a presumption of the Western nature and origin of the books. However, this is a West in which Turkey, unlike Sweden, is not firmly located. Prevailing Turkish understandings of national identity uncritically associate the West with modernity, progress, and civilization, upholding the West as a model for Turkey. Turkey is generally differentiated from other Islamic and Middle Eastern countries as being more modern and Western. However, the aspirations for a Western identity come up against the fact that Turkey is not unequivocally recognized as a part of the West. Hence, in Turkey, all sorts of encounters with the West—products, people, and ideas—become occasions to demonstrate the Western credentials of the country.[29]

The Harry Potter books have posed some difficult challenges for the positioning of Turkish national identity between the West and the East. On the one hand, as the latest example of Western children's literature, the Harry Potter books are seen as a model to be emulated. On the other hand, the books contain elements that clearly contradict what the West is understood to be. For instance, reviewers note that Harry Potter is a retreat to the pre-modern literary form of the fairy tale and beliefs in superstition, magic, and witchcraft. Such allegedly pre-modern elements are seen as Eastern rather than typical of Western literature. The discussions of Potter demonstrate uncertainties about how to portray Turkey as Western in relation to Harry Potter. Hence, Turkish commentators maintain an uneasy relationship with Harry Potter, fluctuating between admiration and mockery, identification and resistance.

## *Imitating, Mocking, and Resisting the West*

In dealing with the challenges posed by the elements of witchcraft and magic in Harry Potter, some commentators salvage the West by characterizing the superstitious elements as "more typically Eastern." Sevin Okyay, the translator of the Potter books to Turkish, argues in an interview that "actually this book is not so novel to us. We are a nation with genie men. The Eastern culture is more at home with these."[30] Similarly, the main daily paper *Hurriyet* reports:

> The adventures of the little wizard Harry Potter have been around us for centuries. From the pig fat spilled on beds to separate lovers, to the prayers read on 41 chickpeas to win hearts. There are the tales with genies and fairies, and the "*elemtere fis kem gozlere sis*" [a saying to ward off evil]. [Our wizards] do not learn about these at the Hogwarts School of Wizardry and Witchcraft. They hide their identities, they do not appear on TVs. But whoever needs them can find their numbers even in corner stores.[31]

Such comments uphold the superiority of science to superstition and present the West as more "advanced" than the East. In identifying Harry Potter as familiar to Turkey because of the magic and supernatural ingredients, they underscore that what is purely fiction in the West becomes a lived reality in Turkey. As long as the superiority of the "West" and "modernity" are established in this fashion, the identity of Turkey as a nation that aspires to a Western identity can be maintained.

Other news items present Turkey as superior by ridiculing the West. The negative reactions to Harry Potter in the West, for example, always become news stories in the Turkish press. The news that "a church in New Mexico is preparing to burn Harry Potter books because they challenge the belief in God" appeared in all major papers in Turkey in December 2001. Pointing out the irrational and pre-modern behavior of U.S. actors, *Hurriyet* likened this to the witch hunts of the Middle Ages.[32] In January 2003, at least two such stories made the news: a Baptist church had accused Harry Potter of moving children away from religion and toward the devil,[33] and a Greek-Cypriot church sought to ban the Harry Potter movie because it promoted evil, wizardry, and fraud.[34] There is no mention of the many banned political books in Turkey in conjunction with these news stories. The publication of these news items thus helps present Turkey as more Western and tolerant, as nobody in Turkey has resorted to such measures against Harry Potter.

Yet others find in Potter the occasion to underscore the richness and distinctiveness of Turkish culture. An interview with the author of the Turkish fantasy novel *Kral Suban* in the conservative daily *Zaman* is a good illustration. In the interview, the author of the novel objects to the charge that fantasy is not characteristic of Turkish literature: "We actually have the richest sources of fantasy literature, from *Deli Dumrul* [a character in Turkic legends] to stories in the Quran."[35] Such comments presume that the fantasy genre constitutes something new to Western literature, and they do not call into question what such presumably pre-modern features might tell us about the West. Instead, the fact that Western literature has currently embraced fantasy is presented as evidence of the inherent richness and value of Turkish culture, which was not duly appreciated before.

There are, finally, those who see the Potter books as a threat to Turkish identity and culture. In January 2004, the Harry Potter phenomenon was brought before the Turkish Grand National Assembly by the opposition party deputy Basoglu. He contended:

> The Anatolian culture has been neglected for the last 50 years. Now it is under cultural imperialism's attack with movies and books. We need to defend our culture. In 1950, we took a proposal to the US to shoot the movie of *Keloglan* [Turkish folk child character]. Even though we were going to pay for the costs, our proposal was rejected thrice. This calls for thinking. It is because they have Walt Disney. Economic imperialism is coming with cultural imperialism.[36]

It is interesting that to defend Turkish culture against cultural imperialism, Basoglu proposes to replace Western heroes with Turkish heroes. In the interpretations above, the defense of Turkish identity entailed tolerating and even imitating Harry Potter. In this case, however, it necessitates the rejection of Potter.

## Potter and the Challenges to Inequality

A striking contrast with the reception of Potter in Sweden is how the class and gender themes are interpreted. From newspaper reviews to Internet fan sites, the class theme is what is most readily noticed by Turkish readers. There is, on the other hand, a general silence about the gender relations in Potter. In a country with one of the worst income distributions in the world, commentators do not question class inequality as such. Instead, they commend the book series for conveying to children that while prevalent, class and status do not determine everything. One commentator argues that "class within class" is a prevalent theme in Anglo-Saxon children's literature, contending that the books are so popular around the world precisely because they show that solidarity and friendship are possible across classes and various other classifications.

> It is not a pure coincidence that the fair and reasonable Harry happens to fall into the same class with the common, red-haired and freckled Ron and

the brainy Hermione, and refuses the friendship offer of the proto-fascist squat aristocrat Malfoy. . . . When Harry took the side of his friend, Ron, against the "bad" Malfoy, I am sure all children (and some adults) murmured a "good-for-you" and this is exactly what I mean.[37]

The Turkish children who respond to the question "Why do I like Harry Potter?" in an Internet fan site also lend support to such comments. For example, a female reader notes that:

[Harry] does not discriminate among his friends (as an example, he is friends with Ron whose family is not that rich). He stands up to people regardless of their rank and status.[38]

In addition, Potter is associated with and cherished for the possibility of class mobility. Inequality is not necessarily permanent, in other words, as Potter and Rowling herself show that it is possibly to move from poverty to wealth. J. K. Rowling's ascent from poor single motherhood to riches is likened to the orphan Harry's magical move from the muggle world to Hogwarts. That Rowling is now richer than the British queen has made the news in top newspapers across the country.[39] A local version of this rags-to-riches story has been produced for the translator of Harry Potter books to Turkish, Sevin Okyay. Turkish newspapers report that while previously only a poor writer, she has been able to afford to buy an apartment with the money she has received from the Harry Potter translations.

Data on the class backgrounds of Potter readers in Turkey is not readily available. However, it would be safe to assume that the participants in the Potter Internet fan sites are overwhelmingly from middle- and upper-class families. Among these fans, there is a discernable discomfort with the social implications of income differences within Turkish society. There is an appreciation for the fact that Harry Potter and J. K. Rowling are both self-made. "We also want to exist only with our own talents," a female reader declares.[40] Another reader makes explicit that she, like Harry, does not choose her friends on the basis of class: "It is as if Ron is the son of our upstairs neighbor, and Hermione is the daughter of the doorman whom I regularly play with." Sevin Okyay, the translator of the Potter books, agrees: "Harry became a hero although he was condemned to be a loser. He is the hero of our times. He has not inherited this from someone."[41]

If the interpretation of class inequality differed dramatically between Sweden and Turkey, the Potter books were nonetheless seen as products of commercialism in both countries. In Sweden, this commercialism was mostly upheld as typical of Great Britain, but many commentators pointed to the spread of global capitalism as a precondition for the success of the Potter books. In Turkey as well, the books have also become subject to discussions of the implications of globalization and global capitalist relations. Readers and commentators all agree that Harry Potter owes a big portion of its success, both globally and locally, to its effective promotion strategy. For example, the first company that published the Harry Potter books in Turkish could not sell more than ten thousand copies. When the current publisher, *Yapi Kredi Yayinlari*, took over, however, the sales soared as a result of successful marketing and promotion.[42] The aggressive promotion campaigns of the Harry Potter books engender feelings of being targeted and lead commentators to note that

> We are being bombarded with brands, not with books. It is apparent that children are the new targets of the publishing sector. For the last few years, women were the main targets. All stories, novels, memoirs, biographies, etc. were written for the female reader. Now the target age has declined, but apparently, the sphere of influence has widened.[43]

A reader, commenting on a promotional news article on Harry Potter over the Internet, also complains:

> Isn't profit the only motive behind the serialization of these books? The middle-income Turkish families, who do not spare any money from their kids' education, are being deceived with advertisements and marketing.[44]

In another very sophisticated commentary, a commentator links the global popularity of the Harry Potter books to the rising consumerism in the new world order:

> What does it indicate that the whole world is reading the same tale(s)? It is not enough to just say it is globalization. What we need to talk about is how tales have become the central discourse in our global village, incorporating magical elements, the absolute good and evil, and promoting infancy as the main identity for their readers. In today's information society and global communications age, literature is returning to its pre-history, to the tale, a product of oral culture and communal order. The oral tale, with all its mystery, magic, and wizardry, serves to unite the community and reproduce the belief, knowledge, moral, and ideological structures that the community is based upon. In the new world order, we are retreating to the age of the tales. How befitting for the Consumers International![45]

Interestingly, the critical undertone disappears when Turkish newspapers report, with surprise and pride, their finding that the global Potter has

Turkish influences. *Radikal* reports that a carpet manufacturer from Turkey is producing the Harry Potter theme carpets for Warner Brothers. The report proudly underscores how Turkish companies are now successfully participating in the global webs of production.[46] It also turns out that the shoes used in Harry Potter movies are traditional Turkish *cariks*, handmade in a three-square-meter store in the traditional coppersmiths' bazaar in Kahramanmaras, Turkey.[47] This provides the occasion to discuss the negative impacts of technology and industrialization on traditional crafts, which are continued by a dwindling number of dedicated artisans.

Finally, with regard to the theme of gender relations, there is barely any discussion of gender in the Potter books in Turkey. This is surprising since Turkey, like Sweden, routinely uses the "status of women" to distinguish itself from other states. Turkey claims cultural and civilizational superiority by having "advanced" gender relations specifically in relation to the Arab states and the rest of the Islamic world. However, because of the Western origin of the Harry Potter books, and because of the automatic association of the West with modernity in Turkey, the gender relations within Potter books are simply *presumed* to be advanced. Had the books been of Middle Eastern origin, their gender relations would have been subjected to closer scrutiny in Turkey. However, the media's depictions of J. K. Rowling have evoked at least the following commentary, which criticizes how the established hierarchies of class and modernity/tradition configure gender roles in Turkey:

> Every news story about the [Harry Potter] book stresses this about its author: "Seven years ago, [J. K. Rowling] was an unemployed single mother. She would sit in cafes and take notes while her baby slept. Now she is one of the richest women in England." Why is everyone so surprised by this? Because in our repository, we do not carry such an image of a "mother." In our minds, a successful working mother hires a full-time nanny from Moldova, dresses herself up in suits, and works. . . . What surprises me is that the whole world thinks that a woman cannot produce anything worthwhile while raising a baby. Most probably Ms. Rowling did not have a leather briefcase while writing Harry Potter. Most probably, she carried a bag full of diapers and baby wipes. Now tell me; has not Ms. Rowling shattered our established stereotypes?[48]

## Conclusion

In selecting the divergent national settings of Sweden and Turkey for comparative analysis, we have elucidated how a global artifact like Harry Potter can be interpreted and handled in states that are differently situated in international society. In Sweden, the Potter books are seen as a Western body of literature and in that sense apparently something so shared and familiar that its Western nature needs no elaboration or commentary. Instead, the discussions of Harry Potter construct a sharp boundary between the Swedish self-image of egalitarianism and the class and gender hierarchies seen as characteristic of Britain. Indeed, and in rather dramatic contrast with the reception in Turkey, the gender and class dimensions of the books are interpreted not only as oppressively archaic but as symptomatic of *foreign* forms of repressive social relations.

In Turkey, on the other hand, reviews of Harry Potter manifest the postcolonial tendency to simultaneously mimic and mock the Western Other. The foreignness of Harry Potter is negated and de-emphasized when Turkey is to be depicted as Western, and pronounced when the West is to be criticized and ridiculed. A systematic analysis of reviews and news about Potter shows that international cultural products, like Harry Potter, rightly constitute a terrain of international politics—not only of cultural politics, but also the politics of identity-formation around class and gender.

## Notes

1. See, for example, David Campbell, *Writing Security* (Minneapolis: University of Minnesota Press, 1992) and Bahar Rumelili, "Constructing Identity and Relating to Difference: Understanding the EU's Mode of Differentiation," *Review of International Studies* 30, no. 1 (January 2004): 27–47.

2. For an extensive review, see Phillip Darby and A. J. Paolini, "Bridging International Relations and Postcolonialism," *Alternatives* 19 (1994): 371–97.

3. See the contribution of Patricia Goff to this volume.

4. Nira Yuval-Davis, *Gender and Nation* (London: Sage, 1997).

5. Ann Towns, "Norms and Inequality in International Society: The International Politics of Women and the State," PhD dissertation. University of Minnesota, 2004.

6. Per Beskow, "Fenomenet Harry Potter" [The Harry Potter Phenomenon], *Signum* 9 (2000): 36–39.

7. Beskow, "Fenomenet Harry Potter" [The Harry Potter Phenomenon].

8. Billy Ehn, "Kamouflerad försvenskning" [Camouflaged Swedenization], in *Försvenskningen av Sverige: det nationellas förvandlingar* [*The Swedenization of Sweden: The Transformations of the National*], ed. Billy Ehn et al. (Stockholm: Natur and Kultur, 1993), 234–67.

9. Maja Lundgren, "Hatet mot de vanliga" [Hatred of the Common People], *Aftonbladet,* 26 March 2001.

10. Andrew Casson, "Det väsentliga är hur frågorna ställs" [Importance Lies in How the Questions Are Posed], *Svenska Dagbladet,* 13 December 1999, 13.

11. Aase Berg, "Smygauktoritärt under trollkarlskappan" [Veiled Authoritarianism behind the Wizard's Cloak], *Göteborgs-posten,* 11 January 2000, 40.

12. Lundgren, "Hatet mot de vanliga" [Hatred of the Common People].

13. Lundgren, "Hatet mot de vanliga" [Hatred of the Common People].

14. Berg, "Smygauktoritärt" [Veiled Authoritarianism].

15. Lundgren, "Hatet mot de vanliga" [Hatred of the Common People].

16. www.harrypotter.nu/besokarnas/veckansbrev.html.

17. Lundgren, "Hatet mot de vanliga" [Hatred of the Common People].

18. Kristin Hallberg, "Potter—dragplåster mellan jul och rea" [Potter—Attraction between Christmas and the Sales], *Svenska Dagbladet,* 24 January 2001, 54.

19. Hallberg, "Potter."

20. Maria Sundvall, "Sagolikt år för pojkar" [Dreamy Year for Boys]. *Expressen* 29 December 2001, 2.

21. Sundvall, "Sagolikt år för pojkar" [Dreamy Year for Boys].

22. Sundvall, "Sagolikt år för pojkar" [Dreamy Year for Boys].

23. Hallberg, "Potter."

24. Hallberg, "Potter."

25. Ann Towns, "Paradoxes of (In)Equality: Something Is Rotten in the Gender Equal State of Sweden." *Cooperation & Conflict* 37, no. 2 (2002): 157–79.

26. Pia Huss, "Rowling uppfinner sagan på nytt" [Rowling Reinvents the Fairytale], *Dagens Nyheter,* 22 January 2001, B03. Note that the Swedish term used, *omoderna,* means un-modern.

27. Huss, "Rowling uppfinner sagan på nytt" [Rowling Reinvents the Fairytale].

28. Jesper Lindau, "Ny Harry Potterbok—samma story för femte gången" [New Harry Potter Book—Same Story for the Fifth Time]. *Sveriges Radio— Nyhetssidan,* 4 January 2004.

29. These identity dynamics demonstrate themselves clearly, for example, in Turkey's relations with the European Union. See Bahar Rumelili, "Producing Collective Identity and Interacting with Difference: The Security Implications of Community-Building in Europe and Southeast Asia." PhD dissertation, University of Minnesota, 2002.

30. "Çevirmen Sevin Okyay ile Söyleşi" [Interview with the Translator Sevin Okyay], *Milliyet,* 23 June 2003.

31. *Hürriyet,* 9 February 2002.

32. *Hürriyet,* 27 December 2001.

33. *Zaman,* 7 January 2003.

34. *Hürriyet,* 16 January 2003.

35. *Zaman,* 29 July 2004.

36. *Milliyet,* 9 January 2004.

37. Fatih Özgüven, "Sınıf İçinde Sınıf" [Class within class], *Radikal,* 6 February 2002.

38. www.harrypotter.gen.tr.

39. "Kraliçe Bile, Harry Potter'ın Yazarından Fakir Çıktı" [Even the Queen Is Poorer than Harry Potter Author], *Sabah*, 19 April 2004.

40. www.harrypotter.gen.tr.

41. "Çevirmen Sevin Okyay ile Söyleşi" [Interview with the Translator Sevin Okyay], *Milliyet*, 23 June 2003.

42. *Hürriyet*, 2 February 2002.

43. Zeki Coşkun, "Madonna, Pınar, Harry Potter . . . Markalardan Marka Beğen" [Take Your Pick among the Brands], *Radikal*, 27 June 2003.

44. Reader reaction to "Harry Potter Nasıl Öpüşür?" *Radikal*, 7 September 2003. www.radikal.com.tr.

45. Zeki Coşkun "Şenlikli Cenaze" [The Joyful Funeral], *Radikal*, 8 February 2002.

46. "Atlas Halı Hollywood'da" [Atlas Carpets Is in Hollywood], *Radikal*, 23 February 2002.

47. "Harry Potter'ın Ayakkabıları Maraş'tan" [Harry Potter's Shoes Come from Maras]. www.bilgitukiye.com/join/Default.asp?ID=News&Nid=196.

48. Sebnem İşigüzel, "Ambalaj ve Algılama Bozuklukları" [Packaging and Perception Defects], *Radikal*, 11 May 1998.

# Children's Crusade                                   4
## The Religious Politics of Harry Potter

MAIA A. GEMMILL AND DANIEL H. NEXON

*ϟ*

IT DIDN'T TAKE LONG FOR J. K. ROWLING'S TALES of witches and warlocks to arouse religious passions. A number of Christian conservatives
in the United States soon attacked the novels for, in their view, promoting witchcraft and Satanism. In 1999, the *New York Times* reported on
the growing controversy. "In their formal complaints asking school districts
to remove the materials, parents argue that because witchcraft is a religion,
books about it do not belong in public schools, and they say that Harry's
flirtations with death and disaster are troubling story lines in light of recent
school shootings."[1] Prominent conservative Christian publications, such as
*Citizen* and *Family Voice*, ran articles condemning Harry Potter for promoting occultism and undermining Christian values.[2]

Although J. K. Rowling does not describe the witchcraft in Harry Potter as demonic in origin (or intend it to be), it should not be surprising that
her writing has engendered a great deal of religious criticism. In crafting the
Harry Potter universe, Rowling clearly draws on medieval mythologies
about witches. Thus, far from being irrational, religious critics of Harry
Potter correctly note the degree to which the books valorize activities long
condemned in Christian tradition. Indeed, as of 2002, the Harry Potter novels ranked among the most frequently challenged works in American public
libraries and schools.[3] Religiously motivated opposition to Harry Potter is a
worldwide phenomenon, with important incidents in Australia, Canada,
Russia, and Thailand. Elements within the Russian Orthodox church, in
fact, number among the most vociferous denouncers of Harry Potter.[4]
Although the controversy within the American Christian Conservative

movement has been supplanted by other concerns, it is not difficult to find examples of conservative Christians still condemning Harry Potter.

The religious attack on Harry Potter within the United States took place in the broader context of increasing political assertiveness by the Christian Right. Christian conservatives believe that the political and social landscape in the United States is dominated by groups hostile to Christian beliefs and values. Their goal is to reclaim that landscape; popular culture represents one of the major fronts for their efforts. As one commentator explains, "American pop culture, while promoting a lot of great music and entertainment, is also the world's most corrosive influence on traditional morality."[5] Indeed, a recurrent theme of the movement is that parents must constantly struggle against a hostile mass media, lest their children fall prey to the un-Christian and anti-Christian influences that are peddled daily on television, radio, in the bookstores, and in public schools.[6]

In a global context, the religious politics of Harry Potter echo a broader theme: that of traditionalist responses to the cultural dimensions of globalization and modernization. Put simply, in the United States the attack on Harry Potter came from a traditionalist religious movement. In raising objections to the implied message of the Harry Potter phenomenon, they responded to an element of popular culture that was, itself, part of a process of cultural globalization. At the same time, the mobilization against Harry Potter followed trends in the nature of collective action under conditions of globalization. The ways in which different Christians have viewed Harry Potter, in turn, reflect varying ways in which those holding traditional beliefs adapt to elements of secular modernity. Indeed, many of the most influential critics of Harry Potter take carefully considered positions that represent mixtures of accommodation and resistance to global forces antithetical to their beliefs and values.

We proceed by tracing the various trajectories that come together in the religious politics of Harry Potter. We begin with globalization and secularization. Here we draw a connection between Harry Potter itself and these two processes. We also argue that aspects of the backlash against Harry Potter reflect dynamics of globalization. Next we examine the traditionalist trajectory of the Harry Potter debate. We examine how the Christian Right is a self-consciously traditionalist movement, and then turn to an exploration of the historical development of Christian traditions about witchcraft, both in the European and more recent American context. This exploration reveals the enduring strength of these traditions. It also highlights how Rowling, by drawing on more benign aspects of these traditions in crafting the world of Harry Potter, ran afoul of the concerns of Christian conservatives.

In the final sections of this chapter, we examine the tenor of the religious debate surrounding Harry Potter. We argue that the debate reveals different strategies of accommodation and rejection of secular popular culture, and therefore provides insights into the complexity of the relationship between globalization, secularization, and traditionalism.

## Globalization and Secular Modernity

*Globalization* is an amorphous concept that describes a variety of different economic, social, and cultural processes. For example, scholars of globalization write about the increasing speed of communication and transportation technologies, growing trade interdependence and capital mobility, shifts in processes of production that bring multiple countries and regions into single supply chains, the erosion of national borders through increased immigration, and the growth of global public goods problems relating to environmental degradation, transnational crime, and transnational terrorism.[7]

Processes of globalization also create new promises and pitfalls for social and political movements. The Internet, mass media, and other elements of global and national communications can, as suggested above, make it easier for actors to activate common identities and to coordinate movements.[8] The fact that local events may be, and frequently are, reported across the globe creates conditions for responses, protests, support, and emulation by individuals and groups in other nations and localities. Those who make effective use of increasingly fast and far-reaching communication media can enhance the prospects for social mobilization aimed to change policies at regional, state, and global levels. Globalization can imply either "a proliferation of localities that communicate through transnational media and defend themselves against both each other and states" or "a consistent homogenizing of sociocultural process through which transparent, rational norms provide boundaries to human behavior the world over."[9] Processes of globalization appear to be simultaneously enhancing, on the one hand, forces of localism and particularism and, on the other hand, globalism and regionalism.[10] Indeed, those aspects of globalization that empower political movements—in regional, national, and transnational forms—create opportunities for various identity-based groups to expand their recruitment, access to resources, and ability to garner attention.[11]

Globalization brings together a wide variety of different cultural orientations and worldviews, some of which are compatible and some of which are contradictory. Most scholars stress that globalization is not simply the spread of "Western" modernity. Nevertheless, one of the most significant sources of cultural hybridization and contestation at stake in globalization is the dissemination of nineteenth- and twentieth-century Western ways of life. Of these, secularism numbers among the most politically charged, not only in the developing world but also in Europe and America.

In general, secularization is the process "whereby sacred traditions and certainties lose their sacredness; 'secularity' is the victory of the profane world."[12] Analysts associate secularization with a number of developments, such as the replacement of traditional and charismatic authority with legal-rational principles of legitimacy, the triumph of the state over religious institutions, the expansion of scientific knowledge and procedures at the expense of religion, the differentiation of society such that religion, for example, is compartmentalized in increasingly narrow spheres, and the diminishment of the influence of religion in individual consciousness and choice.[13]

Early theorists of secularization argued that there was a fundamental contradiction between religion and modernity: modernization necessarily and inevitably involves the diminishment of the importance of religion and religiosity. This view has foundered on the continued vitality, even in the advanced industrialized world, of religious movements and religious beliefs. Although secularization can no longer be viewed as inevitable, it does not follow that secularization is a useless concept for understanding aspects of global modernity. If secularization is located as part of a broader set of processes related to institutional differentiation, then we can empirically assess the factors that shape the relationship between aspects of modernity and the reduction of the sphere of religious influence in social and political life.[14] The claim that religion "acts far less intimately with governing institutions than it once did" is more or less accurate for a good many countries and regions.[15] We can detect trends, most powerful in western Europe, but also present elsewhere, whereby religion is a less significant source of authority than it used to be.[16] These trends, however, are frequently challenged by organized religious movements, who see secularization as a threat to not only their beliefs, but the vitality of the social order.[17]

Disenchantment is a particular manifestation of secularization. In Weber's famous formulation, the "disenchantment of the world" is the consequence of rationalization, which itself is driven by a host of larger social processes. "The fate of our times is characterized by rationalization and intellectualization and, above all, by the 'disenchantment of the world.' Precisely the ultimate and most sublime values have retreated from public life either into the transcendent realm of mystic life or into the brotherliness of direct and personal relations."[18] Disenchantment is the retreat of the mysterious and magical in the face of scientific and technical-rational explanation:

> It means that principally there are no mysterious incalculable forces that come into play, but rather that one can, in principle, master all things by calculation. This means that the world is disenchanted. One need no longer have recourse to magical means in order to master or implore spirits, as did the savage, for whom such mysterious powers existed. Technical means and calculations perform the service.[19]

The world is disenchanted to different degrees for different individuals and social groups. For some, god (or gods), demons, witchcraft, and magic are omnipresent and very real, for others they are rare, for others nonexistent. God may be dead, may operate somewhere outside of the unfolding of human history, or may be actively at work in the world. Secularists, such as Carl Sagan, bemoan or mock the "demon-haunted world," but those who do not see the world as disenchanted may themselves view secularists with a mixture of pity and contempt.[20]

The relationship between globalization and secularization is, as we have suggested, complex. On the one hand, globalization spreads secular outlooks. On the other hand, globalization also involves the clash between secular modernity and religious traditionalism. Significant aspects of world politics—from the confrontation between the United States and various militant Islamist movements, to political struggles in countries such as India, Israel, and Iran, to tensions over identity and religion in Europe—involve challenges of religious traditionalists to the elements of globalization, particularly secularization.[21] The stakes in the Harry Potter debate are not as great as they are in such conflicts, but they do involve this central question of how globalization plays out in the context of adaptation, confrontation, and adjustment between secularism and religious traditionalism.

At one level, Harry Potter is merely an extremely successful literary franchise aimed at children and young adults. But Harry Potter is also a vector in the cultural dimensions of globalization. As numerous chapters in this volume make clear, the Harry Potter novels are particularly British works of literature. They reflect a genre of boarding-school novels that describes a set of experiences largely confined to the British cultural milieu. More generally, the images of magic and sorcery that Rowling borrows from are highly specific to European folk culture; so much so that the Chinese adaptations actually altered the content of the volumes to fit the particularities of Chinese supernatural traditions.[22] In this respect, the global success of the franchise reflects how globalization involves the export of genres rooted in national and regional cultures to other cultures with differing traditions, as well as the ways in which cultural themes are adapted and hybridized as they are spread, via popular culture, throughout the globe.

As Patricia Goff argues in chapter 1, we should understand the marketing and success of Harry Potter as part of broader trends in globalization and mass media, in which firms with an international presence and a transnational orientation make money by selling aspects of popular culture throughout the globe. Indeed, Harry Potter challenges the often conventional view that globalization is simply Americanization—that the United States is mainly an exporter of popular culture, whether in the form of McDonald's, hip hop, or Hollywood action films to consumers throughout the globe. America is just as much a consumer of global mass media as a supplier; it is an object, as well as an agent, of cultural globalization. Although many of the companies involved in the Harry Potter phenomenon are based in the United States, Harry Potter is, in the final analysis, a work of British literature that, after its initial wave of success, was appropriated by the multimedia giant Time Warner.

The importance of globalization to the controversy is reflected in the global nature of religious criticisms of Harry Potter. But the nature of the mobilization against Harry Potter has elements of the changing dynamics of movements under conditions of globalization. These elements are reflected in the role of the Internet, grass roots activism, and interest-group participation in the backlash against Potter. In the United States, the backlash spread very quickly, fed by direct mail, the Internet, and television reporting. Robert Knight, the director of Concerned Women for America's Culture and Family Institute, says that "Concern" over Harry Potter, "was across the board from the grassroots to the policy analysts at the national level because of the incredible popularity of the books." Concerned Women for America received a "tremendous amount of mail regarding [Harry Potter], because we thought of it as part of a larger cultural issue involving popular culture and [its] treatment of Christianity, or lack thereof."[23] As objections to Harry Potter garnered more and more attention, increasing numbers of worried parents and religious officials took stands on the books: not only in the United States, but worldwide.

In the United States, Rowling's works were thrust into a more general confrontation between secularism and religious traditionalism, with the latter side most visibly represented by the Christian Right. As Clyde Wilcox explains, "the Christian Right is a social movement that attempts to mobilize evangelical Protestants and other Orthodox Christians into conservative political action. . . . Like all social movements, the Christian Right is composed of social movement organizations, leaders, activists, and members, and it seeks to attract support from a broad constituency." The movement is not singular or monolithic but includes a number of different interests and agendas, including ending abortion, promoting homeschooling, and restoring prayer to schools. Its membership contains evangelicals, fundamentalists, Pentecostals, and charismatics.[24] Membership in the Christian Right—and the number of people who self-identify with the movement—have remained relatively stable over the last decade.[25] At the same time, the Christian Right has emerged as one of the most powerful forces within the Republican Party, and prominent members of the movement have shifted their orientation increasingly toward traditional coalitional politics.[26]

Members of the Christian Right generally view themselves as under siege from cultural, social, and political forces that favor secularism and disdain Christianity. The mass media, popular culture, and the educational system figure prominently among the institutions they perceive as undermining Christian values and identity.[27] For example, Concerned Women for America lists among its major issues the "failure of our government to recognize the God-given, inalienable rights of individuals," "the declining quality of education in public schools and the increasing emphasis on a Godless philosophy such as secular humanism, new age philosophy, and so-called value-neutral sex education in classrooms and textbooks," "the potential loss of religious liberty as a result of increased governmental intervention," and the "morally deteriorating impact of the entertainment industry on our country and the increasing emphasis on violence and sexual exploitation."[28]

The movement is self-consciously traditionalist—aimed at restoring "traditional" Christian values and morality, which are seen as lying at the bedrock of American political and cultural identity. It is also, to varying degrees, anti-secularist—aimed at opposing attempts to overly secularize society and government. Not only is the movement anti-secularist in its political objectives, but self-identified members of the Christian Right are likely to view religious actors and religious texts as sources of political authority. They are "much more favorably disposed towards religious-based political activism" than most other subpopulations.[29]

All of this helps explain why elements of the Christian Right targeted Harry Potter. First, the books portray magic—and particularly witchcraft —as morally neutral. Hence, they contravene elements of Biblical scripture and Christian tradition which hold that all magic emanates from demonic forces. Second, the books subvert "traditional hierarchical power structures where there is a single 'right' or 'true' source of power." Many Christian critics of Harry Potter see within the books both the promotion of occultism *and* an ethical orientation that is secular in nature—in which individuals are answerable only to their own conscience.[30] Third, the aggressive marketing and broad popular appeal of the Harry Potter franchise places it squarely within a basic frame of the Christian Right—that they are an embattled minority fighting against large-scale commercial and cultural forces intent on undermining their values and corrupting their children. As Michael Ostling notes, Harry Potter's widespread popularity made it a "primary marker in the culture wars."[31] Moreover, the degree to which educators latched onto the Harry Potter series—in an attempt to promote reading among their students—played into fundamental concerns among members of the Christian Right about the existence of an anti-Christian agenda in public education.[32] Each of these sources of opposition to Harry Potter locates the Christian anti-Potter movement within the frameworks of "globalization against localism" and "secularism against traditionalism."

## Christianity and Traditions of Witchcraft

What is particularly interesting about the traditional elements of the anti-Potter worldview is that they are not recently manufactured or "invented"[33] but have a long lineage in Christian beliefs. Although modern secularists often hold a particular image of the medieval witch—a village wise woman who dispensed fertility and good luck charms, along with the occasional hex, as well as herbal remedies and pagan folk wisdom[34]—witchcraft meant something very different to medieval Christians, particularly to the church hierarchy. Witchcraft represented a potent religious threat to Christianity. It was not perceived as a pagan alternative, however, but rather as a profound perversion of Christian doctrine, ritual, and practice.

Most modern knowledge about medieval perceptions of witchcraft are derived from inquisitorial records. The inquisitorial bureaucracy kept detailed transcripts of interrogations, including the accused and the witnesses against them.[35] Although some testimony was given voluntarily and extemporaneously, it was much more common for the questioner to ask the respondent a series of leading questions, probing for assent to propositions matching an existing script of witchcraft and heretical practice. Individuals who confessed and repented were punished severely with lengthy, punitive penances, long prison sentences, or sometimes, turned over to the secular authorities for a quick death (such as by strangulation or hanging). Those who continued to assert their innocence could be held in prison indefinitely and subjected to all manners of physical deprivation and psychological manipulation.[36] Church authorities might decide, however, that a recalcitrant prisoner was unrepentant. Under those circumstances, the prisoner could be tortured and even burned alive.[37] Given the alternatives, it is not surprising that many of the accused confessed to all sorts of wildly outrageous acts. While inquisitorial transcripts are a singularly unreliable source for the beliefs of those who were accused of witchcraft and heresy, they do represent an excellent account of the beliefs of the *accusers*, particularly the representatives of the church.

The core ritual of witchcraft, according to these accounts, was the black mass, or the witches' sabbat. Descriptions of the black mass vary, but there are some common elements. The witches (male and female) gathered at a particular location (sometimes in a church), where they engaged in a variety of activities that perverted Christian practice. Often these rituals were presided over by a mysterious dark man—who was sometimes explicitly the Devil, complete with goat's feet—or a hooded woman.[38] The demonic leader required witches to renounce Christian beliefs, particularly the Eucharist, and to trample on a cross. Animals associated with the Devil, such as goats, toads, snakes, asses, and black cats, were often present and played a sexual role; sometimes the Devil would demand that witches kiss the animal on the mouth or the anus. Human sexual perversions were also common elements in the confessions, including frenetic dancing, orgies, and homosexual activity. Animal and human sacrifice played a large role as well. Witches reputedly cooked and ate children—sometimes their own, but often those they stole from strangers. They preferred, or so sources claim, unbaptized children. The corpses of ritually murdered babies were an important ingredient in a magical ointment that was applied to new witches (a perversion of the application of holy chrism during certain sacraments); sometimes this ointment was used to initiate metamorphoses into animal shape or to grant the power of flight. In some accounts, orgies took place with the express purpose of producing babies for later sacrifice.[39] Pope Gregory IX describes the deviant sexual practices in which witches engaged in great detail, as well as the ceremonial adoration of the Devil, in his papal Bull Vox in Rama, issued in 1232.[40] Similar depictions can be found in other contemporary witch-hunting manuals, including the (in)famous *Malleus Malifaricum,* written in 1486, which also affirmed that witches cooked and ate their own children, as well as in political theorist Jean Bodin's *Demonomanie des Sorciers,* published in 1580.[41]

Accused witches also confessed to numerous other offenses, some major and some minor. They flew through the air to and from witch gatherings, sometimes through the use of a magical ointment, sometimes on the backs of enchanted animals such as mice, hares, dogs, goats, pigs, or cows; broomsticks begin to appear as a mode of transportation in the late fifteenth and early sixteenth centuries. Others transformed themselves into animal form in order to travel to the sabbat or to wreak other mischief. Many witches confessed to casting curses that caused children and livestock to fall ill or even die, and to spoiling crops or the wine in the cellar of others' houses. Witches also commonly confessed to spirit possessions—allowing themselves to be possessed or possessing other victims.

Witches were not the only ones accused of these sorts of activities. In fact, there is a much older tradition by which heretics and other religious deviants were purported to engage in devil worship, nocturnal gatherings, orgies, and human sacrifice. The first well-documented application of this tradition to Christian heretics occurred in Orléans in 1022, among the canons of the church of the Holy Cross. The core beliefs of these heretics seem to be gnostic in origin—membership was conferred by a laying of hands, which relieved initiates of all sin and gave them a full understanding of scripture. Believers also denied the sacraments and the divine birth of Christ and partook of a "heavenly food" that bestowed them with visions. The chronicler of these events, a monk named Paul writing about fifty years later, added a number of additional layers to this. The heavenly food, he claimed, was made of the ashes of murdered babies, which were, in turn, the progeny of the group's secret nocturnal orgies. This heresy was discovered, rooted out, and authorities burned the accused on the orders of the French king, Robert.[42]

Similar accusations were made against the ascetic Christian sect of lay preachers known as the Waldensians (after their founder Valdes or Waldo) who first appeared in France around 1170.[43] Much like the later Franciscans, the Waldensians took a vow of extreme poverty; however, they also viewed the existing church structure as corrupt and therefore illegitimate.[44] As such, they presented a grave challenge to the church. During the early fourteenth century, Frederick of Austria and the local bishop launched a campaign to root out suspected Waldensians; a contemporary chronicler provided a summary of Waldensian beliefs and practices that included devil worship and incestuous orgies in underground caverns.[45] In Arras in 1459, a group of five alleged Waldensians was accused of devil worship, including attendance at a black mass, complete with "the banquet, the profanation of the crucifix, devil worship, and sexual orgy."[46] A Dominican inquistor, Antonio di Setto, gave a similar account of Waldensian ritual in Italy in the later half of the fourteenth century: the Waldensians gathered at a secret location and engaged in a breaking of bread in mockery of the Eucharist. An old woman then poured each attendee a sip of special drink that would bind them irrevocably to the sect; this drink allegedly contained the excrement of a large toad. The members agreed to obey the preacher and to worship Satan. Finally, they engaged in a great, incestuous orgy that lasted until dawn.[47]

Although the Franciscans managed to obtain official papal sanction, the order fractured in the fourteenth century over the meaning of the vow of poverty. Rome declared the extreme ascetics, who became known as the Fraticelli, heretics; by the late fifteenth century they had been nearly stamped out. However, in 1466, Pope Paul II decided to launch a new campaign against the Fraticelli. Several dozen were arrested and interrogated in the great fortress Castel Sant'Angelo in Rome. Under torture, several prisoners admitted that the sect engaged in orgies and ritual infanticide: "From the babies born, they take one little boy as a sacrifice . . . later they make powders from the body. They put these powders in a flask of wine . . . each drinks once from the flask by way of communion."[48] Another contemporary account for the source of the child sacrifice reads: "A most wicked woman voluntarily confessed to him [that] when as a result of this diabolical copulation, she had given birth to a child, she carried it to the cave . . . and she stayed to watch her son . . . being roasted."[49]

These same allegations appear during the French crown's campaign to suppress the Templar crusading order. In 1307, on the orders of King Philip IV of France, Templars throughout the kingdom of France were arrested and charged with heresy and devil worship. After interrogation and torture, many members of the order confessed to a litany of familiar offenses: sexual perversions (particularly homosexual activity within the order), denial of Christ, desecration of crucifixes and the Eucharist, as well as adoration of a demonic cat.[50] Barber argues that this set of allegations was deliberately designed by Guillaume of Nogaret, Philip's leading minister, to invoke earlier heresy and witchcraft accusations, thus clearing the path for the French crown to seize the assets of the extraordinarily wealthy Templar order.[51]

Most modern scholars emphatically agree that although heretical groups definitely existed (although not likely as Satan worshippers), there were no organized groups of witches.[52] Cohn argues that much of the standard accusations leveled at heretics and witches dates from pre-Christian Roman narratives associated with religiously or socially deviant groups, noting that participants in the Catiline conspiracy in the first century B.C.E. were supposed to have ritually murdered and eaten a child.[53] He also points out that Roman authors applied this same narrative to early Christians (possibly as a result of misunderstanding the ritual of the Eucharist), while also claiming that Christians regularly engaged in orgies and other forms of sexual libertinism.[54] In Alexandria, Jews were widely rumored to worship a donkey's head as well as conduct human sacrifices. Cohn locates the source of these allegations as a desire to place these deviant groups (conspiratorial and mysterious religious groups) outside of the realm of acceptable human behavior: "In most societies, therefore, to say that a group practices incest, worships genitals, kills and eats children, amounts to saying that it is an incarnation of the anti-human. Such a group is absolutely outside of humanity."[55] The projection of these narratives onto heretics and witches, then, places them outside the realm of socially accepted practice.

Carlo Ginzburg, however, takes a different (although not necessarily contradictory) view, arguing that the archetypes of the witches' sabbat are based on ancient folkloric traditions, that while not satanic per se, are clearly pre-Christian in origin. While examining sixteenth-century inquisitorial records for the northern Italian region of Friuli, Ginzburg discovered evidence of a group that called themselves the *benandanti*. The benandanti believed that they were marked from birth with a duty to engage in a spiritual battle to ensure a bountiful harvest. In this, they seem to be a remnant of a pre-Christian agrarian cult that was blended syncretically with Christianity. The benandanti understood themselves to be in the service of Christ fighting against evil witches who, if undefeated, would destroy the harvest. Periodically the benandanti would travel in spirit, either flying or riding animals, to a great battleground, where they would meet an angelic figure who served as their captain. After tipping their caps to the captain, the benandanti would begin a ritual battle against the witches, using bundles of fennel as weapons against the witches' bundles of sorghum.[56] The inquisitors, naturally, were quite perplexed by this tale and quickly began to attempt to fit it into the known categories of witchcraft. Certainly, significant portions of this story fit existing narratives: the spiritual journey to a secret meeting place (particularly through flight and on animal mounts) and the presence of a mystical captain or leader. However, they initially declined to prosecute the benandanti they interviewed. Only four years later did the benandanti who first attracted inquisitorial attention received minor sentences for heresy.[57] Later benandanti were not treated with such leniency, as the church sought to shape the benandanti's practices and beliefs to their own understanding of witchcraft as a demonic force. In the eyes of the church, there was no independent space for this type of spiritual activity—mystical power could only be understood as derived from canonically approved sources (such as miracles performed by saints) or as demonic in nature. Descriptions of the benandanti's gatherings in inquisitorial records took on a greater and greater resemblance to the witches' sabbat described above, until by the mid-seventeenth century, they were indistinguishable.[58]

Even after the witchcraft craze died down in the early eighteenth century, rumors of mysterious cults that engaged in ritual murder, human and animal sacrifices, bisexual orgies, and demon worship persisted. During the nineteenth century, this narrative was most commonly directed against the Masons; a French journalist in the 1890s, Léo Taxil, created a panic with claims of an international Masonic conspiracy of Satan worshippers based in London, with chapters as far-flung as Charleston, South Carolina.[59]

To many readers, the allegations made against witches and heretics may seem like the product of a vivid medieval imagination, thankfully left in the mists of the distant past. However, fears about Satanism have resurfaced periodically in popular discourse; Harry Potter is far from the first pop culture phenomenon to feed these fears, particularly with regard to the occult's appeal to children and teenagers. During the 1970s and 1980s, the success of bands such as Black Sabbath and Iron Maiden sparked a wave of concern about occult themes in popular music. At the same time, the sudden popularity of the role-playing game Dungeons & Dragons, in which participants imagine themselves as characters wielding magical weapons and spells in a fantastical world inhabited by strange creatures (many drawn from pagan mythology) also fed this anxiety about the seductiveness of Satanism.[60]

Folklorist Bill Ellis has argued that traditions of folk magic have persisted in popular culture, pointing, for example, to the popularity of the Ouija board (first sold through the Sears Roebuck catalog in 1898).[61] In the United States, the continued vibrancy of the Pentecostal and evangelical tradition has also played an important role in preserving belief in supernatural power manifested through the Holy Spirit; this supernatural power may take forms such as miraculous healing, prophesy, or speaking in tongues.[62] Because these practices are sanctioned by the churches in which they are observed, they fall within the realm of acceptable belief rather than being deemed superstitious or occultist.[63] For believers in supernatural good, belief in supernatural evil is a natural—and perhaps necessary—corollary.[64]

The most dramatic evidence of the persistence of beliefs about Satanism can be seen in the Satanic ritual abuse scare of the mid-1980s and early 1990s. During this period, many therapists began using techniques of hypnosis to unlock repressed memories of trauma and abuse. Some patients, however, claimed that the hypnosis therapy unlocked memories of abuse at the hands of Satanic cults, including "raising babies for sexual torture, ritual murder, and cannibal feasts"[65]—these accusations were remarkably similar to those made against medieval heretics and witches.[66] In some cases, the accusers even made conscious claims of continuity for Satanic ritual abuse to medieval witchcraft and pre-Christian paganism: the psychiatrist Lawrence Padzer, coauthor of *Michelle Remembers,* one of the first published accounts of Satanic ritual abuse, writes: "Most people think they're strictly Dark Ages, but the fact is, the Church of Satan is a worldwide organization. It's actually older than the Christian Church."[67]

These stories spread rapidly through American mass media, particularly via popular television talk shows hosted by Geraldo Rivera, Oprah Winfrey, and Sally Jesse Raphael. In 1994, a national survey published in *Redbook* magazine found that 70 percent of Americans believed these stories of abuse by Satanic cults to be true. The panic over Satanic ritual abuse was not limited to the United States. Thematically similar accusations of Satanic abuse of children occurred in the United Kingdom, Norway, Sweden, Germany, New Zealand, Canada, Australia, and the Netherlands.[68]

In some cases the alleged Satanists were the victim's parents; however, in many of the most sensational cases, the abusers were day-care workers. In many of these instances, social workers and prosecutors interviewed small children (sometimes as young as three) about their interactions with the day-care workers. Small children are notoriously difficult to interview, since the realms of fantasy, make believe, and reality often overlap. In addition, children are very suggestible and will often give answers that they perceive will please the adult questioner.[69] Thus, their allegations were sometimes wild and often stoked by psychologists and social workers investigating ritual abuse. One English psychologist wrote about Satanic cults in which "children were caged, hung, chained, whipped, burnt, tortured, drowned, buried alive, and strapped to inverted crosses and assaulted."[70] In the most notorious case in the United States, the McMartin preschool trial, the proprietors allegedly forced a child to "watch the sacrifice of animals and human infants, to ingest urine, blood, and feces, and to accompany his teachers on airplane flights to Palm Springs and into a labyrinth of underground tunnels where one of the accused 'flew in the air' and the others 'were all dressed up as witches'"; ultimately the number of alleged victims rose to 369.[71] Similar accusations were made at day-care centers in North Carolina, Massachusetts, New Jersey, and elsewhere. Although the defendants in the McMartin case were ultimately acquitted at trial, in some of the other cases, the accused day-care workers were convicted and sentenced to lengthy prison terms.

## Harry Potter's Cauldron

The religious politics of Harry Potter bring together three mutually implicated trajectories: globalization, secularization, and traditionalism. In the preceding sections we trace each of these trajectories, and discuss how they converge in the American context such that Harry Potter, itself a product of globalization, became an element of the broader struggle between secularism and local traditionalism sometimes referred to as America's "culture wars." In this section, we focus upon the actual terms of the debate over Harry Potter. Two things are striking about this debate. First, they explicitly echo the broader intersection we identify. Defenders of Harry Potter rely upon assumptions derived from worldviews that are more or less disenchanted, while many detractors operate from traditionalist beliefs in which magic and demonic forces really do exist and operate in the world. Many religious critics of Harry Potter focus on the ways in which the works contribute to a broader assault on Christian beliefs found in popular culture and society at large. Second, between the most extreme views on Potter one can find more sophisticated positions, ones which weigh, from a conservative Christian perspective, the virtues and drawbacks of Rowling's stories.[72]

Christian reactions to witchcraft in Harry Potter range from outright condemnation to strong affirmation. The Vatican, for its part, weighed in on the controversy by declaring that the books are "benign and nonthreatening to the faith."[73] Critics tend to agree that the books teach disrespect for authority—for parents, for institutions, and so on.[74] In this sense, the books constitute part of a broader assault on traditional authority by a secular, "anything goes" popular culture.[75] Yet Christian critics offer differing assessments of the magic and witchcraft in Harry Potter. Many believe that Rowling's use of occult themes is troubling, but they disagree about the implications of Harry Potter's witchcraft and wizardry for the ultimate value of the books.

The most extreme position holds that the books directly affirm Satanism. For people who believe that witchcraft and Satan cults are real, the magic in Harry Potter cannot easily be treated as mere childhood fun. As one Christian website claims, "anyone who has researched witchcraft and talked with contemporary pagans will see the alarming parallels between contemporary occultism and Rowling's seductive message to children."[76] Another argues, "Adults, as well as children, find great obsession with scary ideas that speak of the forbidden realm. The devil and his demons, along with the witchcraft ideas out of his evil characters, are quickly becoming the highest ideal of intellectualism. It is Satan's day to say the least."[77] A primary school principal of a small school in England banned Harry Potter from her school, saying, "The Bible is consistent in its teachings that wizards, devils and demons exist and are real and dangerous, and God's people are told to have nothing to do with them."[78]

Other critics take a less extreme position, acknowledging that witchcraft, occult, and Satanism may not be identical. However, magic never comes from God and hence is always malevolent. Richard Abanes, for example, dismisses the notion that Harry and his friends use their power for good: "Biblically speaking, Harry and all the other 'good' characters are simply using one set of sinful behaviors to defeat another set of sinful behaviors."[79] Another critical website makes a similar point: "God is clear in Scripture that any practice of magic is an 'abomination' to him. God doesn't distinguish between 'white' and 'dark' magic since they both originate from the same source."[80] There is no room for good magic, since all magic that is not a miracle performed by God can only have a demonic origin, much in the way that the seventeenth-century church could not perceive the benandanti as anything other than witches. The fact that Harry and his friends use magic to defeat a clearly evil foe is not exculpatory.

The upshot is that, while J. K. Rowling may not intend to draw children into the occult, her writing risks seducing children into occult practices because it portrays magic in a good light. Indeed, the degree to which Rowling borrows from traditional accounts of witchcraft—without, of course, the sexual orgies and Satanism—is striking. Wizards and witches have the power of flight, cast spells via incantations, and brew complex herbal potions. Wizards duel by casting curses and countercurses. Many of the students keep animal familiars, such as toads, rats, and cats—all animals commonly associated with Satan in medieval witchcraft lore. Some powerful wizards can change themselves into animal form. Harry has the ability to talk to snakes (which are a common demonic symbol), as do the dark wizards Lord Voldemort and Salazar Slitherin. Lord Voldemort spiritually possesses others, such as Ginny Weasley (CS), while a human sacrifice plays a crucial part in Voldemort's full resurrection (OP).

Thus, John Murray writes in *Citizen*, "by disassociating magic and supernatural evil, it becomes possible to portray occult practices as 'good' and 'healthy,' contrary to the scriptural declaration that such practices are 'detestable to the Lord.' This, in turn, opens the door for less discerning individuals—including, but not limited to, children—to become confused about supernatural matters."[81] Abanes makes a similar critique, drawing heavily on the scriptural prohibitions against spell-casting, divination, fortune-telling, potion-making, and other magical techniques that Harry and his friends learn at Hogwarts.[82] He argues that although the "countless references to ancient and modern occultism . . . certainly do not teach the precise doctrines of witchcraft, nor do they instruct children to purchase a step-by-step guide to Wicca . . . the allusions could stir a child's curiosity about occultism—perhaps enough for that child to one day dabble in it."[83]

As such, Harry Potter can be understood as a training manual of sorts for witchcraft. Abanes and similar critics acknowledge that no child is going to be able to cast spells or mix potions based on the instructions in any of the Harry Potter books, but they worry that children may be encouraged to seek out real spell books, such as those used by Wiccans.[84] This effect is exacerbated by the marketing machine surrounding Harry Potter, which encourages children to play-act being wizards and witches. Harry Potter-branded items currently available in stores include a Harry Potter dress-up set (which includes a cape and a wand), Harry Potter wizard chess, the Sorting Hat, the Harry Potter Levitating Challenge Game, Harry Potter Legos, and more.[85]

Rowling herself has called these accusations "absurd," stating that "I have met thousands of children now, and not even one time has a child come up to me and said, 'Ms Rowling, I'm so glad I've read these books because now I want to be a witch.'"[86] In an interview, she said that "I truly am bemused that anyone who has read the books could think that I am a proponent of the occult in any serious way. . . . I don't believe in witchcraft, in the sense that they're talking about, at all." Moreover, Rowling argues, "I think it's a source of great fun, drama. Magic is going to be a theme of children's literature as long as the human race exists."[87]

Rowling's defense of her work, of course, presupposes that one views the world as, to at least some degree, disenchanted. Since magic, as such, does not exist, then it follows that tales of witchcraft cannot possibly be dangerous; they are "mere fantasy." Interestingly, a similar impulse can be found even among some Christian defenders of Harry Potter. Christian defenders of Harry Potter generally argue that the magic in the books is clearly not real, or that it is mechanical and disenchanted.[88] Chuck Colson of Breakpoint Ministries dismisses magic in Harry Potter as "purely mechanical, as opposed to occultic. That is, Harry and his friends cast spells, read crystal balls and turn themselves into animals—but they don't make contact with a supernatural world . . . .contrast the mechanical magic in the Potter books to the kind of real-life witchcraft the Bible condemns—the kind that encourages involvement with supernatural evil."[89] Colson is not alone in this position. Alan Jacobs observes that in Harry Potter's world, "magic simply works, and works as reliably, in the hands of a trained wizard, as the technology that makes airplanes fly and refrigerators chill the air—those products of applied science being, by the way, sufficiently inscrutable to the people who use them that they might as well be the products of wizardry."[90]

Neither Colson nor Jacobs are secularists. Colson takes pains to distinguish between genuinely occultic literature and the way magic is presented in Harry Potter, while Jacobs complains that technological disenchantment is a greater threat to religiosity than *Potter*. But even the act of drawing such distinctions represents a kind of *modus vivendi* between a completely traditionalist worldview and one informed by logics of disenchantment. In general, Christian defenders of Harry Potter argue that their coreligionists should overlook its use of witchcraft and recognize that the books affirm Christian principles and morality.[91]

Indeed, whether or not members of the Christian Right agree with these defenses depends, of course, on the degree to which they can accept some form of disenchantment. As one critic of Colson's contends, "part of the problem is that witches and magicians do exist. They DO cast spells and read crystal balls. A few even work on the discipline of lycanthropy—shapeshifting into animals. Thus, there is nothing fictitious about any of this, except in the minds of head-in-the sand Christians."[92] Nor do these critics accept that Rowling has merely created a fantasy world: "The truth is that Rowling has succeeded in blurring the lines between fantasy and real-life occultism. Actual occultism is incorporated into her books in staggering amounts and is recognized by occultists."[93] Jacobs himself notes that his argument will not persuade those for whom witchcraft is a very real threat.[94]

Many religious critics of Potter attack its portrayal of witchcraft but also draw distinctions between those who are mature enough to compartmentalize the magic as "fantasy" and children who may not be able to do so. As

Robert Knight explains, Christians should "worry about the books' impact on children who are taking everything in, often uncritically and could be swayed to see witchcraft and self-empowerment as more powerful than that of the Christian gospel." Indeed, "with all of Harry's virtues the 'pride of self-empowerment' is still the ultimate message, which is a bad one especially in an era in which educators believe that self-esteem is the key to achievement. In fact, the self-esteem movement runs smack up against Christian gospel." The idea that the magic in Harry Potter is merely technology, Knight argues, may be appropriate for mature readers who can draw such distinctions, but it doesn't answer the real danger that the books pose for impressionable children.[95]

What all of this suggests is that the controversy of Harry Potter is more complex than a simple clash between modernity and tradition, globalization and localism. Within it one can find a variety of ways in which individuals and groups respond to a world in which globalization—and global popular culture—increasingly pits differing beliefs and perspectives against one another. Viewing the religious debate over Harry Potter as symptomatic of broader global processes, we believe, gives us better insight into its dynamics. It also reminds us that the often contentious interaction between religion, traditionalism, and globalization is not simply a feature of the developing world but is also playing itself out in the advanced industrial economies of the West. Most importantly, the religious politics of Harry Potter force us to recognize the degree to which this interaction produces heterogeneous and nuanced responses, even within movements that self-consciously seek to defend "traditional values." To the extent that the religious politics of Harry Potter are a microcosm of broader global political processes involving these trajectories, they teach us something about the complicated world we live in.

## Notes

1. Wildoren 1999.

2. Murray 2000; Kleder 2001. *Citizen* is a publication of Focus on the Family. *Family Voice* is an organ of the Concerned Women for America. Both are major forces in the Christian Conservative movement and Republican politics.

3. Peace 2002.

4. *Straits Times* 2000; BBC News 2003b; *Pravda* 2003; *The Mirror* 2003; Desira 2004.

5. LaBarbera 2003.

6. Focus on the Family, for example, lists "are kids really as influenced by popular culture as they say?" among its frequently asked questions. The answer is in

the affirmative, and their family.org website provides numerous resources for conservative Christians seeking to limit the dangers posed by mass media to their children's moral development. See http://family.custhelp.com/cgi-bin/family.cfg/php/enduser/std_adp.php?p_faqid=944.

7. Rodrik 1998; Barbieri and Schneider 1999; Brooks 1999; Cha 2000; Evans 2000; Walby 2000; Hardt and Negri 2001; Steger 2002.

8. Guidry, Kennedy et al. 2000.

9. Guidry, Kennedy et al. 2000, 30.

10. Rousenau 2003.

11. Robertson 1992; Pieterse 2004.

12. Bolle 1970, 242.

13. Weber 1946; Bolle 1970; Carroll 1984; Chaves 1994; Thompson and Sharma 1998.

14. Martin 1978, 1991.

15. Philpott 2002, 68.

16. Chaves 1994.

17. Philpott 2002, 68.

18. Weber 1946, 155.

19. Weber 1946, 139.

20. Sagan 1996.

21. Juergensmeyer 1993, Philpott 2002, Buruma and Margalit 2004.

22. See Patrick Jackson's and Peter Mandaville's chapter in this volume.

23. Interview with Robert Knight, conducted by Daniel Nexon, April 12, 2005.

24. Woodberry and Smith 1998, 27–30; Wilcox 2000, 5–7.

25. Gonzalez-Servin and Torres-Reyna 1999, 594.

26. Moen 1996; Bolce and Maio 1999, 32.

27. Stephens 2003, 60; Leege 1992, 203; Wilcox 2000, 10.

28. www.cwfa.org/goals-concerns.asp.

29. Bolce and De Maio 1999, 32.

30. Stephens 2003, 56–57.

31. Ostling 2003, 4.

32. One could also argue that, at a minimum, controversy over Harry Potter could serve as an effective means of disseminating the Christian Right's message and broadening connections between its organization and like-minded individuals.

33. Cavanaugh 1986; Gellner 1973; Hobsbawm and Ranger 1992.

34. Some scholars dispute whether this stereotype of the witch represents an even remotely plausible description, arguing that it is an entirely modern, syncretic view. Although some of those accused of witchcraft did dabble in magical healing, there was nothing consciously pagan about these practices. Furthermore, they argue, medieval accounts of witchcraft, including the black mass and devil worship, were entirely fictional. See, for example, Briggs 1996, 5–6. Carlo Ginzburg, on the other hand, argues that while much of the standard inquisitorial account of

witchcraft is fictional, these fictions rest on a foundation of Eurasian folklore and shamanistic practices stretching back into the mists of prehistory, Ginzburg 1991, 9–11.

35. See Given 1997, 25–39, for a detailed discussion on record-keeping by medieval inquisitors. The records kept by Jacques Fournier, Bishop of Pamiers and later Pope Benedict XII, provided the material foundations for Emmanuel Le Roy Ladurie's famous microhistory of the Provençal town Montaillou, Le Roy Ladurie 1975.

36. Given 1997, 52–65.

37. Cohn 1973, 43 and 71. Technically, by canon law, church courts were forbidden to shed blood; however, the church courts simply "relaxed" or handed defendants over to the secular power for the administration of such punishments.

38. Ginzburg 1966, 28; Cohn 1973, 136.

39. Cohn provides a concise summary of the commonly accepted sabbat rituals, Cohn 1973, 146–47.

40. Kors and Peters 1972, 48–49.

41. Barstow 1994, 171–72; Briggs 1996, 34.

42. Cohn 1973, 39–40; Lambert 1977, 9–12.

43. Despite the ascetic doctrines of the Waldensian heresy, Waldensians became strongly associated in the popular mind with witchcraft; at one time "*vauderie*" was synonymous in France with sorcery and magic.

44. Audisio 1999, 11–13.

45. Cohn 1973, 53.

46. Audisio 1999, 75.

47. Cohn 1973, 57.

48. Cohn 1973, 65.

49. Cohn 1973, 71.

50. Cohn 1973, 91–92; Barber 1978, 59–61.

51. Barber 1978, 181–82.

52. Cohn 1973, 161; Briggs 1996, 6.

53. Cohn 1973, 6.

54. Cohn 1973, 8–10.

55. Cohn 1973, 12.

56. Ginzburg 1966, 1–16.

57. Ginzburg 1966, 14.

58. Ginzburg 1966, 120–45.

59. Ellis 1993, 14.

60. Lancaster 1994, 70–73.

61. McLemee 2003.

62. Clark 2003, 27.

63. However, to outside observers (even those who are strong religious believers) faith-healing, prophesy, snake-handling, and other similar rituals may very well appear as superstitious or suspiciously deviant, Clark 2003, 27–28.

64. Clark 2003, 28–29.
65. Crews 2004, 37.
66. This comparison is readily evident to historians of religion, Frankfurter 2001, 352–53.
67. Frankfurter 2001, 357.
68. Victor 1995.
69. Watters 1991; Bruck, Ceci et al. 1997.
70. Webster 2002.
71. Talbot 1999, 27.
72. See, e.g., Neal 2001, 2002.
73. *Pittsburgh Post-Gazette,* "Side of Right," 1999.
74. Interview with Robert Knight, conducted by Daniel Nexon, April 12, 2005.
75. Stephens 2003.
76. Kjos, n.d.
77. Chambers 2004.
78. *The Guardian,* "School Puts a Hex on Harry," 2000.
79. Abanes 2001, 137.
80. James 2001.
81. Murray 2000.
82. Abanes 2001, 89–96.
83. Abanes 2001, 24.
84. Abanes 2001, 58–59. Although conservative Christians hold varying opinions on the dangers of Wicca, they do generally view it as subversive to Christianity and prohibited by Biblical teachings.
85. This is a selection of Harry Potter-branded merchandise available as of August 2005 from ToysRUs. See www.amazon.com/exec/obidos/tg/browse/-/526292/102-1740992-8852937.
86. Giles 2001.
87. MacCormack 2000.
88. Ostling 2003; Bates, n.d.
89. Neal 2001, 15.
90. Jacobs 2000.
91. Killinger 2002.
92. Schnoebelen, n.d.
93. Anonymous, n.d.
94. Jacobs 2000.
95. Interview with Robert Knight, conducted by Daniel Nexon, April 12, 2005.

# CONFLICT AND WARFARE

**II**

# Conflict and the Nation-State
## Magical Mirrors of Muggles and Refracted Images

JENNIFER STERLING-FOLKER AND BRIAN FOLKER

I N WHAT WAYS DOES THE MAGICAL WORLD of Harry Potter mirror the political and international world of muggles? Answering such a question is one way to explore those things that we take for granted as normal in our muggle world of politics and international relations. In this chapter we explore the mirroring of international political and economic institutions in Harry Potter in order to argue that it underscores an important element of human conflict. At first glance it appears that Harry lives in a partially globalized world that is quite similar to our own. Magicals live in nation-states, identify with their countries of origin, have developed state structures that are similar to our own, and participate in rudimentary international institutions and cooperative activities. As with the muggle world, magicals also find themselves in frequent conflict, and warfare is a common occurrence throughout magical history.

Yet one important difference between the worlds of magicals and muggles is that nationalism and the nation-state plays no role in magical conflicts. This is very different from muggle international politics, in which conflict can usually be described according to the parameters of nation-states and national identity markers. Magicals certainly fight one another over identity markers, most notably "race" as it relates to blood purity issues. Yet in muggle international relations these same markers are inevitably linked to politics among nation-states, which are the dominant political organizations of modern global affairs. Human beings tend to self-organize themselves into conflict-oriented groups because resource utilization requires collective effort, which also entails demarcating group boundaries and differentiating group membership. Nationalism and the nation-state have played a central role in defining and demarcating collectives in the modern international system, and so they play a major role in muggle conflict. Yet these elements are absent in the world of Harry Potter, which is essentially consistent with a liberal vision of international politics. In highlighting this absence from Harry Potter's world, our goal is also to highlight the seminal role that the nation-state plays in muggle affairs and international conflict.

## Muggle International Processes

Magicals carry on their daily lives within the parameters of the muggle political and economic world, which is a world divided into individual nation-states. Nation-states usually have a defined territory with carefully marked boundaries, and a population that sees itself as distinct from the populations in other nation-states (on the basis of a variety of cultural identity markers discussed later). Nation-states also have governments that make decisions for their particular populations, so that choices regarding political structures, leadership, and policies are made within the territorial boundaries of nation-states.

Yet nation-states are also interconnected, because most participate in a global capitalist-market system in which goods and services are traded across their borders. Nation-state governments coordinate a great deal of their economic activities so that trade can be relatively "free" from encumbrances. To assist in this process, and to address other transnational problem areas that cut across nation-state boundaries, nation-states have established a variety of international organizations such as the United Nations (UN), the World Trade Organization (WTO), and the World Health Organization (WHO), to name only a few. These have been supplemented over time by nongovernmental organizations established by private citizens or professional organizations.

International relations scholars often refer to the modern, global, political and economic system as "Westphalian," in reference to the treaties signed in Westphalia in 1648 that ended Europe's Thirty Year's War and signaled what international relations scholars often refer to as the "birth" of the nation-state. Historically, human beings organized their political, economic, and social affairs in a variety of institutional ways, such as tribes, kinship groups, or city-leagues. Empires are actually the more common institutional variant throughout human history. Yet after the seventeenth century, the nation-state gradually displaced all other institutional competitors. Today the nation-state is the globe's dominant political unit.[1]

## Mirroring Nationalism and the State

On the surface there are a number of ways in which the magical world of Harry Potter replicates or mirrors existing nation-states and hence this modern Westphalian world. Magicals share distinct nationalities and identities linked to particular sporting teams, languages, and educational systems. The nationalities referenced are ones with which we are already familiar. The Quidditch World Championship brings sports teams from Ireland and Bulgaria to England, as well as contingents of witches and wizards from around the world. Ludo Bagman complains that he is unable to communicate with the Bulgarian representatives given their foreign language.[2] Different nation-states in this magical world have their own educational institutions, such as Beauxbatons or Durmstrang. And magical governing structures, with missions similar to that of muggle governments, are apparently replicated within nation-state borders around the globe.

As a representative of these governing structures, the Ministry of Magic in Great Britain exists alongside the governing structure developed by muggles within Britain's borders. The head of the Ministry, the Minister of Magic, has contact with the leader of the muggles' government, the British prime minister, as situations warrant.[3] But the main job of this Ministry is, as initially described by Hagrid, "to keep it from the Muggles that there's still witches an' wizards up an' down the country," otherwise "everyone'd be wantin' magic solutions to their problems."[4] Many of the Ministry's departments and the tasks they undertake are directed at hiding the wizarding world as a result. Wizards from the Ministry are regularly wiping muggle memories clean of magical encounters. The Ministry maintains departments for accidental magic reversals, magical law enforcement, magical catastrophes, improper use of magic, magical transportation, and a committee for muggle-worthy excuses.

Yet as Harry's story unfolds, it becomes clear that regulation to prevent muggle detection is not the Ministry's only responsibility. The Ministry also regulates intramagical behavior in ways that are similar to the regulation of muggle populations by their respective national governments. The Ministry's Department for the Regulation and Control of Magical Creatures, for example, regulates the conduct of goblins and uppity house elves, and it enforces the Code of Wand Use that "no non-human creature is permitted to carry or use a wand."[5] The Ministry also requires that Animagi be registered, and, according to Myrtle the ghost, the Ministry can regulate the behavior of ghosts by preventing them from haunting particular victims.[6] In a similar fashion, muggle governments may establish different conduct rules (and rights) for different subgroups within their territories (Indian tribes are accorded a different legal status by the American state, for example).

Muggle governments also regulate the possession and use of particular types of weapons within their population. They are particularly careful to regulate the use of dangerous substances (such as weapons-grade plutonium or cyanide), just as the Ministry of Magic does with regard to Hermione's use of a time turner or Snape's use of the truth potion Veritaserum.[7] Muggle governments might regulate and monitor communications across phone lines or the internet, just as the Ministry's Floo Regulation Panel monitors the use of fireplaces within the magical world,[8] as well as ensuring that muggle and magical fireplaces are not connected.[9] And the Ministry requires wizards to pass a test and obtain a license in order to apparate, just as muggles are required to obtain driver's licenses from their governments before operating an automobile.

The Ministry's powers are apparently relatively far-reaching as a result, which is consistent with the powers and responsibilities of most muggle governments found around the world. The Ministry can, for example, direct educational institutions and expel students from school if they do not abide by Ministry laws, such as the Decree for the Restriction of Underage Wizardry. The Ministry has a wizard high court, the Wizengamot, which tries individuals and can fine or punish them. It maintains a prison, Askaban, where the worst offenders of magical laws can be incarcerated. And, as with many muggle governments, the Ministry has the authority to order and carry out executions. A Committee for the Disposal of Dangerous Creatures oversees executions of magical creatures. Magical humans who are condemned to death by the Ministry's court system are executed by the Dementors who guard Askaban. Although some muggle governments have purposefully eschewed the death penalty in response to human rights concerns, many muggle governments retain the right to make corporal punishment decisions for their particular populations. Given the Ministry's wide-ranging responsibilities, it is no wonder that there is a desire among the politically ambitious, such as Percy Weasley, to climb its ranks and become the Minister of Magic.

## Mirroring Capitalist Economics and International Cooperation

In mirroring the muggle world, magicals also have a capitalist-market system with characteristics that are similar to the capitalist-market systems of most modern muggle nation-states. The magical economic system provides goods and services in exchange for magical currency. The students of Hogwarts must purchase school supplies in Diagon Alley, which is the magical equivalent of a muggle shopping mall, and the Weasley twins' long-standing ambition is to open a joke shop where they can sell their wares. The background of the best-selling author, Gilderoy Lockhart, and the annual purchasing of schoolbooks suggest that there are magical publishers who operate as muggle publishers do, by supplying books for purchase and profit in a market catering to the magical community. To support the magical capitalist-market system, the magical community has its own wizard banking system, Gringotts, which is run by goblins and has international interests.

Why magicals cannot simply conjure the items they need at will is unclear, as is the magical desire to replicate these historically specific forms of muggle economic exchange. The sign above Ollivander's indicates that they have been "makers of fine wands since 382 B.C."[10] This means they have experienced a wide variety of economic exchange forms that have also varied historically in their relationship to the dominant political institutions of any period. Yet magicals seem intent upon closely mirroring the political, economic, and social expectations of the present muggle world. This is most obvious in the magical expectation that humans must work for wages and benefits, and a career path must be chosen in the fifth year of study.[11] These expectations are entirely bound to the present capitalist-market system and have no counterparts in other historical periods (medieval peasants did not have a career with wages and benefits, nor would a Roman merchant have known what such terms meant).

Magicals also share the muggle expectation that those with lower-paying jobs will have lower standards of living. This results in a hierarchy of classes which Tammy Turner-Vorbeck notes could be examined from a neo-Marxist lens.[12] Constant references to the Weasley family's relative poverty are often linked to Mr. Weasley's job in the Ministry's relatively unimportant Misuse of Muggle Artifacts Office. When the Malfoys taunt the Weasleys, it is often related to Mr. Weasley's job. Lucius refers to Mr. Weasley's need to be "paid overtime,"[13] for example, or his inability to pay for good Quidditch Cup seats.[14] Similarly, Professor Lupin's shabby appearance is frequently attributed to his inability to find steady employment, made particularly acute after the Ministry passes "Anti-Werewolf Legislation" that denies werewolves access to jobs in the magical community. The Malfoys, on the other hand, represent a class of aristocrats who do not appear to need to work.

As with the muggle world, the magical capitalist-market system extends beyond nation-state borders. There is international trade between the separate national communities of magicals. As with the governing structures of the muggle world, the Ministry of Magic is intimately involved with international cooperative efforts to regulate and harmonize trade across distinct national political units. Percy Weasley's first job in the Ministry's Department for International Magical Cooperation has him negotiating with his institutional counterparts in other nation-states to harmonize trading standards. This mirrors similar muggle efforts in Europe and the WTO. There is a need to standardize cauldron thickness, he asserts, because "foreign imports" often leak, and "unless some sort of international law is imposed" the British market will be flooded with poor quality, dangerous products.[15] And as with muggle trade, particular magical items have been deemed too dangerous to import freely and have resulted in a collective ban across national magical communities, such as flying carpets.[16]

The existence of magical international organizations, international laws and agreements, and cross-national sporting events encouraged by departments of international cooperation are a final way in which muggle activity is mirrored in the magical world. There is an International Federation of Warlocks, which has been holding conventions since 1289,[17] an international court of wizards, and an International Confederation and Code of Wizarding Secrecy.[18] The Quidditch World Championship attracts wizards from all over the world who must simultaneously be kept hidden from muggles. In order to host the Cup, the Ministry works with the International Association of Quidditch, an intergovernmental organization that allows the Ministry to coordinate with its counterparts elsewhere and establish portkeys across five continents.[19] Percy's Department of International Magical Cooperation is also in charge of organizing and overseeing security for the Triwizard Tournament. This international event is similar to muggle Olympics and foreign student exchange programs, because it is a "way of establishing ties between young witches and wizards of different nationalities."[20]

## Conflict, Power, and the State in the Muggle and Magical Worlds

Magical politics and economics occurs within the established realm of muggle international relations, yet an interesting exception to this magical mirroring may be found in conflict and the role that governing institutions play in it. Obviously, violent conflict and warfare occur in both worlds.

Muggle history is replete with examples of warfare among different groups and nations of people. Not surprisingly, the study of warfare is of ongoing interest to international relations scholars, particularly among realists, who tend to focus on issues of power and violence.[21] Similarly, there are many references throughout the Potter series to wizards waging wars among themselves, as with the case of Voldemort and his Death Eaters, or against other magical creatures, such as giants, goblins, and trolls. The reasons for conflict in the magical world are also all too human, involving the specific goal of racial purity and oppression that have their counterparts in the Westphalian system and world politics in general. Xenophobia, or the intense hatred of another group of people on the basis of nationality, race, ethnicity, religion, and other attributes, played an important role in World War II. And xenophobia remains a basic feature of contemporary international politics, as violence in Yugoslavia and Rwanda–Burundi in the 1990s reminds us.

Racial purity is not the only reason for conflict in the muggle world, however, and it is here that interesting differences between the two worlds begin to emerge. Differences over political ideology or economics, and over control of territory or resources, can also lead to violent conflict among muggles. Such conflicts can either be internal to nation-states, as is the case of civil wars, or between nation-states, as is the case of international wars. Warfare in the magical world, on the other hand, seems almost solely connected to issues of racial purity among wizards and the oppression or containment of other magical creatures. The Death Eater's obsession with blood purity is as old as Salazar Slytherin's participation in the creation of Hogwarts, and it seems to have been the central division among wizards and witches since that time. In wizard relations with other magicals, there are references to historical goblin rebellions against wizard rule, and Ministry Aurors were responsible for killing giants during Voldemort's original reign of terror.[22] As Dumbledore notes, the "Fountain of Magical Brethren" in the atrium of the Ministry of Magic was a misnomer since "wizards have mistreated and abused our fellows for too long."[23] What the fountain actually celebrated was not a common magical heritage, but the triumph of wizards and witches over other magical creatures such as centaurs, goblins, and house elves.

These magical conflicts are not easy to categorize according to the parameters of muggle international relations. The conflict with Voldemort might be characterized as a civil war among wizards, with one of its epicenters being Great Britain, since Hogwarts is an important site of resistance and is located there. Prior conflicts between wizards and goblins or giants might also be characterized as a form of magical civil war, in that all parties involved share a common characteristic of being magical and are fighting over who will have sovereign control over whatever shared territory they might occupy. But we could also characterize magical conflict as international instead, since other magicals are not specific to Great Britain, and prior magical conflicts, as well as the present conflict with Voldemort, have both worldwide dimensions and ramifications for *all* magical creatures as well as muggles. In addition, various sides in these conflicts have sought alliance partners in foreign countries, which is a characteristic of international warfare.[24] Ultimately it may be more appropriate to characterize magical warfare as transnational, which means that it does not occur along standard Westphalian lines. In other words, it is not strictly or even primarily inside the nation-state, nor is it strictly or even primarily between nation-states. Rather it occurs outside of, beyond, or in spite of standard international political categories.

## The Role of the State in Muggle Conflict

Alternatively, our muggle world of territorially bounded nation-states shapes the scope and conduct of muggle war to a large extent. Certainly muggles have crosscutting identities, just as the identity of being a wizard or witch cuts across nation-state boundaries, and many liberal scholars argue that national identity and its loyalty to the state is declining.[25] Yet the nation-state itself remains a primary point of identification for its population in the Westphalian system, and realists are quick to point out that transnational identities that cut across nation-states are not the primary fault-lines for international conflicts in the modern era. As Franke Wilmer puts it, "the state today makes claims on individuals on the basis of their identity as citizens which trump all other claims, past and present, based on all other group identities."[26] The possible exception to this is international terrorism, which can involve transnational identities and may attempt to operate transnationally outside and against the nation-state system. But it is important to remember that not all terrorism is global in scope, nor are transnational identities always involved. In addition, terrorists must still find safe havens with*in* nation-states in order to operate, because every inch of the habitable globe belongs to some nation-state.

In the case of civil wars, such wars often bleed into neighboring states or, depending on a variety of factors, have international ramifications. Yet the existence of nation-states can also prevent civil conflicts from spreading, because what is being fought over is control of specified territory, which is bounded by the protected territory of neighboring nation-states. If the internal conflict spills across those borders (whether in actual fighting or an outpouring of refugees), then neighbors might directly intervene in the conflict. When such spillage does not occur, however, neighboring nation-states are just as likely to let the conflict run its course without interference. This had advantages after Europe's Thirty Years' War in the seventeenth century, since it meant that different political and economic units would not interfere in one another's affairs on the basis of transnational identities or interests. But it also means that genocides during civil wars are common to the Westphalian era, since transnational identities and political conflicts are not shared across boundaries and so other nation-states do not intervene to end them. In both instances, of modern international war and civil war, it is still possible to conceptualize warfare according to parameters that relate to the attributes of the nation-state, and hence the very foundation of the modern international system.

The ability of a nation-state's government to make decisions for its population without the interference of other governments and populations is referred to as "sovereignty," and it is a topic much discussed and analyzed by international relations scholars.[27] Sovereignty does not mean that nation-states are isolated from one another, or disinterested in one another's political and economic affairs, or do not try to sway and affect one another's political and economic policies. Because there is an entwining or "interdependence" among nation-states in particular transnational issue areas (such as environmental degradation or capitalist-market economics), the policies enacted by one nation-state can have serious ramifications for the environmental or economic health of its neighbors or trading partners.[28] The nature of such transnational problems is not amenable to either a violent or unilateral solution. There is a great deal of effort among nation-states to coordinate policies to one degree or another as a result.

The final decision as to whether to cooperate still rests with the governing structures unique to each nation-state, however, and much of the international cooperation that occurs today is coordinated by and between the governments of these nation-states. Sovereignty is often defined as a legal right to noninterference. As such, it is the legal basis for most international treaties. Yet this definition can be confusing since, as with any right, it can be violated by those who have relatively greater power. I have the right not to be murdered, and yet this right can easily be violated by a criminal with a gun. In a similar vein, nation-states have the right to sovereignty within their own borders, yet neighboring nation-states with relatively greater power may attack and occupy them. Who guarantees a right is just as important as the content of the right itself, which is why nation-states often obsess over one another's relative power and go to great lengths to correct perceived imbalances.[29]

In the absence of a higher authority over nation-states, the nation-state both guarantees *and* violates the rights of their own populations and those of other nation-states. In other words, in the anarchic environment of international politics, nation-states can only enjoy the right of sovereignty within their own borders if they can also guarantee it themselves and with respect to other nation-states.[30] Unfortunately, the governments and leaders of many nation-states have taken this basic truism of the modern era to mean that they must conquer and subjugate their own populations, as well as those of neighboring nation-states, in order to ensure their own national sovereignty. The outcome is tantamount to an "organized hypocrisy," according to Stephen Krasner, because nation-state governments spend a great deal of time talking about the importance of sovereignty while simultaneously violating one another's sovereignty when they believe it is in their own interests to do so.[31] It is probably more appropriate to think of nation-state sovereignty less as a solid legal wall and more as a "mental horizon" that shapes the decisions and actions of leaders, governments, and populations.[32] It justifies one's own actions, even when those actions violate the general principle that all nation-states should have the right to sovereignty within their own borders. As a result, invasion has been a common practice among nation-states, as recent examples of Iraq's 1989 invasion of Kuwait or the United States' 2003 invasion of Iraq illustrate.

The nation-state is also pertinent to how war, as an organized, collective activity, is waged in the modern era. Muggle warfare has always involved complex battlefield planning and strategies, which must include the movement of large numbers of people, weapons, equipment, and other materials. Even more complex planning and coordination is involved in waging war in the modern era, due to technology advances and large population growths. Such coordination only comes about with the intervention of leadership and collective governing structures. In other words, a nation-state's population does not suddenly rise up in a fit of passion to attack its neighbors. Instead, waging war involves encouragement and coordination by a nation-state's governing institutions and its leaders. The result is that "those who make the momentous decision to lead a state into war do not themselves do the fighting on the battlefield," and "those who actually engage in battle are likely to have had little or nothing to do with the actual decision to fight."[33] Because "war is a matter of political decision, which can be the result of rational as well as irrational processes," muggle governments always figure prominently in the activity of warfare.

International wars in the Westphalian system are waged between populations whose activity is coordinated by their respective governments and directed at *both* the population *and* government of their enemies. The close identification of populations/nations and governments/states is one of the reasons why modern warfare can be so deadly for muggle civilians and noncombatants. The nation-state's governing institutions are also seminal to civil wars, because the immediate goal of the factions that are fighting one another is typically the seizure of state power. Regardless of the specific causes of the fighting, whether it is for racial purity, resource control, or economic ideology, the goal of each side in a civil war is to gain control over or create a government in order to impose their preferences within the nation-state's boundaries. Warfare in the muggle world has always been a collective endeavor, then, and in modern times it has required and depended upon the state in order to be waged. The state is ruthlessly efficient at it, too. As Bruce Falconer notes, "the rise of the modern bureaucratic state . . . simplified the task of identifying and tracking target groups and provided an institutional cloak behind which executioners could hide."[34]

The state as a whole remains a relatively powerful instrument in the muggle world. This also makes it extremely dangerous, which is something that international relations scholars of all theoretical stripes generally agree upon. Obviously terrorists acting alone or in small groups are capable of killing relatively large numbers in short periods of time, as the Oklahoma City bombings or the airplane hijackings of 9/11 demonstrate. But terrorist death tolls since the nineteenth century, which can be measured in the thousands, pale in comparison to the casualties achieved by states in that same period of time. Rudolph Rummel has compiled statistics on state-sponsored killings, or democide, and compared them to battlefield deaths.[35] He estimates that between 1900 and 1987 democide was responsible for 170 million deaths as compared to 34.4 million battlefield deaths from *both* international and civil wars combined. In other words, more people died at the hands of their states in the twentieth century than they did in terrorist attacks, international wars, and civil wars combined. The state can be ruthlessly efficient at genocide in either international or civil wars. It can also produce massive lethal results that individuals working alone or in small groups simply cannot achieve.

## The Absence of the State in Magical Conflict

Alternatively, the nation-state does not play a central role, either as the co-ordinator of mass conflict or the goal of it, in the conflicts of Harry Potter. The Ministry of Magic does not appear to figure prominently in accounts of prior magical wars, nor is the desire to gain control over it a motivation in the conflict with Voldemort and the Death Eaters. Certainly Voldemort has sought to destroy the Ministry's ability to thwart him, but he and his followers do not appear bent on either controlling existing governing institutions or creating their own in its place. Given that the state is such a powerful and dangerous entity in the world of muggles, it is all the more curious that Voldemort and the Death Eaters do not seek to create or control such an institution. The answer to this curiosity may lie in the observation that, unlike muggles, magicals do not seem to need political governing structures and institutions in order to obtain their preferences, particularly if those preferences involve violent conflict.

Voldemort appears to have no interest in taking over the Ministry of Magic and becoming simply a malignant state official. Voldemort wants to, variously, eliminate mud-bloods, kill Harry Potter, and "become the greatest sorcerer in the world."[36] By the fourth novel we learn that one of Voldemort's ultimate objectives reflects his pseudonym: to "conquer death" and pursue "immortality."[37] As he claims in Order of the Phoenix, "there is nothing worse than death."[38] His goals, at least as we understand them through the Half-Blood Prince, have little to do with seizing control of the organs of the state.[39] Certainly one of Voldemort's ongoing desires is to kill mud-bloods and achieve blood purity, which is what he has in common with the Death Eaters. Yet hereto these goals do not appear to require magical governing institutions in order to be pursued or obtained. Certainly the Ministry might serve as a bulwark against blood purity activities, but it is constantly thwarted and undermined by the magical abilities of individual wizards and witches.

For all its powers of oversight and regulation, then, the Ministry of Magic is not a particularly powerful entity within the magical community itself, and when compared to the relatively greater powers of the muggle state. While there are apparently no institutional political competitors to the Ministry (with the possible exception of Hogwarts), the Ministry's powers are checked by the magical power of particular individual wizards, such as Dumbledore or Voldemort. It is no surprise, then, that none of the major characters seeks to lead the Ministry, and those who do, such as Cornelius Fudge or Percy, are buffoons with relatively little magical power. The Ministry is necessary for the maintenance of law and order, but it is a mere shadow image of the muggle state it is meant to reflect.[40] It is not a location or site of power in its own wizarding world. Power is instead the wand used at times jointly and simultaneously by Death Eaters or members of the Order of the Phoenix, but more often by individuals battling one another. In fact, collective conflict in the wizarding world usually involves individuals fighting one-on-one with their wands. It resembles multiple, simultaneous duels rather than the sort of complex coordination required for muggle conflicts.

The real "powers" of the wizarding world are individuals such as Voldemort, Dumbledore, and Harry, who have followers but do not seem to need them when encountering one another. Thus power in the magical world ultimately derives from the individual's own innate capacities. It does not appear to derive from the pooling of those capabilities into institutional governing structures as it does in the muggle world. Even when pooling does occur, as when the Death Eaters appear after the Quidditch World Cup to torment the muggle camp owners, such activity does not require complex coordination. Nor can collective pooling stand up against the powers of particular, individual wizards, which is underscored by Dumbledore's appearance in the Ministry in the fifth novel, which effectively ends the fight between the Death Eaters and members of the Order.[41] The state is simply not as necessary for accomplishing large-scale collective violence among magicals as it is for nonmagicals. It is instead individuals who determine outcomes and represent the real power to achieve, unmake, protect, and kill in Harry Potter's world. As a result, the world of Harry Potter is very liberal in an international relations theoretical sense. It associates power with individuals rather than with collectives or their governing structures. It does not assume, as realist international relations scholars do, that collectives and conflict necessarily go hand in hand.[42]

# The Social Construction of Identity Difference in the Muggle and Magical Worlds

The absence of the state in the magical conflicts of Harry Potter would not be so notable if it were not for the presence of socially constructed identity differences in that same world. Intimately connected with the muggle need for governing institutions to accomplish collective goals is the need to identify group boundaries in the muggle world. Who participates in collective decisions, who reaps the benefits of collective action, and on whose behalf governing institutions will act are basic questions of muggle polities. National membership is a boundary that determines who will and will not receive the full benefits of citizenship, such as education, access to health care, the right to vote, or a passport. Less benignly, it is also a boundary that determines against whom it is acceptable to use collective violence. Where such boundaries come from is a matter of social construction.[43] That is, they are determined by the social construction of shared characteristics among group members. The most obvious characteristics include a common language, religion, political or economic ideology, culture, history, racial characteristics, and blood lineage.

A great deal of conflict in muggle affairs revolves around what qualities unite a collective, because the delineation of collective identity involves exclusion. As Iver Neumann puts it succinctly, "there is no inclusion without exclusion."[44] The elements necessary to claim a common identity and membership in a group also determine who should be excluded because they lack those characteristics. This can lead to marginalization, exclusion, or forced assimilation within collectives. In asking "what is the basis for group solidarity within the state," Franke Wilmer notes that "the creation of real states has been an enormously violent process," because "state-making conquers the 'Others' within imagined boundaries."[45] Differences over shared characteristics and the exclusions they entail can pull nation-states apart, particularly when subgroups within a collective demand purity of an identity marker, whether it is of blood, race, religion, ethnicity, or language. And the juxtaposition of one's own national collective "self" against that of "other" national collectives often serves as the justification for intercollective violence. Hence how collective identity is socially constructed is a subject of inquiry for both liberal and realist international relations scholars, with the former focusing on the role of identity in cooperation and the latter focusing on its role in violence.

While the imposition of a collective identity is often a violent process, violence is not innate to the *content* of any particular identity marker or configuration. A notion of racial or ethnic difference does not necessarily mean intolerance or lead inevitably to policies of violence and the oppression or slaughter of others who are different. It is perfectly possible to eschew identity difference or accept it as mere difference and nothing else. But socially constructed identity difference, as a fundamental feature of human collectives, is frequently used by leaders and states as triggers for collective violence against other collectives who do not share the same socially constructed identity. The exploration of group identity boundaries, and the triggers that lead to violence or the conditions that promote tolerance, are an important part of international relations scholarship.[46] Under the right conditions, the notion of "blood" purity, as a significant but ultimately socially constructed identity marker, can become the source of intracollective intolerance and violence among muggles.

## *The Social Construction of Magical Collective Identity*

This dynamic of socially constructed intolerance and violence can be seen at work in the magical world of Harry Potter.[47] Much of the conflict in the magical world revolves around the fact that wizards and witches have supposedly been regularly fraternizing with muggles at the most basic level of sex and marriage. The result is that much of the magical community has a muggle in the family tree. "Most wizards these days are half-blood anyway," Ron asserts, because "if we hadn't married muggles we'd've died out."[48] Sirius makes similar assertions.[49] This genetic mixing provides the basis for the "pure blood" claims of the Death Eaters (although not for Voldemort himself), who have not fraternized with muggles and so can claim that they have not been "tainted" with muggle genetic material.[50] Both claims, that there is a need to procreate with muggles and to maintain a standard of "pure blood," are problematic, just as they would be in the muggle world. It is possible for two muggles to spontaneously give birth to wizards and witches, as is the case with Hermione and with Harry's mother, Lily. Thus the claim that human magicals needed to intermarry with human muggles to continue producing human magicals is erroneous. Both Hermione and Lily are also accused of being mud-bloods by Death Eaters, but if their parents were muggles then there was no magical blood to begin and it is unclear how their blood could be "muddied" in any biological or physiological sense.

Squibs such as Filch and Mrs. Figg represent an alternative situation in which offspring of a witch and wizard have no magical powers. It is unclear why such individuals are not simply called muggles, but the point is that pure bloodlines are no guarantee of magical ability. Nor are they a guarantee of relatively exceptional magical power. Hermione's apparently tainted blood does not prevent her from having exceptional magical powers or Neville's pure blood from having relatively less magical ability. The same is true for Harry as well as for Voldemort who, despite his obsession with pure blood, is actually a mud-blood himself and yet one of the most powerful wizards of his age. Magical abilities associated with blood ties do not even need a direct parental linkage in the wizarding world in order to become manifest. Harry enjoys protection from Voldemort due to his mother's sacrifice and his genetic relationship to Aunt Petunia, whose "blood became your refuge," Dumbledore tells Harry.[51] Yet Voldemort is actually able to steal this protection to some extent, by using Harry's blood to resurrect himself.[52]

Thus there is no correlation between the purity of one's blood and one's magical abilities. Nor does it appear that either the mixing or purity of blood makes a difference as to whether you have magical powers in the first place. If magical abilities are rooted in biological, physiological, or genetic differences, they appear to occur at random and do not need the social engineering of either genetic mixing or separation to continue. This makes the pureblood mania of the Malfoys and Blacks, with the latter's pureblood family tapestry, all the more ridiculous.[53] Yet it is simultaneously consistent with our own world of human collectives, who obsess over blood purity by tracing it back across many generations and using percentages of blood purity as cues to citizenship rights. As J. K. Rowling herself notes, "the Nazis used precisely the same warped logic as the Death Eaters" with regard to blood distinctions, and there are parallels between Voldemort's obsession with blood purity and Hitler's obsession with a pure Aryan race.[54]

## *Why Not Oppress Muggles Instead?*

What is interesting about Rowling's reliance on blood purity as a source of conflict in Harry's world, however, is that it deflects attention from the more obvious potential conflict that exists in that world between magicals and muggles. Based on innate abilities, one can readily identify which individuals are magical, and hence part of the magical collective "self," and which are not, and hence part of the nonmagical "other." Why, then, haven't *all* magicals seized upon what is apparently a tangible genetic difference with an alternative collective (rather than socially constructing a difference within their own collective) and united to oppress muggles? After all, if magical humans develop collective identity markers and configurations to delimit who they are versus who they are not, just as muggle humans do, then it's not clear why the difference between magical ability and muggle inability would not serve as an obvious collective identity marker to justify the political and economic domination of muggles.

We are led to believe that most magicals want muggle coexistence and hide themselves so they will not be bothered by constant requests or demands for magical assistance in muggle affairs. This implies that exposed magicals would be forced to do muggle biddings, but magicals certainly do not fear muggles, as Harry's essay on "Witch Burning in the Fourteenth

Century Was Completely Pointless—Discuss" indicates.[55] The fact that Mr. Weasley's job entails ongoing efforts to stop or clean up after various magical acts of "muggle-baiting" suggests that magicals do not have a very high regard for muggles.[56] When magicals use the term *muggle* it is not meant as a compliment, and the term is similar to the derogatory word, *nigger,* used by bigots to describe African Americans. Even among magicals who profess a fondness for muggles, there is an effort to disassociate from them. When Ron Weasley admits that there is a muggle in the family tree, he also notes, "but we never talk about him."[57] Mr. Weasley's constant afterthought to "bless them,"[58] because muggles are completely unaware that their behavior is shaped by magicals, is highly paternalistic. And the wizarding treatment of house elves, goblins, and giants, as well as the Ministry's "Fountain of Magical Brethren," underscores a pattern of wizarding domination that makes the absence of systematic muggle oppression all the stranger.[59]

The extent to which there is no overt conflict between muggles and magicals may simply be a literary device to preserve the fantasy that any child could be swept up in a magical world at a moment's notice.[60] After all, the essence of Harry's appeal to the young adolescents who constitute Rowling's principal audience is obvious. Harry is a skinny loser with thick glasses. As a despised stepchild in direct competition with a physically stronger and favored natural son, his position in the highly regimented social world of the Dursley family is hopelessly inferior. For him, life is an unbroken string of humiliations that reinforce his essential powerlessness. All of this changes, however, when he learns another world exists; one in which, far from being obscure and insignificant, he possesses a measure of honored and even heroic fame. And most importantly, he possesses power. The very marks of his inferiority at home are in the magical world of the badges of his special superiority. Harry represents a fantasy of escape from a well-ordered social world, in which he feels marginalized and insignificant, to a world of unrestrained individual power. Voldemort is a much darker version of the same fantasy: a powerful individual who threatens to plunge a nascent and fragile social order back into Hobbsian anarchy. Both are orphans and as such represent the ultimate fantasy of individualism, in which there is no debt owed to or constraints from a collective, such as the family, and power may be wielded as the individual alone sees fit.

These themes can be highlighted by comparing the Harry Potter series to another "fantasy" series, the Marvel comic book series the *X-Men,* which mirrors the power and constraints of human collectives in a way that

Harry Potter's world does not. At first glance the similarities between the two series are remarkable. In both cases, our world of human limitations and frailties exists alongside a world of human beings with extraordinary powers. Which human beings are born with and develop such powers is a mystery in both series. Both also contain powerful individuals, such as Dumbledore and Professor Xavier, who want peaceful coexistence with "regular" humans and are pitted against other powerful individuals, such as Voldemort and Magneto, who would victimize or oppress them instead. Our ability to sympathize with both positions, to both restrain and wield power, is explicitly encouraged in the *X-Men* series. We can all too readily identify with both the fear of unchecked power and the glorious possibility that we might possess power unknown. Similarly, Harry's regular return to the Dursleys, as though he were awakening from a self-gratifying dream, underscores the tensions between checked and unchecked individual power. Even if Harry continues to chafe under the conditions of life during the summer, he has the satisfaction of knowing that the Dursleys' contempt has been replaced by fear once his magical powers are acknowledged.[61]

In the case of the *X-Men*, however, both types of humans are well aware of one another and this serves as the thematic catalyst for the entire series. Those born with extraordinary powers are referred to as "mutants." They are born into a world where regular humans dominate political, economic, and social structures but also fear the mutant's potentially destabilizing power. Unlike muggles and magicals, regular humans in the *X-Men* series do have some capacity to control mutants, and mutants are regularly rounded up and contained. In order to escape this oppression, mutants must band together. Professor Xavier is a leader among mutants who encourages peaceful coexistence and the use of mutant power to protect and serve all humankind. Magneto is Xavier's opposite, who refuses to accept his inferior and hunted status, instead leading mutants who would use their powers to dominate and oppress. Thus the conflict in *X-Men* involves the relationship between two sets of collectives, mutant humans and regular humans, who have crosscutting allegiances.

The Harry Potter characters, on the other hand, do not have crosscutting allegiances and their goals relate largely to one another but not to nonmagical humans. In other words, the conflict between Dumbledore and Voldemort is over how to socially construct the magical collective, not its relationship to that of the nonmagical collective. Nonmagicals can certainly be victims of Voldemort and his Death Eaters, but they are usually bystanders and not the intended targets, who are instead other magicals who have failed to live up to the Death Eaters' standards of collective identity difference. Obviously the Potter series is a fantasy that most of us can enjoy because it allows us to retain the normalcy of our daily lives while acting out the very thing that is not possible in that life—an individual who does not need human collectives in order to wield power. It is the ultimate fantasy of liberal philosophy. But this very attribute is also what makes the need for collective identity within the magical world of Harry Potter so inexplicable from a realist theoretical perspective. In a world in which power is innate to individuals and governing structures are not necessary for the achievement of collective goals, the relevance of collective identity markers should be less important as well. It should not matter who is or is not a member of the magical collective if the pooling of individual resources is not necessary for achieving larger collective goals. There should be relatively little cause for collective conflict among wizards and witches themselves as a result.

## Concluding Remarks

That Rowling does not have a logically consistent understanding of either human genetics or human conflict is not the point. In fact, the absence of tangible genetic distinctions within the magical world is consistent with our own world, in which differences between groups of humans are socially constructed and not innate. There is nothing natural or transhistorical about any of the standard identity markers or specific configurations of them relied upon by humans in constructing their collectives. *Homo sapiens* constitute a single species, there is no single "true" religion, ethnicity is always a combination of historical myths and truths, and languages evolve like anything else. Human beings cling dearly to the fiction that these collective identity markers and configurations are stable and real, because doing so gives their lives purpose and meaning. Yet identity is always fluid and indeterminate in its content and boundaries. It always involves an imaginary sense of collective "self" in juxtaposition to an imaginary collective "other." The construction of such markers ultimately involves the determination of who is a member of one's collective and who is not. Ethnic or racial hatred needs no actual genetic grounding to produce collective violence and genocide, only the collective belief that such differences exist and matter. Hence the social construction of identity and its linkage to self-other in Harry Potter mirrors the way in which the goals of racial oppression and blood purity continue to plague our own world.

Yet the important linkage between identity and collective political structures, and hence to resource control and power, is missing in the world of Harry Potter, as it is in most liberal international relations scholarship. In the muggle world it is identity "that secures the social cohesiveness necessary to create and maintain the boundaries of inclusion and exclusion among those who identify themselves as 'members' of the social group or 'citizens' of the state."[62] When nationalism, ethnic identity, and racial bloodlines are at issue in muggle conflict, the touted identity characteristics often parallel the nation-state as the main political/economic and collective unit of the modern era. This is one of the central insights of realist scholarship. In other words, muggles with xenophobic tendencies who seek to obtain pure blood forms of nationalism usually pursue their goals via the state, by seizing the reins of power that the state embodies, by directing it toward these particular aims, and by using it to mobilize the population and a configuration of identity markers to violent collective ends. Hence the seizure or control of the state is the means whereby muggle collectives can obtain goals such as racial purification and oppression that involve violence en mass. Even if identity formation is irrational and internally inconsistent, then, realism argues that it still has a rational external motivation in the muggle world: It makes collective action possible in a world where collective action is necessary.

Alternatively, the Harry Potter story involves a nation that is pulling itself apart on the basis of identity politics and the delineation of collective boundaries. Yet neither the Death Eaters nor those who would stop them need a state in order to realize their goals. This is because in the wizarding world collective action is not necessary, so its formation is all the more transparently absurd. The Potter series is a story of individuals who are free from the constraints of and responsibilities to collectives, and yet choose to differentiate themselves as collectives nonetheless. The delineation of collective characteristics among wizards and witches is very much a social fabrication. This tells us less about J. K. Rowling's world of Harry Potter, of course, and more about our own simultaneous need for collective identity efforts that ultimately divide us. In the modern era, those divisions are manifest in territorially based nation-states that involve efforts within specified territories at delineating a collective identity of "self" that is juxtaposed to "other" nation-states and their collective identities. This Westphalian system is a historical construct and, as with any global system, will change and be replaced by other foundational concepts and governing structures over time.[63] Yet the impetus to form collectives and so divide and differentiate ourselves in some way will remain a fundamental attribute of any future global governance system.

# Notes

1. Considerable attention has been given to the question of how the nation-state came to dominate global politics. Many scholars argue that the nation-state displaced other institutional competitors because it was more efficient at raising revenues in order to wage war and/or participate in capitalist-market endeavors. See, for example, Desch 1996; Rasler 1989; Spruyt 1994; and Tilly 1975, 1990.

2. GF, 89.

3. The escape of prisoners from Azkaban is deemed such a situation, although in the case of Sirius Black's escape, the Minister at the time, Cornelius Fudge, was also criticized by the International Federation of Warlocks for having done so (PA, 37–38; See also OP, 544).

4. PS, 81.

5. GF, 98, 132, 449.

6. GF, 465.

7. GF, 517.

8. OP, 612.

9. GF, 45.

10. PS, 102.

11. Alternatively there is some discrepancy as to whether nonhuman magicals can expect wages and hence what their role is in the capitalist-market system. Hermione's ongoing attempts to raise awareness of house elf servitude, and their right to expect wages and benefits instead, are met with incredulity by everyone, house elves included but with the exception of Dumbledore. Yet presumably Gringott goblins work for wages, and when the Fat Lady's portrait is attacked, Dumbledore "hires" security trolls to guard her (PA, 269). The difference in treatment may derive from the less obsequious natures of goblins and trolls, but it is a mirror of the historical development of the muggle's capitalist-market system which, as it developed in Europe and the Americas from the fourteenth century on, depended on the African slave trade to provide non-wage-earning labor. See, for example, Smith, Collins, Hopkins, and Muhammad 1988 and Wallerstein 1979.

12. Turner-Vorbeck 2003, 16. More extended analyses of capitalism and class in Harry Potter may be found in Goodman 2004; Mendelsohn 2003; Park 2003; and Turner-Vorbeck 2003.

13. CS, 77.

14. GF, 101.

15. GF, 56.

16. GF, 91.

17. CS, 189.

18. GF, 425 and 482.

19. GF, 91.

20. GF, 187.

21. A sampling of this literature includes: Bueno de Mesquita 1981; Gilpin 1981; Jervis 2002; Kugler and Lemke 1996; Levy 1998; Midlarsky 2000; Vasquez 1993, 2000; and Wright 1942.

22. PA, 77 and GF, 234.

23. OP, 834.

24. See, for example, Hagrid and Madam Maxime's travel to contact the remaining Giants (OP, 426–33), the foundation of the international confederation of wizards and troll-hunting (OP, 725–26), and the refusal of the centaurs to enter into an alliance with either side in the pureblood wizarding conflict (OP, 602–3, 756).

25. This argument may be found in Ferguson and Mansbach 1996; Held 1996; Shapiro and Alker 1996; and Rosenau 1992.

26. Wilmer 2002, 11.

27. See, for example, Bartelson 1995; Biersteker and Weber 1996; Campbell 1993; Jackson 1999; Krasner 1999: Sørensen 1999; Thomson 1994; and Weber 1995.

28. These points are elaborated in works such as Keohane and Nye 1977; Rosecrance 1986; Zacher 1992; and Young 1989.

29. See, for example, Christensen and Snyder 1990; Ikenberry 2002; Schweller 1998; Vasquez and Elman 2003; Walt 1987; and Wohlforth 1993.

30. As a result, scholars often refer to the international system as one of "self-help," as a means of explaining why all nation-states arm themselves, protect their borders, seek to balance the relative power of their neighbors, and often avoid cooperation with one another. As Waltz (1979, 105) argues, "in any self-help system, units worry about their survival, and the worry conditions their behavior." Yet there is also considerable controversy over what a self-help, anarchic system actually means for the behavior of nation-states. See, for example, Buzan, Jones, and Little1993; Holsti 1992; Keohane 1984; Onuf 1989; Ruggie 1998; and Wendt 1992.

31. Krasner 1999.

32. Reus-Smit 1999.

33. Dougherty and Pfaltzgraff 1997, 263.

34. Falconer 2003, 5.

35. Rummel 1994, 1997.

36. CS, 396–98.

37. GF, 653, 656.

38. OP, 814.

39. Certainly many muggles have sought to lead states in order to both control events and obtain a sense of figurative immortality, that is, by shaping human political and economic affairs so that they may claim a place in human memory after their deaths. But Voldemort seeks to overcome death itself and to bend it to his will, as the very name "Death Eaters" suggests, and this is not a goal that leadership of either a muggle nation-state or the Ministry of Magic can attain.

40. Hall 2003.

41. OP, 805. When Dumbledore appears, Harry thinks "they were saved," as if Dumbledore were a one-person cavalry, and Dumbledore effortlessly dispels a Death Eater who a regular member of the Order had not (OP, 805).

42. The difference between these two theoretical positions has been examined in a variety of texts, including Kegley 1995; Keohane 1990; and Zacher 1992.

43. The international relations literature on the social construction of identity is considerable, but a sampling of seminal pieces includes Hall 1999; Kublakova, Onuf, and Kowart 1998; and Wendt 1992.

44. Neumann 1998, 15.

45. Wilmer 2002, 122. See also Anderson 1991.

46. See, for example, Fearon and Laitin 2003: Hechter 2000; Horowitz 1985; Kaufman 2001; Petersen 2002; and Wilmer 2002.

47. Other essays that explore the social construction of identity and its relationship to blood purity in the Potter series include Anatol 2003 and Ostry 2003.

48. CS, 146.

49. OP, 113.

50. Harry's muggle Aunt Marge is similarly obsessed with blood purity, asserting that "bad blood" is the cause for attributes such as weakness and underbreeding (PA, 27–28).

51. OP, 836.

52. GF, 657.

53. OP, 111–12.

54. "J. K. Rowling Official Site" at www.jkrowling.com, 2004.

55. PA, 1.

56. CS, 48.

57. PS, 123.

58. CS, 148 and GF, 96.

59. It also makes the wizarding ability to subjugate these alternative magical creatures questionable. House elves are assumed incapable of acting against the wishes of their masters and cannot leave their houses without permission. They are, as a result, treated like the "dregs of the magical world" under Voldemort (PS, 226), and Sirius Black's treatment of his own house elf, Kreacher, as "a servant unworthy of much interest or notice" (OP, 834) is probably typical of wizards. Yet when Dobby is freed, he is capable of repelling an attack on Harry by his former master with the mere flick of his wrist (CS, 428–29), Winky has a "brand of magic" that is capable of binding wizards to them (GF, 687), and Kreacher proves perfectly capable of leaving Gimmauld Place when the occasion suits him. Similarly, wizards have supposedly managed to drive giants into uninhabited wilderness, yet six wizards working collectively are unable to subdue Hagrid, who is only a half-giant (OP, 720–23). And then there are the goblins, who have rebelled against wizard control throughout history, and whom Hermione asserts are "quite capable of dealing with wizards" and are unlike house elves "who never stick up for themselves" (GF, 449). All of these examples raise the question of whether

wizards ever really had control over these magical creatures, or if this control was not simply a collective self-delusion, with the desertion of the Dementors from Azkaban, because "Voldemort can offer them much more scope for their powers and their pleasures," being a case in point (OP, 707). The pivotal role of the goblins in the financial system of the wizarding world is also strange given the extent to which goblin rebellions have occurred in the past. It underscores *either* the extent to which mirrored institutions are probably relatively unimportant in the final analysis *or* the possibility that goblins have a great deal more power than wizards would like to acknowledge.

60. See the essay by Hall in this collection, as well as essays by Grimes 2003 and Nikolajeva 2003.

61. From this perspective, neither the *X-Men* nor the Harry Potter series are particularly pleasant fantasies. One might wonder, after all, what a child like Harry is likely to become? It is not far-fetched to suppose that he would inevitably grow into something like Magneto or Lord Voldemort, who would both concur with Quirrell that, "there is no good and evil, there is only power, and those too weak to seek it" (PS, 361). Both Magneto (in some versions of the *X-Men* storyline) and Voldemort represent the same fantasy as Harry, but they are versions in which all of the dark implications of unchecked individual power are made manifest.

62. Wilmer 2002, 126.

63. Buzan, Jones, and Little 2000; Sterling-Folker 2005.

# Quidditch, Imperialism, and the Sport-War Intertext

**6**

DAVID LONG

> Quidditch . . . is a fictional sport.
>
> ALBUS DUMBLEDORE

> A foolish consistency is the hobgoblin of little minds, adored by little statesmen and philosophers and divines.
>
> RALPH WALDO EMERSON

IN THIS CHAPTER I EXAMINE THE RELATIONSHIP of the game of Quidditch to the conflicts in Harry Potter's world. I consider the simple rendition of a parallel between Harry's exploits on the Quidditch pitch and his battle with the evil Voldemort. And I explore the more complex sociological and psychological function of games in schools like Hogwarts. The purpose of this discussion is to uncover the ways in which Quidditch and games relate to the international and the political relations of the magical world of Harry Potter. In this regard I argue that a concentration on the good versus evil narrative does not serve us especially well in understanding the significance of the game that Harry is playing or the international relations of his or our world.

The idea of games has been used in many ways in international relations scholarship. The most common association these days is certainly game theory, a rationalist modeling technique that highlights and clarifies the importance and subtleties of strategies in international interactions. This is not and has not been the only way of drawing on games to understand international relations, however. For instance, in his influential study of different approaches to conflict resolution, Anatol Rapoport distinguishes between fights, games, and debates, arguing that there are significant differences in the goals, rules, and structures in each. In debates, the disputants try to persuade each other of their respective case. The aim is to convert the other, the means are rhetoric and other methods of persuasion. Each party in a debating contest respects the bodily integrity of the opponent and also observes the rules of the debate. For Rapoport, fights are contests where opponents try to destroy or harm the other. Any means to do this are appropriate and the ultimate goal is the elimination or subjugation of the opponent in the fight. Games come between these two extremes. While opponents try to outwit each other, they are not trying to convert the other. While they are trying to win, winning is within the set of rules and conventions that make up the game, unlike the ruleless context of fights.[1]

Rapoport's purpose in drawing the distinction among fights, games, and debates was to secure but also delimit the use of game theory as an approach to studying conflict. Only where the context allowed us to portray the activities of opponents as games could we readily use this metaphor. Since then, however, analysts have happily moved beyond Rapoport's limits and the whole world of international relations has been studied as a game using mathematical methods. It has been argued that international relations theorists need to move beyond the simple deployment of the game metaphor and be more theoretically rigorous.[2] Indeed, the models and methods have advanced in sophistication beyond the simple models used, for example, in early products of the field, such as Robert Axelrod's *The Evolution of Cooperation* (1984: chaps. 1–2, esp. pp. 6–7) or in Kenneth Oye's *Cooperation under Anarchy*.[3]

In *The Nature of International Society*, Charles Manning suggests that international relations can be understood as a game but takes a different approach to game theorists. *Contra* Snidal, Manning encourages us not to attempt to surpass the use of metaphor but to play with it; to think of international relations as (among other things) a game or "pseudo-game" of cricket or of chess. But Manning is not content with the simple analogy; rather, he suggests that the choice of game analogy conveys different aspects of international relations—chess, for instance, relates the notion of the importance of territory "wherein it shows its peculiar affinity also with war" and also at once respect for and challenge to the opponent's king.[4] We are on the field in cricket, above it in chess; in a two-sided contest in cricket with a clear sense of the opponents capability, in a many-sided one in poker with lack of information about the other players' strengths and weaknesses. Furthermore, Manning argues of international relations that "*It's Only a Game.*" But he is not only nor even primarily highlighting the playlike elements of international relations such as can be found in its diplomatic niceties. He is also drawing our attention to the character of international relations which, "though dubbed the international 'anarchy,' [is] not those typical of the jungle, but rather a kind of quasi-game."[5] What Manning as a proto-constructivist means by this is that international society is rule-bound and that only in the context of the rules of the game is it possible to understand international relations. Meanwhile Manning is aware that the players may be playing more than one game, that there is no referee, and that rules can easily be broken. Indeed it was the breaking of the rules of the game of international society that preoccupied Manning.

While the game might be an insightful device for understanding certain aspects of international relations, there are a number of difficulties with the distinctions that Rapoport makes, the theories Snidal wants to build, and the analogies Manning draws. Most importantly for this chapter, while sports are games, they are particular types of games. I show in this chapter that the competitive, physical nature of sports, and in particular sports with a combative element like Quidditch, readily fade over into what Rapoport categorizes as fights. For this reason, as well as a number of others, we might want to take more seriously the connection rather than the distinction of fights and games, or more specifically, war and sport. Similarly, focusing simply on the playful game aspect of Quidditch obscures its important place in the construction of identity and difference, solidarity and enmity, as well as its social function in the generation of individual and international competitiveness and the legitimation of a world of dramatic inequality.

While gaming language is often applied to international relations, the language of war frequently infuses that of the sports that we play, particularly in terms of strategies for defense or attack, winning or losing a competition. This suggests there is a more complex, intertextual relationship of sports and international relations, a connection explored by Michael Shapiro.[6] For instance, sport and war are not simply linked through the ancient origins of sports in preparation for and the development of skills readying for war, Shapiro observes, but also in the way that the text of sport that is so prevalent in our world at once obscures the politics and legitimates violence of international relations. Intertextuality of sport and war is evident in the use of sports analogies in war and vice versa, but more than that, the social function of playing and watching sports contributes to a depoliticization of the use of violence internationally. Shapiro points in particular to the use of the game analogy in Brzezinski's *Game Plan*, where international relations is reduced to a contest between the United States and U.S.S.R. for global domination. Furthermore, insofar as the purpose of sports has in part been the preparation for conflict, this preparation is influenced by the development of gaming technology. Whether it be fencing or running or soccer, the requirements of skill and physical fitness map on to the requirements for fighting or strategy needed for fighting. Today's video and computer games, flight simulators most notoriously but also many versions of RPGs (role playing games), similarly map onto the high tech world of virtual war.

Shapiro's analysis, like many, reads sports as a cultural event considered in terms of display, that is, as a form of entertainment or even as a sort of art form. This is an important characteristic of sports like Quidditch, as we see especially in the Quidditch World Cup. There are team and player posters, collectible playing cards, rosettes, cheerleaders, and national leagues and international tournaments—all familiar paraphernalia of sports as entertainment. But in the Harry Potter stories this display element is largely subordinate to Harry actually playing Quidditch himself. Indeed, the Quidditch World Cup is unique in the Harry Potter stories because it is one case of sport where Harry is a spectator. The rest of the time Harry is a participant, except when he is forced to the sidelines by injury or detention. He is a player, and his school friends and we are the spectators. As a player of a game, Quidditch fulfills a number of sociological and psychological functions for Harry. At the same time, the institutional practice around Quidditch, at school and in the wizarding world, helps structure Harry's world. Harry's discovery of the international relations of the wizarding community derives largely from his participating in and playing games, specifically Quidditch and the Triwizard Tournament.

When we read the Harry Potter stories, we can read them as fantastic tales of Harry's (and to a lesser extent his friends, Ron and Hermione's) heroism in the face of growing evil and danger. In doing so, one can seek recourse to the myths and legends that are drawn on by other literary figures such as Tolkien and Lewis, and link the stories to others in the muggle universe such as more recent children's fantasy writers like Philip Pullman and William Nicolson. This sort of reading encourages us to see Harry's playing Quidditch for Gryffindor as a metaphor for his struggle against the Dark Side, particularly when playing against Slytherin or less directly in winning the Quidditch and House Cups for Gryffindor (and in beating Hufflepuff and Ravenclaw houses in the process).

But why focus on Tolkein and Lewis rather than the just as obvious parallels to Enid Blyton whose *Mallory Towers* stories mirror the seven years of high school at Hogwarts and in which the role of sports is also prominent? I am tempted to offer an ad hoc response to this question to the effect that there is a selection bias in the children's literature international relations scholars refer to or will admit to reading! More seriously, there is a masculinist bias at work here. Comparisons of Harry Potter to *The Lord of the Rings* is masculinist in inspiration and in outcome: it is inspired by a concentration on male authors writing on masculine topics, dealing with grand themes, war, nobility, kings, and the like; and the comparison results in a masculinist reading that emphasizes precisely those elements of the Harry Potter tales. This reading surrenders to what Richard Ashley has called the blackmail of the heroic practice.[7] Seeking the grand themes, the foundations and manifestations of good and evil, the attempt to expose the underlying structures and forces of the magical world of Harry Potter considers Harry and his friends and enemies in black and white terms. Such explanations are themselves rehearsing the heroic practice in their focus on the dichotomies of good and evil and the location of responsibility in the sovereign individual, in this instance, for the most part, Harry himself. Looking for the origins of good and evil in this way this approach actually re-presents, reinforces, and even generates the dichotomous representations it seeks to undermine. Such analyses must, it seems to me, be irretrievably mundane. They reduce Quidditch and Harry Potter's magical world to a masculinist two-dimensional timeless algorithm and omit the complexities, pluralities, and contradictions of gender, class, and history.[8]

As a sport enjoyed by Harry Potter and his wizard friends (and enemies), Quidditch is a focal point for a consideration of Harry's heroism and illustrates the ways in which he (and the author J. K. Rowling) deals with conflict. It also provides a portal into the wider world of the international relations of the wizarding community. Reading Quidditch through a dichotomous "good versus evil" narrative of Harry's heroism and the battle between Harry and Lord Voldemort obscures the history and function of Quidditch as a sport-as-social-activity which is just like any other sport-as-social-activity. For example, this magical sport, played by wizards apparently for hundreds of years, happens to have a history that maps closely to muggle, and specifically British imperial, history.

Unsatisfied with a simplistic reading of Quidditch as a metaphor for Harry's heroism, in this chapter I present a double reading of the magical problematic in Harry Potter particularly as it pertains to Quidditch. After a brief presentation of a mundane analysis, I attempt a "magical" reading of Quidditch considered as a social practice located in specific historical and geographical space-time. This reading requires that we suspend our muggle disbelief about the magical world, abandon the dichotomies of the heroic practice, and instead consider the wizarding world as a social and cultural system, focusing our attention particularly on the role that Quidditch plays in that magical world. In short, our reading must not stop with Harry's leading the good team but should interrogate the place of Quidditch in the magical world and its meaning for wizards and for muggles. As a combative team sport, Quidditch at once provides the context for the rehearsal of skills important to war but it also features in the social hierarchy at Hogwarts and beyond. The history of the development of Quidditch and the contours of its current global reach also suggest a link to European imperial history very much like that of modern-day muggle sports such as football, rugby, and cricket.

Just as Dumbledore tells us that Quidditch is fictional, yet in the same sentence wishes the best to Puddlemere United, the magical reading begins on the understanding that "there is always an ineluctable debt to interpretation such that there is nothing outside of discourse": all social relations are representations and thus to varying degrees fictitious and at the same time real.[9] Before presenting the double reading, however, we need first of all to be clear on what Quidditch is, as well as the way it connects Harry to the international relations of the magical community.

## Quidditch, Sport, and War

*It's our sport. Wizard sport.*

RUBEUS HAGRID (PS, 6)

*The game of Quidditch continues to thrill and obsess its many fans around the world.*

KENILWORTH WHISP

Quidditch is a sport played at school at once very familiar and very strange to us muggles. Its familiarity begins for some of us in the resemblance of the name to the game of cricket. This association is an important one insofar as it connects Hogwarts and the wizarding world with a particular view of an England of the days of Empire. The traditional connection is one that resonates with the class aspects of Hogwarts as an old English aristocratic academy. I have more to say on this below. Nevertheless, of all the sports usually played at such English private schools, Quidditch is most un-like cricket.

When Harry is first introduced to Quidditch, he asks: "So—that's sort of like basketball on broomsticks with six hoops, isn't it?" (To which he re-ceives the reply: "what's basketball?" see PS, 124). The other associations are rounders (PS, 125) and football (soccer) (PS, 138). In all cases, we are informed that Quidditch is not like any of them. First of all, Quidditch is played with four balls: the Quaffle, about the size of a baseball, which is the ball that the teams score with; two Bludgers, shaped, sized, and made of iron like cannonballs which can be used to attack opposing players and which are thus the focus of the Beaters on each team who attempt to hit them toward the opposing team and away from their own players, espe-cially their Seeker; and the Golden Snitch, which is the smallest of the balls and short of agreement between the two teams the capture of which is the only way to end a Quidditch game. Each team has seven players: one Keeper, minding the goals of the team in order to prevent the other team scoring; two Beaters who deal with the Bludgers and generally try to pro-tect the other players on their team; three Chasers who are responsible for scoring with the Quaffle; and the Seeker whose sole responsibility is to find the Snitch and thus end the game. The aim of the game is to amass the greater number of points by scoring with the Quaffle before the game is ended when either side's Seeker catches the Golden Snitch.

Superficial similarities to other sports aside, there are a number of unique aspects to Quidditch. The surfeit of balls is likely indicative of wiz-ards' superior capabilities, whereas muggles find it difficult enough to fol-low or control one ball in their team sports, let alone four. Quidditch is also unusual in there being essentially two games going on simultaneously on or rather over the same pitch: the contest to score the most goals runs parallel to but separate from the duel between the Seekers in the hunt for the Snitch.

Another aspect that is unique is that Quidditch is played in the air—you have to fly in order to play the game, and therefore you need the ap-titude to be able to control your broom before you play the game. This is important in a couple of respects for Harry Potter. First, his very strong ability to fly marks him out from his peers and makes him already a good prospect for his house Quidditch team. Second, flying is important to Harry from a psychological point of view. It gives him a sense of freedom; the literal loosening of the physical bonds holding him to earth is a metaphor for his release from the cares of the world, at least briefly. Fur-thermore, Harry himself feels that this is something he is good at and this is an important bolster to his self-esteem. In the requirement that one learn a skill prior to being able to play the game proper, Quidditch is special but not unique among sports. Ice hockey or water polo are impossible to play without the prior ability and training to be able respectively to skate or swim well, with speed, agility, power, maneuverability, backwards and forwards.[10]

Another unusual characteristic of Quidditch is that it is played by both girls and boys and that they play together. Or at least they can play together. At one point, the Gryffindor team has three girls: Katie Bell, Alicia Spinnet, and Angelina Johnson, who are the Chasers on their team, while Ginny Weasley later also plays for the team as Harry's replacement as Seeker and Angelina becomes team captain. Harry's one-time romantic interest, Cho Chang, is the only girl playing for Ravenclaw. Interestingly, this is not regarded as a disadvantage by Gryffindor or Ravenclaw for whom Katie, Angelina, and Alicia's or Cho Chang's participation seems to be simply on merit. By contrast, Slytherin's team is all male, adding a gender dimension to the singular evil already represented by purity of blood and the aristocratic connections. Interestingly enough, the co-ed character of Hogwarts and its sports teams deviates from the traditional hierarchical and gendered organization of equivalent muggle academies, which have generally been single-sex institutions.

Interestingly, other than flying on a broom and the fact that the balls are charmed, there is notable lack of magic in Quidditch of the sort that George Gmelch is referring to in his "Baseball Magic."[11] In this regard the magic of Quidditch is, like that of wizard's chess, rather ordinary, and the magical elements are as well rather stereotypically technological.[12] Happily, this ordinariness makes comparison to muggle sports easier and facilitates a consideration of the nature of Quidditch as a sport and the sport-war intertext using muggle analysis.

Quidditch is a sport, which is a form of play and a type of game. Understanding the sport-war intertext in Quidditch requires an understanding of the characteristics of Quidditch as a sport. Sports first of all are a form of play. According to Guttmann, play is "non-utilitarian, physical or intellectual activity pursued for its own sake."[13] Play is a realm of freedom, something that is done for the pure enjoyment of doing it. The play aspect of Quidditch is important to Harry. We are told at one point that Harry leaves his cares behind when he is flying and playing Quidditch. He feels more free playing Quidditch than at any other time: "In a rush of fierce joy he realized he'd found something he could do without being taught—this was easy, this was *wonderful*" (PS, 111; see also PA, 225).

Play can be spontaneous or organized. In organized play we are in the realm of games. Games limit the freedom of play by the requirement that there be rules. The aim of the rules is simply to give structure to the game. Rules structure games in different ways, and Guttmann points to the critical distinction between competitive and noncompetitive games. When we think of games, we generally think of contests like chess or poker or golf or football that are structured competitively and in which there are winners and losers.[14] Harry and his friends play a variety of games besides Quidditch that are contests, such as Exploding Snap and Wizards Chess. While in each of these there is a physical element, both are marked by the intellectual rather than physical characteristics of the competition (although this is rather clearer with Wizards Chess than in Exploding Snap, in which once a snap is recognized it is a matter of reflexes and speed who wins [PS, 159]). Harry is aware of the competitive aspect of Quidditch and regards it as an important part of his identity. When asked by Moody what he is best at, on reflection he replies, Quidditch. Harry's conclusion reflects his sense that he excels relative to others: he is the best Seeker (and the youngest in over a century), not merely that it is the thing he does better than other activities, including schoolwork and so on.

Quidditch clearly falls into the category of a contest; each side aims to score more goals and catch the Snitch first (if they are ahead in points). On a number of occasions the supreme importance of winning is stressed, not only by Harry but Hermione Grainger and Oliver Wood. (See PS, 164; CS, 131, as examples.) For example, at one point, Gryffindor's captain Wood implores Harry, "Get to that Snitch before Malfoy or die trying, because we've got to win today, we've got to" (CS, 126; see also PA, 181). According to Guttmann, contests such as Quidditch are already associated with war. Unlike cooperative games like leapfrog and ring-around-the-rosie, competitive games such as chess and baseball are also contests like legal proceedings, examinations, or elections (HBP, 178). Sharing the characteristic of being a contest, games like Quidditch are also prescribed analogues for war because they share the same discursive universe of competition and contest.

But sport is also like war in other regards. Sport is a predominantly physical rather than an intellectual contest. As Guttmann notes, because they involve strategy and tactics, both of which entail planning and thus are intellectual to some extent, sports are always to some degree intellectual pursuits. Nevertheless, sports and war are physical contests where it is agility or strength or speed that is the basis for winning. Unlike war, for most sports, physical damage to the participants is not a legitimate part or objective of the game, although it is in many games a routine, predictable, and accepted (although proscribed by the formal, written rules) outcome or result.[15] Sports can be either individual or team sports, instances of the former being golf or tennis, while the latter includes basketball or lacrosse. In addition, sports can be more or less combative, where damage to the opponents is a greater or smaller part of the game. The most combative of modern muggle sports is boxing and in the magical world it is dueling, where the purpose is to render the opponent in some way incapacitated to the point of knocking them out, and thus making them unable to continue the bout.[16] By contrast, in tennis while there can be attrition, hoping to outlast an opponent, damaging the opponent is generally prohibited. Similarly in baseball it is not permissible to pitch at the batter, although this does occasionally happen. The range of permissible combativeness in sports seems to be almost infinite, from the bodyline bowling of cricket through the physical contact of football, to the hitting and checking of ice hockey and the "mock fight" of rugby and American football.[17] Clearly, the more combative a sport is, the more it resembles a fight in Rapoport's terms where the goal is damage to the opponent, bringing it closer of course to war. At the same time, team sports and war resemble one another in their collective and organized character. But similarity is not identity and the comparison can obscure the difference of the two concerning the centrality of damage to the opponent as a means to a political objective. Thus, Shapiro is correct in his suggestion that the intertextuality of team sports and war can serve to depoliticize the latter insofar as the game element is emphasized over other aspects of war.

Quidditch is an extremely combative team sport where violence is formally prohibited but is in actuality rife in practice and where damage to an opponent if not a goal in itself is seen as a means to the end of victory in the game. Compared to other combative team sports, Quidditch seems to closely resemble ice hockey and American football in the central part that hitting plays in the game, although it is only allowed in limited circumstances compared with the continuity of physical contact and the brute force used in rugby and football. We are told that a few players have died playing Quidditch but at Hogwarts the worst that has happened is a broken jaw or two. Of course, during one game, Harry's arm is broken. Quidditch is a physical, combative, even violent contest, and as a result it is hardly surprising that the language of war should appear. As well as the preparations, planning, strategies, and tactics, we find that Harry's first appearance as Seeker is kept quiet so that he will be Gryffindor's "secret weapon" (PS, 133), that the Weasley twins "dive-bomb" each other (PS,

159), that the brooms of the Slytherin team are like "jump jets" (CS, 94—the reference is to a British military aircraft, the Harrier Jump Jet). The warlike atmosphere is even higher in Fourth Year when Ron accuses Hermione of fraternizing with the enemy in her flirtation with the international Quidditch player, Viktor Krum (GF, 367).[18]

## A Mundane Reading: Quidditch and the War of Good against Evil

The mundane reading I present here refers to nothing more than a non-magical understanding of the world of Harry Potter, although I recognize that this choice of terminology is far from innocent because of the derogatory associations of mundane and because the technical usage I deploy is derived from wizard rather than muggle usage. A mundane reading focuses on the grand themes in Harry Potter and his world and reads them as a work of fiction seeking parallels in the great works of literature. The grand theme in the Harry Potter stories is the contest between good and evil. Quidditch, then, becomes a metaphor for and even a part of that contest.[19]

A mundane reading presents Harry as the hero fighting for the good, as the Chosen One, with Lord Voldemort representing the ultimate in evil. Interestingly, Harry is regarded as a hero by his peers at numerous points in the stories, but usually in connection with his exploits on the Quidditch pitch or in getting points for his house, rather than for his infamous scar, which is often a source of envy and fear, at least until Harry's sixth year when Voldemort's return is finally acknowledged officially by the wizard community. By contrast, we are regularly reminded of the false heroism of those on the Dark Side. Tom Riddle frames Hagrid and takes credit for exposing the monster in the Chamber of Secrets, and Peter Pettigrew makes himself a "posthumous" hero by faking his death at the hands of Sirius Black. While Harry actually breaks his arm playing Quidditch, Malfoy suffers a small scratch from a Hippogriff and uses it to avoid facing Harry and his Quidditch team. Later, Harry suspects Malfoy is using Quidditch matches as a cover for and distraction from his suspicious activities. Surrogates for Voldemort as the Bad Guy include Draco Malfoy and his father Lucius Malfoy, as well as for a time, Snape, the Head of Slytherin House, and Sirius Black, Harry's godfather.

This reading highlights and reinforces a series of dichotomies: besides good and evil, there is Harry/Voldemort, Harry/Malfoy, Gryffindor/Slytherin (Harry's choice of Houses when he first arrives at Hogwarts), and the matching trinities, Harry, Ron, and Hermione versus Malfoy, Crabbe, and Goyle. Rowling lets us know whose side we should be on in the use of language of names—mort, mal, black—and the way in which Gryffindor players are called by their first names (conveying the sense that they are our friends) while Slytherin are presented by surname only, creating a sense of formality and distance. In case we missed it, the Slytherin symbol is a snake and the Gryffindor symbol a lion.

Throughout, Quidditch plays a central role as a vehicle and metaphor for Harry's heroism. Harry is the important Seeker and in his sixth year, and significantly, shortly before Dumbledore dies, he becomes captain of the team. In Quidditch, Harry is placed directly opposite the "anti-Harry," Draco Malfoy, who becomes the Slytherin Seeker by buying his way onto the team. Malfoy neatly satirizes Harry as "the Chosen Captain—the Boy Who Scored" (HBP, 386). Harry plays for Gryffindor, the good, brave House, and while he and his team also play Ravenclaw and Hufflepuff, the main focuses of attention are Gryffindor's games against Slytherin, the bad, ambitious House. Harry is victorious and honorable in victory on the Quidditch pitch while Slytherin either avoid playing when weather conditions are poor or resort to cheating or other underhand methods in their thirst for victory (PA, 126, 224–30). These cheating methods are in vain as we know, and Harry usually wins. The one time Harry appears to have cheated, he has simply deceived his friend Ron in order to bolster his confidence (HBP, 274, 279–80).[20] He has won all but twice indeed, once when Harry was being impeded by a rogue Bludger and in this instance the opposing victorious Seeker, Cedric Diggory, subsequently dies, and once when the team is squabbling Harry is accidentally hit by a Bludger from one of his own teammates (HBP, 389). Harry's house, Gryffindor, has won the House Championship each of the years that Harry has been at the school when the championship has run. But one of the high points of Harry's victory over the representatives of the dark forces comes when Slytherin Malfoy, Crabbe, Goyle, and Flint pretend to be Dementors in order to put Harry off his game. Harry summons his patronus (in an illegal move I would note, since players are not allowed to use their wands on the Quidditch pitch) to knock out his tormentors (PA, 134–35). Indeed, Gryffindor has never lost to Slytherin while Harry has been playing.

In its search for a grand theme, the mundane reading leads us to consider the Harry Potter stories in terms of comparable literary forms and techniques. In this regard, we are pointed to Tolkien and Lewis, among others, and the common technique of children's fiction and fantasy more generally wherein there is a contest between good and evil. The similarities between the Harry Potter characters and stories and *The Lord of the Rings* are of course manifold—Frodo/Harry, Dumbledore/Gandalf, Voldemort/Sauron, Wormtail/Wormtongue,[21] as is the circumstances of the conflict where there is good within and evil without.

As well as making the links to other mythic children's literatures such as *Lord of the Rings*, the mundane reading's emphasis on the literary character of Harry Potter, Quidditch, and so on highlights the dichotomies of author and subject. It considers not only where the author Rowling drew her conscious and unintended inspiration for Quidditch. It highlights the origins of Harry Potter in the writing of once impoverished single parent, Joanne Rowling, in which she creates a magical world populated by wizards, giants, dragons, werewolves, and the like. The mundane reading reinforces the distinction between author and text as we are invited to think of the influences on Rowling, and between fact and fiction (which itself conflates the dichotomies of true and false and of nonfiction and fiction). A magical reading refuses these categories.

The mundane reading reduces the magical world of Harry Potter to a series of mundane dichotomies. Populated though it is with wizards and other magical creatures, we are instructed to read the story as a stylized tale about an individual hero fighting the good fight. Yet this reading, as hidebound as it is, neglects not only the many categories Rowling challenges in the traditional stories of heroism and glory but also omits those elements of Harry's world that are rendered in a rather traditionalist way by the author. This applies particularly to international relations and the way that the world of sporting nations is portrayed. Rowling is often sensitive and thought-provoking when it comes to questions of intercultural, intergenerational, and even interspecies relations, certainly in comparison to the grand literature to which she is compared in the mundane reading, yet when international relations crops up, it is a world of given identities where otherness is suspicious and conflictual.

# A Magical Reading: Quidditch, the Civilizing Process, and International Relations

The mundane reading is idealist and paradigmatic rather than a historical and sociological understanding. Structuring Harry Potter's world according to the axis of good and evil, Quidditch is subordinated to this narrative and becomes a focus for the conflict between good and evil. Among other problems with this reading, it neglects the historical and sociological aspects of Quidditch as a social practice in the wizarding world. Conducting what I style a magical reading involves suspending our disbelief about the unreal qualities of Harry Potter and his world and instead entering that world as if it is our own. Such a magical reading points our attention to the actual social practices of Quidditch and what they tell us about society and international relations in the wizarding world. Rather than a black and white world that mimics international relations' realism and idealism, we find a world of unequal and exploitive relations, a world of internationalism and imperialism. Quidditch plays an ambiguous part in this world, normalizing these inequalities while providing a locus for challenging the established categories of the wizard's world.

The cultural studies of sport have highlighted not only the historically increasing dominance of display over play, the rationalizing shift from ritual to record (as Guttman puts it), but also the patterns of class dominance in modern sports.[22] This centralizing, rationalizing, and routinizing of sport has been presented as part of the civilizing process where violence in society at large is increasingly diminished and displaced onto the realm of leisure activities.[23] The history of Quidditch matches this development very well.

In the early record of the games recorded by Whisp, Quidditch was already an international sport insofar as a Scottish player was present and there were some later Norwegian reports on games resembling Quidditch.[24] However, the early informal development of the sport lacked consistency of rules and seems to have been prone to outbreaks of violence. This early version of the game was also absent the most notable part of the game with which Harry Potter is associated, that is, the Golden Snitch. The origin of this fourth ball was a cross-fertilization of game hunting with the original form of Quidditch reported in the Museum of Quidditch as taking place in 1269.[25] The association of Quidditch in its very early stages with a particularly ruthless and violent social practice is indicative of a certain gladiatorial element that the sport maintains in Harry's time. The diminution of the level of violence matches that in contact sports like rugby and football, but also even such apparently noncontact sports as cricket.[26]

Quidditch has folkloric origins, being played in an early form by wizards and witches in a variety of locales, with modifications made to the game through happenstance, necessity, and changes in technology.[27] The intervention of the Wizards Council, however, marks the beginning of the familiar schism in the sport between its origins in play and the locality, on the one hand, and the increasingly centralization and regulation of Quidditch, on the other. This resonates with the process that Shapiro notes occurs with muggle sports, where local control is usurped by central authorities as a way of pacifying the magical populace. Specifically, the development of Quidditch looks like the history of rugby. In *Barbarians, Gentlemen and Players*, Dunning and Sheard show that rugby emerges in localities and is played by people according to locally established rules.[28] Progressively, however, centralized rules come to predominate, and Dunning and Sheard note that this process parallels the social control of industrial workers. The rules that come to predominate are those associated with the upper (that is, the ruling) classes. In the case of rugby, we find that the sport splits along class lines with rugby union being the aristocratic "amateurs" and rugby league the working-class professionals.

The centralization, routinization, and the de-escalation of violence in present-day Quidditch extends to its international dimensions. Although Quidditch is a magical wizard sport, the ordinariness of its bureaucratic organization is striking. Like muggle sports, it is a sport that is played in an organized way at school, is played by "professionals" or at least those who specialize in playing the sport (it is not clear that anyone is paid for playing the game), and is played in an informal way by Harry and his friends (CS, 39; HBP, 103). Like muggle sports, Quidditch also involves the paraphernalia of "professional" and national teams, with its attendant cultures and cultural products of fan support. There are posters of famous players and teams, figurines of Quidditch players, rivalry over who supports which team, and so on, all of which would be familiar to muggle sports fans.

While Harry is initially relatively ignorant of the international relations of the wizarding world, it is through Quidditch that he begins to learn about it. Before the start of his fourth year, Harry goes to the Quidditch World Cup final. This event highlights the role of sports in the political and international shape of the wizarding world. Although he was presumably aware of the international dimension of the muggle world, Harry had apparently not thought about there being foreign schools of magic (he had not thought of schools other than Hogwarts, indeed) until the international competition involved in the Triwizard Tournament (GF, 165–66). Before the Quidditch World Cup final, the countries with wizards that Harry would be aware of are predominantly European.[29] Southeastern Europe figures because of the existence of a certain variety of dragons. The only other reference to a country outside Europe before the World Cup Final is Egypt (where Bill Weasley is employed by Gringotts Bank). The Cup Final, however, presents a veritable bonanza of international variety, although it becomes clear that the geography of Quidditch centers on the British Isles first of all, then Europe, and then a collection of countries that are part of the British Commonwealth. Thus, at the Quidditch World Cup Harry watches Ireland defeat Bulgaria, but the crowd is made up of wizards and witches from around the world. The color and variety of the event is exemplified by the different dress and demeanor of wizards and witches from foreign lands. For instance: "Three African wizards sat in serious conversation, all of them wearing long white robes and roasting what looked like a rabbit on a bright purple fire" (GF, 76). This event is also the only occasion at which Americans are mentioned, when Harry passes "a group of middle-aged American witches [who] sat gossiping happily beneath a spangled banner stretched between their tents which read: *The Salem Witches Institute*" (GF, 76).

While there are national Quidditch leagues around the world, Kennilworth Whisp (2001) focuses on the league in Britain and Ireland which has thirteen teams. This league includes teams from across the United Kingdom but also Ireland. This is unlike, for instance, English football, where Welsh teams play in the same league with English teams but Scottish and Irish teams do not. At the national team level, however, Quidditch more closely resembles the world of football, rugby, and cricket as there are separate national teams for England, Scotland, and Wales as well as Ireland. The political geography of the muggle world intrudes into the description of the teams' locations, as while the Ballycastle Bats are described as coming from Northern Ireland, the Kenmare Kestrels are simply from Ireland and their players are reported to have represented the Irish National Team.[30] Generally, the exotica of the magical world is embellished here by the association of Quidditch teams with the Celtic parts of the British Isles, along with names resembling village names of southern England.

If sport is a way that Harry discovers international relations, it also provides insight into the institutional character of those international relations. For example, chairwizard of the International Association of Quidditch, Hassan Mostafa, referees the Cup Final (GF, 96). Both the major sporting events that Harry participates in or watches, the Quidditch World Cup and the Triwizard Tournament, are overseen by the Ministry of Magic, specifically the Department of International Magical Cooperation, which is essentially the Foreign Ministry, although the title suggests that it is itself an international body, as well as the Department of Magical Games and Sports. In comparison with muggle sports institutions, the magical community seems to be equally bureaucratized but more internationalized. The influence of the international association is matched by the control that the Ministry has over national associations for Quidditch. The Department of Magical Games and Sports, as well as being an apparently quite significant part of the Ministry, also incorporates the headquarters of the British and Irish Quidditch League.[31] This prominence of games and sports in the bureaucracy of the wizarding world is unmatched in the muggle context. Nor do we see the level of governmental and international penetration in muggle sports, which are for the most part managed and self-regulated by national and nongovernmental associations.

One might from a commonsense point of view expect wizards' and witches' superior magical skills to free them from the constraints that we muggles face in terms of speed and ease of travel, and in being able to provide for themselves. Yet we know that there are still inequalities in wealth (and as a result, in social status) among wizards and witches and that wizards share nationalities with muggles. The magical community is clearly not cosmopolitan. While there is not one global wizard community, there is international cooperation among wizards, much of which seems to have been a response to a combination of Quidditch and relations with muggles. Whisp (2001) tells us that Quidditch is a significant reason why muggles associate witches with brooms, and before long there were rules to keep Quidditch games from the prying eyes of muggles. These rules were apparently not enforced until the International Statute of Wizarding Secrecy of 1692 mandated that all Ministries of Magic were responsible for the sports played within their territories. In Britain this led to the creation of the Department of Magical Games and Sports. Interestingly, this account of the development of Quidditch rules suggests that international regulation changed the character of national regulation of sports. Among the very few rules of Quidditch that appear in *Quidditch through the Ages*, the sixth indicates that wands can be taken onto the pitch but may not be used against other players. A footnote indicates that this rule has less to do with Quidditch than the wizarding world in general. At the time this rule was instigated, there were concerns about muggle persecution and wizards were permitted to carry wands at all times for protection. This provision, ratified by the International Confederation of Wizards, has definite hints of the right to bear arms, although the focus was muggle outsiders rather than their own or another government. It should be noted that the perceived threat from muggles is belittled by Adalbert Waffling in his *A History of Magic*, where he suggests that persecution by muggles was in fact unlikely to harm witches and wizards (quoted in PA, 7).

The hierarchical character of the magical community is further highlighted by the provision that Departments of Magical Games and Sports could disband Quidditch teams that were not following the agreed rules. While muggle Ministries of Sport have emerged in various countries, this has not been as a product of an international regulation, organization, or international confederation. Rather, muggle Ministries of Sport were a by-product of the pressure of the Cold War competition between East bloc countries and the West. Just as there was a race into space, there was a competition not only of political systems politically but also in terms of athletic prowess. It was this competition rather than an international impulse that created Ministries of Sport. It is also interesting that these Ministries were set up very early in the life of the sport of Quidditch, and are now hundreds of years old. By contrast, muggle Ministries of Sport are generally late twentieth-century vintage.[32] All this suggests that while the national competition among wizards was serious business, it was not the driving force behind centralization and control in Quidditch or in the international relations of the wizard community more generally. Indeed, it seems that the need to separate and remove themselves from the prying eyes of muggles is the operative factor, and this seems to suggest a particular external threat as the determining element. But this is surely not persuasive, since short of some persecution wizards and witches have little to fear from muggles. A more compelling argument seems to be the overwhelming need to control the massive levels of violence that wizards can visit on one another as well as on muggles. This interpretation reads the internationalization and institutionalization of Quidditch as part of a civilizing process.

As Elias notes, however, this controlled reduction of violence is never complete. The displacement of violence within Quidditch is as ambiguous as it is in muggle sports. Thus, sport is the basis for managed international competition among wizards, although this seems to be a somewhat precarious balance. On the one hand, one of the goals of the Triwizard Tournament is to promote international cooperation through sport in a manner similar to the Olympics, and we read that "[t]he tournament [is] . . . generally agreed to be a most excellent way of establishing ties between young witches and wizards of different nationalities" (GF, 165). Percy Weasley remarks to his brother Ron, "Excellent! That's the whole point you know—international magical cooperation" (GF, 368). However, we are invited here to ridicule the pompous social climber and it is clear that sports also reflect the conflictual aspect of international relations. Hermione observes about interhouse competition at Hogwarts, "That's the trouble with Quidditch . . . it creates all this bad feeling and tension" (OP, 507). Harry feels strongly that Hermione does not understand Quidditch, especially when, reacting to the histrionics of some of the school Quidditch players, she declares, "It's only a game, isn't it." For Harry and for many of his friends, nothing could be further from the truth. When Hermione suggests that the Triwizard Tournament is "supposed to be about getting to know foreign wizards and making friends with them," Ron responds, "No, it isn't. . . . It's about winning" (GF, 368). Hermione points to the gendered aspect of Quidditch—"Is that all boys care about?" she snipes in sixth year, but Ginny Weasley later suggests that Hermione does not understand the game (HBP, 298, 496).

Quidditch is a realm of competition in which conflict and cooperation mix in unequal and rather unpredictable measure. Barnier argues that the competitive aspect of sport reinforces national identity formation, building a bond between those on and supporting one team and reinforcing the strangeness of the other team and its supporters.[33] International relations as a realm of strangeness is reinforced during the Triwizard Tournament, as the visitors from Beauxbatons and Durmstrang are regarded with suspicion, and the teacher and students of the latter are portrayed as surly and somehow untrustworthy. They look and sound foreign, to begin with. In the case of Durmstrang we also know that students not only practice Defense against the Dark Arts but (it is said with rather ominous approval by Draco Malfoy) that they are introduced to the Dark Arts themselves.

## Quidditch, Imperialism, and Violence

Quidditch not only introduces us to international relations and reflects its complex amalgam of cooperation and competition. As a social institution, it also reflects and manifests the social mores of the wizarding community. As such, Quidditch marks out and reinforces social inequality, class conflict, and the imperial heritage among wizards.

I have already mentioned the similarity of the development of Quidditch to the story of rugby; this similarity extends to the social functions it and other competitive sports perform in school. Harry and his fellow wizards are an aristocracy. There is a certain limited social mobility in and out of the wizarding class, but the references to bloodlines and blood purity are class references rather than to an ethnicity. In the aristocratic environment of the wizards and witches, Hogwarts academy is like other private schools in having houses named after glorious heroes.[34] These houses compete for academic and sports honors, and the sports and the competition breed solidarity with the group, a belief in the value of hard work, and a desire to win.

J. A. Mangan suggests that competitive sports were an integral part of the creation of the image of empire among British schoolboys and a key aspect of the export of that imperial regulative ideal.[35] Quidditch seems to operate in a similar way. Indeed, the magical world in a number of ways resembles the muggle world before the fall of the British Empire and the history of Quidditch maps onto the history of British imperialism reasonably well. The similarities to the interwar period are striking, particularly in the sense that we are viewing a world between two wars. There is a sense of impending doom, of approaching conflict, of disagreement over what needs to be done to oppose the gathering dark forces.[36] Having survived a conflict with Voldemort, the wizarding world is facing the prospect of another imminent, perhaps worse, conflict. Even the name of the wizard foreign ministry, the Department of International Magical Cooperation, conjures up the interwar predecessor to UNESCO, the International Institute for Intellectual Cooperation. By the sixth year, with the impending civil war among wizards out in the open (HBP, 17), the tone takes on a distinctly post–September 11 feel with fear of random attacks on wizards and muggles alike.

While international bodies like the International Federations of Wizards and the International Association of Quidditch are important features of the magical world, that world is divided into those places that have adopted Quidditch and those that haven't. According to Whisp, Quidditch spread around the world, fanning out from Britain first to Ireland and then to parts of Northern Europe before reaching a wider audience in Africa and Australia and New Zealand. Quidditch is not very popular in Asia because the preferred method of transportation there is the flying carpet, and thus there is little expertise in flying brooms (Japan being the one exception). We are also told by Whisp that Quidditch is gaining some popularity in North America, with Canada providing a number of good teams and the national U.S. team having performed in the Quidditch World Cup, but that it is not as popular as it might be primarily because of being outcompeted by the rival charms (!) of Quodpot, a variant on Quidditch.[37]

Similarly, the pattern of the development of broom technology emanates from the United Kingdom. Indeed, the development of various advanced forms of brooms is almost exclusively English. The only exception to this appears to be a broom produced by Universal Brooms Ltd., a name redolent of an American multinational enterprise (MNE) rather than a British company. This company produced the cheapest brooms but they didn't work terribly well and the company went out of business.

While there is a coincidence of timing and the geographic extent of the development of Quidditch with its British muggle imperial counterpart, the association of sport with imperialism seems less obviously present

in the case of Quidditch. Some have argued that British sports were introduced not only as distractions but also as the basis for the creation of social
discipline and order. Thus, the export of cricket was not only a product of
expatriates playing the game in front of Indians, West Indians, South
Africans, and so on, but it also performed an important social function of
pacification of the local elite and masses of the subject populations.[38]
However, such a determinist view of the role of sport has been challenged
by, among others, J. A. Mangan who points out that although the export
of sport is clearly a part of cultural imperialism in, for instance, Latin
America, sports are incorporated into and appropriated by national cultures
and tailored to local conditions. Thus, while modern sport is "essentially a
derivative European sport, creatively and imaginatively adapted to North
American cultural needs, inclinations and imperatives," imperialism is not
the end of the story of sport in the postimperial context.[39] This imperial
origin and nationalist response are not easy to reconcile with what we
know of the wizarding community. The analogues to these conflicts, unequal relations, and requirements for control in the magical universe appear
instead in wizards' relations with other types of magical creatures, elves,
giants, dementors, inferi, and so on.

Finally, Quidditch is an arena of controlled violence as is evident in the
persistence of dueling among wizards (CS, 141–45). Thorstein Veblen[40]
argues that:

> Apart from warlike activity proper, the institution of the duel is also an ex-
> pression of the same superior readiness for combat; and the duel is a
> leisure-class institution. The duel is in substance a more or less deliberate
> resort to a fight as a final settlement of a difference of opinion. In civilized
> communities it prevails as a normal phenomenon only where there is a
> hereditary leisure class, and almost exclusively among that class.

The importance attached to Quidditch, where it is a key element in interhouse competition alongside academic excellence, along with the persistence at Hogwarts of dueling,[41] as well as the violent associations of
Quidditch and the cast-off remark that wizards have died in previous Triwizard Tournaments—all these suggest a world like the one Veblen is de-
scribing. There is a common tendency to settle disputes through fighting,
even among the more mild-mannered such as Arthur Weasley who scuffles
with Lucius Malfoy. His son Ron Weasley is routinely being held off pum-
meling Draco Malfoy for his slights of Ron's family. Quidditch seems to
contribute to violence occasionally, as we can see in the fight among Harry
and Fred, George and Ron Weasley on one side, and Malfoy and his

friends on the other, which results in a lifetime ban from playing Quidditch that is later revoked (OP, 371).

In any event as a physical and to some degree combative team sport, we can consider whether we might expect Quidditch to generate, increase, displace, or not affect aggression. Sipes concludes that combative sports are not an alternative to war, that is, such sports do not discharge aggression. He concludes rather that war and combative sports show a direct cross-cultural relationship where the "more warlike [are] more likely to have these sports and less warlike societies less likely to have them."[42] This analysis and that of Guilbert suggest that rather than being a pleasant distraction, sports like Quidditch are reflective of warlike tendencies in the magical world and may even engender aggressive feelings among players and spectators.[43] We see this in evidence in the lead-up to the Quidditch final between Gryffindor and Slytherin in Harry's Third Year: "Tensions between the two teams and their houses was at breaking point. A number of small scuffles broke out," as a result of which a couple of boys are hospitalized (PA, 222). At that time, "the emnity between Harry and Malfoy was at its highest point ever." The upcoming Quidditch game crystallizes and exacerbates the hateful relationship between the protagonists. The violent character of Quidditch suggests, then, that the magical world is a violent one in which Voldemort is remarkable for his ferocity and malevolence rather than his use of force.

But we should be careful in ascribing such a critical role in the fomenting of violence. As Clifford Geertz has observed in his analysis of the Balinese cockfight, while the sport of betting on fighting cocks and the social rules and conventions that surround the sport revolve around a violent practice, it neither seems to stimulate violence among the Balinese nor does the relative equality that is an important part of this sport appear to spill over into the wider, very unequal society in Bali.[44] Sport appears to reflect rather than generate social conflict, and this seems to be the case whether in Geertz's Bali, between rival football fans whether internationally or locally such as Celtic and Rangers in Glasgow, or with respect to Quidditch.

# Conclusion

*The game's over. Harry won. We won.*

HERMIONE GRAINGER

*The game is over.*

GEORGE W. BUSH (QUOTED IN THE *OTTAWA CITIZEN*, FEBRUARY 7, 2003)

Harry Potter has intruded into our world in a number of ways and at a number of levels, whether it be the malicious comparison of Vladimir Putin to Dobby, youngsters likening the newest expensive hockey stick to the Firebolt, or the use of thinly disguised Harry Potter characters by the U.S. army for a military training manual.[45] More generally, the use of game and sports analogies is so common and accepted that we barely notice it.

The quote from Bush, above, illustrates the complicated ways that sports analogies are deployed in international relations. "The game is over" has an air of finality. Not only is the phony war phase of the process over, it suggests, but there is more than a hint here that the United States is ready now to impose its will. In other words, Saddam has lost even before the war (game) has begun. "The game is over" also suggests that the dealings with Iraq have thus far been regarded by at least one party (presumably, the intimation is, Iraq) as a game. International relations is serious business, however, and we now need to get back to the business at hand, the disarmament of Iraq. At the same time, Bush's phrase belittles the process of weapons inspections by suggesting that they are no more than a game.

Similarly, while Harry and his team generally take the game very seriously, he is increasingly distracted and less interested in Quidditch, particularly in his sixth year, and this is echoed at the end of that year when he determines that he will not return for his seventh (HBP, 382–83, 606).

The extent to which sports and violent figures work as efficient explanations of American politics is revealed by the following offhand comment by an official, "You can go up to Congress and you can hit them over the head with a baseball bat once, then you have to allow them a period of time to recover from that before you can hit them again" (unnamed American official quoted by Kingdon 1995: 130–31). By contrast, Hermione Grainger's comment quoted above reflects the joy of victory, the solidarity and collective identification engendered by Quidditch, and the centrality of Quidditch to her and her friends' world.[46] Recently it has been suggested that we have entered a period of international relations in which western populations and their governments engage in "spectator sport war," equating supposedly distant wars with a spectacle. In contrast to the semblance of equality that appears to be essential to most games, spectator sport war is hardly based on equality. Thus, although McInnes is correct to focus on the media presentation and theatrical aspects of contemporary war as it is presented in many Western countries, the connection with sport is weak.[47]

My analysis has suggested that a black and white reading of Quidditch as the parallel of the contest between good and evil will not do. Quidditch

has a rich and varied history. It has a number of associations with war, aggression, a modern form of collective solidarity, and so on. In addition,
Quidditch, like other sports, involves a degree of risk, unpredictability, and
spontaneity. Harry is not, however, a traditional sports hero, a figure that
incidentally has been long in decline as a literary form, particularly the
school sports hero.[48] And the notion that sports are character building is almost universally dismissed these days in the face of criticisms of the impact
on self-esteem, the occasional incitement to violence, and the dubious
consequences of the drive to win (as in the extensive use of drugs and
other cheating).[49] In its place are studies that suggest that sport is manipu-
lated by states as part of their cultural policy and international competition,[50] as well as those that indicate the link between sports and identity
formation, in terms of nation but also of race.[51]

   These considerations, along with the implications of Quidditch as a violent spectacle, suggest that good and bad in the sport are more interwoven
and mixed up than the mundane reading tells us. More generally, the role
of Quidditch as a social institution tells us something of the wizarding
world, a world of aristocratic privilege and inequality, tinged with imperialism. With regard to personalities, if we can abandon our prejudices concerning the goodness of Harry, it is difficult to see why we criticize Malfoy
for having bought his way onto the Slytherin Quidditch team because his
father purchased new high-tech brooms for the team, and yet not similarly
censure Harry when his godfather buys him the most expensive broom
that can be obtained, a world-class broom no less! Surely, if one is purchasing victory in one case, one is doing the same in the other. Snape's assessment of Harry is also apposite: "Famous Harry Potter is a law unto
himself. Let the ordinary people worry about his safety." Comparing Harry
to his father, Snape suggests that "a small amount of talent on the Quidditch pitch made him think he was a cut above the rest of us. . . . Rules
were for lesser mortals, not for Quidditch Cup-winners" (PA, 209). At a
number of points, Harry breaks rules but is forgiven because of who he is.
Dumbledore sends Harry the Invisibility Cloak which is little short of an
incitement to wrongdoing, and the same could be said of Lupin returning
the Marauders Map. McGonagall overlooks Harry's infractions so that he
might win the Quidditch Cup for Gryffindor. And Cornelius Fudge
prefers not to punish Harry for breaking the International Statute on Wizarding Secrecy Regarding Under-Age Wizards.

   Yet, Quidditch is more than a reflection of social privilege and inequality. Most of the time, Harry's concern with Quidditch is playing the
game, although this changes when he is banned from playing during his

fifth year and as he becomes more concerned with battling the intrigues of the Death Eaters during his sixth year (OP, 5; HBP, 391). But in playing the game, as I note above, we are in a realm of play as much as of rules and thus the spontaneous and nonutilitarian elements are what are most important to Harry and his friends. To understand the importance of Quidditch is not only to see the metaphors of good and evil teams nor the cultural context of the sport, it is to appreciate that in the end it is the play itself that matters to the players.[52]

## Notes

1. Rapoport 1960.
2. Snidal 1986.
3. Axelrod 1984, 6–7; Oye 1986, 2.
4. Manning 1962, 207.
5. Manning 1962, 215.
6. Shapiro 1989.
7. Ashley 1988, 230, 238–41.
8. The heroic practice not only reduces Harry's world in this way. It also reduces the stories themselves to the product of a muggle world and a muggle author, to a world that is as disenchanted as ours (Ostling 2003), and represents a reading perpetrated by those unable and usually unwilling to see the magical qualities of Harry's world and ours. On this curious lack of curiosity, see Scamander 2001.
9. Campbell 1993, 8. This means of course that the distinction of fact and fiction cannot be maintained and I consider Quidditch here much as one might consider rugby or cricket in the muggle world. Some may wonder whether I am justified in labelling the consideration of a magical sport in terms parallel to those of a muggle sport as a "magical reading." The point is to avoid the reduction of Quidditch to nothing more than literature and worse still, metaphor. As a muggle myself I can only suggest that in the end the reader must decide whether what I have offered can justifiably be so described, although I think I can defensibly claim that my reading is not mundane. To my social science critics, I hope that even if this paper is not magical it may to some degree be logical.
10. For a children's story featuring the interplay of hockey and international relations, see Roy MacGregor 2001, *Power Play in Washington*.
11. Gmelch 1999.
12. Compared to the games in Lewis Carroll's *Alice in Wonderland* stories, which also feature, among other things, chess. In *Alice*, however, at times the whole world is a chess board and the pieces change into other things. For the magical elements of the games in the *Alice* stories, see Blake 1974, especially on chess at 105. On Carroll's dislike of sport, which he equated with hunting and dueling, and thus as intrinsically violent and destructive, see Blake 1974, 158.
13. Guttmann 1978, 3.

14. Guttmann 1978, 4–9.

15. Weiss 1969, 77–78; McInnes 2002, 149.

16. The most extreme version of this combativeness is hunting (insofar as this can be regarded as a sport at all) where the aim is often though not always the destruction of the hunted. Hunting was common in the wizarding world we are told, and of course persists in various manifestations in our world.

17. Dunning and Sheard 1979, 9.

18. Compare to the reference in Blyton's *In the Fifth at Mallory Towers*: "'You will play well, *n'est-ce pas*? You will win all the goals. I shall come to watch. And for the girl that wins a goal. . . . ' '*Shoots* a goal, Mam'zelle,' said Susan. 'Shoots! Ah yes—but you have no gun to shoot a goal,' said Mam'zelle, who never could learn the language of sports." Blyton 1995 [1950], 94–95.

19. Rather than the grand legends revolving around good and evil, an alternate would highlight the prevailing myth in the magical tales of Harry Potter, of the suburban English life and of school for a reasonably well-to-do English schoolboy.

20. Although Harry does at one point resort to gamesmanship against Slytherin when chasing the Snitch (HBP, 278).

21. At the time of writing, it is unclear whether Snape might be similar to Saruman. This author suspects not, in fact.

22. Although Quidditch reportedly has queer origins. According to the authoritative account of Kenilworth Whisp (2001), the game that became Quidditch was first reported being played at Queerditch Marsh in England in the fourteenth century.

23. Elias 1978; Malcolm 2002, 39.

24. Whisp 2001.

25. The idea for the Snitch came when a Golden Snidget was released into the middle of a game of Quidditch. After that, Snidgets were for a time sought and killed during Quidditch games. Snidgets had been hunted almost to extinction by errant wizards. It appears that there was increasing pressure to end the hunting and killing of the Golden Snidget and a ban was placed on the practice by the Wizards Council. This generated the need for a replacement in the form of a metal Snitch, precharmed to stay on the Quidditch pitch.

26. Malcolm 2002.

27. One aspect of the folklore origins of Quidditch resembles cricket: the length of the game is determined by the teams. Traditionally, especially before the invention of the Snitch, games could last for days.

28. Dunning and Sheard 1979.

29. The references to countries in the first three books are Romania (PS, 80; CS, 40), Transylvania (CS, 122), Africa (PS, 80), England (PS, 126; PA, 61), and Norway (PS, 170), Albania (CS, 242), Egypt (CS, 40; PA, 12), France (PA, 14), Ireland (PA, 43). In GF, the countries referred to in the context of Quidditch are Britain (32 and others), Bulgaria (37, 55, and others), Egypt (96), Ireland (32, 55 and others), Luxembourg, Peru, Scotland, Transylvania, Uganda, Wales (all at 59).

References other than in the context of Quidditch include Albania (58, regarding the disappearance of Bertha Jorkins), Andorra (482), Australia (58, again concerning Bertha Jorkins), Brazil (76), Norway (60), Rumania (48, regarding dragons), and China and Sweden (287, again concerning dragons, this time as used in the first task of the Triwizard Tournament).

30. Interestingly, it doesn't seem as if there is much internationalization of the players on Quidditch teams—that is, there are no mentions of any Europeans or other nationals in British Quidditch teams. The Bosman decision does not seem to have had an impact on the wizard sporting community.

31. And also the Official Gobstones Club and the Ludicrous Patents Office.

32. Allison and Monnington 2002, 114–15.

33. Barnier 2001, 17.

34. In the author's personal experience, these heroes are often drawn from among the imperial conquering heroes and explorers, for instance, Francis Drake and Walter Raleigh. The founders of Hogwarts include women suggesting once again that there is more gender equality in the wizarding community than in our muggle world.

35. Mangan 1986.

36. This narrative not only relates the interwar period but also *The Lord of the Rings*. The connection of these two narratives is made by Alison Lurie 1990, 189–90.

37. Whisp 2001, 43. Quodpot developed from the import of a Snitch from "the old country" by a wizard who accidentally charmed it so that it exploded. In an interesting aside, Whisp notes that the development of Quidditch in North America was also inhibited by "the great intensity of 'anti-wizarding feeling.'" There are parallels of Quidditch and Quodpot to the relationship of rugby and (American) football.

38. Mangan 1998.

39. Mangan 2001, 5.

40. Veblen 1978, 43. Veblen also suggests that "[t]he addiction to sports . . . marks an arrested development of the man's moral nature." Sports are a product of "boyish temperament."

41. In a demonstration of dueling for second years in CS, Lockhart is dealt with severely by Snape, for instance, as a way for Snape openly to humiliate Lockhart in front of his pupils.

42. Sipes 1973, 67.

43. Guilbert 2004.

44. Geertz 1983.

45. At one of my son's recent hockey games, one of his friends showed off his new $200 stick. One parent, looking over the gathered players and parents as they pored over and passed the stick on in turn, remarked, "Just like Harry Potter!" Compare to PA, 171, 184, 188–90. The U.S. army's illicit use of Harry Potter features a character named Topper who attends Mogmarts School of Magic by the

magazine *Preventive Maintenance Monthly*. See *Ottawa Citizen*, 7 February 2005, "U.S. Army Faces Wrath of Harry Potter Creator."

46. One day during the writing of this chapter, my son had what we all agreed was a perfect day. It involved hockey (playing with his Atom House League team and winning), hockey (playing a pick-up game with his mum and a neighborhood kid on the local community outdoor rink), hockey (playing his imaginary game by himself at home), hockey (reading the scores in the newspaper), and hockey (attending an NHL game featuring the Ottawa Senators with his House League team). He slept well in his NHL pajamas . . .

47. McInnes 2002, 148–52.

48. Messenger 1990, 192–208.

49. Rosen 2004.

50. For examples, see Mackintosh and Hawes 1994.

51. Carrington 2004.

52. For a critique of various left critiques of sport and a discussion of practice-communities, see McNamee 1997.

# GEOGRAPHY AND MYTH III

# Naturalizing Geography
## Harry Potter and the Realms of Muggles, Magic Folks, and Giants

**7**

IVER B. NEUMANN

LL THE WAY UP TO THE SECOND WORLD WAR, and particularly since the late 1800s, studies of global politics went hand in hand with the study of geography. Small wonder, since the kind of knowledge production known as geography was born as the handmaiden of the soldier. We still find traces of this in the geographical vocabulary. For example, *region* comes from the Latin verb *regere,* to rule. When the discipline of international relations was institutionalized in the early decades of the twentieth century, it happened partly in conversation with what was known as geopolitics. Geopolitics existed in a number of guises. The term itself was coined by the Swedish social scientist Rudolf Kjellén in 1899.[1] An Anglo-American geopolitical tradition can be traced through works by the likes of Halford Mackinder and Alfred Thayer Mahan.[2] In Germany, Friedrich Ratzel and Karl Haushofer were busy drawing up geographies that would lend themselves handily to various groups of right-wing expansionists. In the wake of the Second World War, geopolitics seemingly lost its luster. It is, however, not hard to excavate geographical presuppositions from the political writings of the Cold War period. Indeed, when geography returned to the study of international relations from the 1980s onward as critical geopolitics, it was exactly as an exercise of this kind.[3] The key argument was that if any politics has a spatial dimension, then it should be worthwhile having a look at how space is configured, where that configuration comes from, and what it does to power relations. One notes how this program is in synch with constructivist concerns (see introduction). Geography is not simply something that exists outside of the signs we use to communicate about it. The techniques we use to categorize space—maps being a key example—and the languages we use to discuss it—for example, dividing space into "regions"—are inseparable parts of our experience of space.

Following the book's introduction, this chapter studies the Harry Potter books with a view to how the category of space is naturalized. I begin by demonstrating how space in Harry Potter is divided into realms, by which I mean dimensions between which only those with privileged access may slip. This is a way of imagining space that is well known from religious discourse. In the Old Norse religion, for example, there is a realm of the gods (*Ásgård*), a realm of humans (*Midgård*), and a realm of giants (*Utgård*). This is a sacred geography, where what happens in certain realms is held to be of more importance than what happens in others. I argue that the sacred geography in Harry Potter is of a special kind, formatted by what is understood as an eternal fight between good and evil. Those who are able to move between realms will have a power advantage in such a world, because they may bring more resources to bear on a struggle in any one realm. Part two of this chapter looks at the question of power and argues that Dumbledore and Harry embody two different principles of power. There is also a third, and perhaps more unlikely, wielder of power in this universe, however, and that is Hagrid. In part three, I draw up Hagrid's family tree or genealogy in European history, and demonstrate how figures such as Hagrid were actually pivotal to early state building. They were seen as embodiments of the land ruled by the king.

All three realms of the Harry Potter universe—those of muggles, magic folks, and giants—are what we may call geographically marked. Hagrid, who is the front man for the realm of giants, has a special rapport with the realm of monsters, to the extent that we may see the realm inhabited by giants and monsters as *one* realm. Hagrid is also marked in terms of geographical directions. Hagrid is of the North and East. Interestingly, in European history, at least up until the nineteenth century, the North was held to be a chaos to the South's cosmos. A key idea was that the North harbored more originary human and nonhuman life forms. From the nineteenth century onward, the east becomes increasingly marked as a political danger. We recognize this in the geographical formatting of the realm of magic folks as well, where Voldemort is marked as eastern. The wizarding school of the east, Durmstrang, has a greater emphasis on the Dark Arts than does Hogwarts, Voldemort and his followers are portrayed as having spent time in the east, etc.[4] In international relations, a number of scholars have drawn on the work by Edward Said and others in order to demonstrate how this has unfolded historically, and what repercussions this way of dividing the world has had on politics.[5] In the world of Harry Potter, these representations of geographical dimensions are still very much present. The geography of Harry Potter's world has been a point of some debate among fandom on and off the net, which is to say that this geography and the representations it consists of uphold a way of thinking about space that has direct bearings on politics, with the North and the East being places where one would find savages and barbarians of all hues.

## Intertwined Realms

The issues involved appear already in the riling question par excellence in fandom debate, which has been where to find Hogwarts. We know that magic places like Diagon Alley and St. Mungo's Hospital are in London, and we know that when the Hogwarts Express leaves London on 1 September each year it aims "due north" out of London, "winding its way past a snow-capped mountain" (CS, 57, 58). We also know that Hogwarts is in Britain, since Hogsmeade, the local village, is said to be the only wizarding village in Britain. In the Britain we know, however, one is hard put to find snow-capped mountains in September. So what kind of symbolic geography may provide for such a situation?

An immediate clue is available in the form of the barriers that magic folks are able to place around Hogwarts and other places of their choice (such as the noted London locations, or the field picked for the Quidditch World Cup). Special attention must therefore be paid to the fact that it is only in wizarding parlance that Hogsmeade is supposed to be in Britain. We do not actually know whether Hogsmeade and Hogwarts are located in *our* Britain. There is an undecidability as to whether our Britain and the entity referred to by wizards as Britain are contiguous. We are talking about different realms here. The symbolic geography of Harry Potter's world features different dimensions that exist side by side. Beings with the special knowledge required may move freely (or not so freely) between the realms. We know about this kind of symbolic geography from numerous other life worlds, many if not most of which share a family resemblance in being thought in terms of the sacred and the profane. Harry's world is, however, not simply a two-dimensional world, consisting of a mundane (or muggle) realm and a magical realm. There exist other realms as well. An immediate clue that presents itself here is the existence of a Forbidden Forest just to the east of Hogwarts. This forest, which younger students are told is out of bounds, is home to a number of magical beings that have intricate relations with the magical world. These beings include monsters such as giant spiders, unicorns, thestrals, and dragons. There are also centaurs. We know, furthermore, that the Forbidden Forest is not alone in harboring such beings; the lake outside Hogwarts features merpeople, trolls and mountain trolls roam in unspecified abodes, and in *Harry Potter and the Order of the Phoenix,* we are introduced to a giant population that lives in mountains somewhere to the east of Britain. We are also told that giants once lived in Britain itself.

What ties the realms of Harry Potter's world together is the cosmic fight between good and evil. It is immediately clear that the principles of good and evil are incarnate to this world. Evil cannot be eradicated. Evil's immanent character in the world is underlined in a number of places, as is the fact that evil is ceaselessly out to ensnare. Indeed, the fight between good and evil is at the heart of this world's politics. Other potentially integrative factors, such as gender, family, and species ties, clearly take a back seat to the clash between good and evil. Indeed, this clash dominates not only group conflicts, but also the political and moral life of each specific being. As discussed in chapter 5 by Folker and Sterling-Folker, every being at least potentially has to choose between the forces of good and the forces of evil.

This is a view of politics that has a history. The idea that the life world may be reduced to only two struggling groups has firm roots in Judeo-Christian tradition, two of which are particularly apposite to an analysis of Potter politics. These are the Hebrews of the second temple and the Manicheans. A quick look at these two groupings should suffice here. Among the ancient Hebrews, Ezra and other leaders of the second temple stand out as particularly fundamentalist in their approach to other groups. They wanted to establish a clearcut boundary between themselves—the Jewish elite which had suffered the Babylonian captivity—on the one hand, and everybody else, including Jews who had stayed behind, on the other. They wanted this boundary to be not only social, but physical, in the sense that the impure should be physically removed from the sacred land of Israel. The way to achieve this was war, and in this war, there were no restraints whatsoever on the use of force.[6] This war was, however, seen as a war between Israel and its enemies, not between a principle of good and a principle of evil. The reason why this framing of the political takes on historical importance lies in its insistence that there exists a clearcut boundary between us and them, between the pure and the impure.

The idea that there is a cosmic dimension to the battle between the pure and the impure crops up with the Zoroastrian sect of the Manicheans, named after their leader Mani. In the early centuries of the first millennium, Manichean thinking strongly influenced early Christians. As Norman Cohn puts it, "All in all, it would seem that amongst the fringe groups in Judaism the Jesus sect was the one that was most exposed to Zoroastrian influence. There is nothing mysterious about that. The Iranian culture is now known to have been long and firmly established in areas into which early Christians moved."[7] As Cohn sees it, this exposure was a fateful one, inasmuch as it has informed the Christian tradition. The key figure here is Augustine, who was closely associated with the Manicheans, to the extent of probably having been one for nine years before becoming a Christian. His *Confessions* is actually our main source on Manicheanism.[8] Augustine is also the man who breaks with the pacifism of the early church, arguing that it is not a sin to kill and commit other acts of violence as long as you do not hate your enemy in your heart. What used to be an ethical ban on actions in the physical world was transformed by Augustine and became a question of the soul, a matter between the killer and his god rather than between the killer, his victim, and other humans. This can only make sense if four criteria are fulfilled. First, there exists an eternal struggle for and between souls—a cosmic battle between good and evil. Second, there is a link between this battle of souls and the battles of men, so that the latter play themselves out as parts of the former. This is to say that the principles of good and evil must be *incarnate*, that is, present in our world either directly (god through his son Jesus; the devil) or indirectly (in human agency). Third, some agency—in this case Augustine himself—must hold a recognized position from which to decide which humans represent good, and which evil. Fourth, this knowledge must be acted upon—somebody must legitimately raise their swords in order to complement by forceful means the spiritual fight for the good.

Harry's world is a world where all these four criteria are fulfilled, and they seem to apply in all three realms. Perhaps they apply in an even greater degree than is realized at first. From a biographical sketch on Dumbledore (taken from the back of a Chocolate Frog card), we learn that he is "particularly famous for his defeat of the dark wizard Grindelwald in 1945" (PS, 77)—a hint that he has defeated dark wizards before, in an intriguing year, including one whose name is not only Teutonic-sounding but also reminiscent of the monster Grendel from the best-known Old English text we have, *Beowulf.* A reading that seems to be invited is that the Second World War may be part of a cosmic battle that also enveloped the wizarding world. Given that the magic realm possesses privileged knowledge and a number of resources that do not exist in other realms, there is a hint here that what happens in that realm is more important than what happens in other realms. This hint is strongly reinforced by the opening of book six, *Harry Potter and the Half-Blood Prince,* which centers on how, in Britain at least, the Minister of Magic duplicates, rounds out, and even supervises the work of the prime minister in 10 Downing Street. It follows that muggle historical knowledge seems to be lacking in depth. We are also invited to think of politics as derivative of the fight between good and evil. Such a politics *must* center on

a) how to separate good from evil. The institution/being who carries out this task will be the linchpin of politics;
b) how to rally allies to the side of good, and how to keep them;
c) when and how to strike out against evil.

I ponder these questions in turn, and I do it from the point of view of wizards, who are the leading species among magic folks and so in a privileged position to form and lead alliances. The alliances that wizards make are fluid. Muggles have periodically persecuted wizards and are not particularly interesting allies. Inside the realm of magic folks, goblins, who run the bank Gringotts, are a key financial asset, but we know that they have rebelled against wizards in the past. House elves are the subalterns of the wizarding world, and so not particularly well suited, either.[9] We do not know much about other species such as dwarves, except that they are introduced as being "raucous" (PA, 57), that they deliver messages that cannot be sent by owl post, and that at least one of their number occasionally drops his aiches (CS, 177). One species that has real potential as allies, however, is the centaurs, but they suffer serious internal fissures over these issues. The scene where they are introduced (PS, 184–89) is heavy with foreboding. Experts in astrology and so eminent soothsayers, the centaurs note that Mars shines brightly—a traditional sign of imminent conflict. The three centaurs we meet take up three different stands on how to react, however. Bane is a fatalist: "Centaurs are concerned with what has been foretold! It is not our business to run around like donkeys after stray humans in our Forest!" (PS, 188). Firenze, on the other hand, acknowledges that the odds are against him but voices the activist stand in favor of an alliance nonetheless: "I set myself against what is lurking in this Forest, Bane, yes, with humans alongside me if I must. . . . The planets have been read wrongly before now, even by centaurs. I hope this is one of those times" (PS, 188–89). Ronan is undecided. Here we see how the fight between good and evil forces everyone to take a stand, and how those stands split a species and may even lead certain members into exile; in book five, Firenze is almost killed when he announces his decision to take a job at Hogwarts.[10]

The division of centaurs on this issue mirrors the deeper undecidedness about whether, and perhaps in what degree, centaurs belong to the realm of magic folks or the realm of giants. It is fitting in this regard that Hagrid is the messenger between magic folks and centaurs, since he is the key channel between magic folks and most of the species that populate the realm of giants and monsters. Indeed, giants themselves are problematic allies. They have been known to ally with evil, both during Voldemort's first appearance and seemingly again upon his return (HBP, 18), but this seems to be the result of bad wizarding politics rather than the result of any immanent quality. Sundry nonhuman species such as veelas (GF, 116), leprechauns (GF, 118), giant spiders (CS, chap. 15), and merpeople are potential flanking allies. The dementors, on the other hand, are said to be the "natural allies" of the evil Voldemort, and sure enough, in book six, they float to his side. The mountain trolls also seem to have a proclivity for the dark side, as do snakes, but most other monsters seem to have no particular leanings one way or the other.[11]

To sum up so far, even in a Manichean world like Harry Potter's, politics make for strange bedfellows, and beggars cannot be choosers. As summed up by a bureaucrat wizard, "you sometimes have to join forces with those you'd rather avoid" (PA, 75–76; also PA, 180). Furthermore, you have to know your enemy and acknowledge that, however cosmically important it may be, the line between good and evil is often razor-thin. In Harry's world, this undecidability is present not only in the character of Snape, but also in the link that was forged when the evil Voldemort tried to kill baby Harry. The idea that good and evil may have a mutually enhancing effect on one another as the struggle between them unfolds is firmly established in tradition. We find it, for example, in the Merlin legend, where Merlin is the offspring of evil and is only salvaged for the children of light by a quick-witted priest who has the wherewithal to have him baptized. Dumbledore and Merlin have a whole swathe of similarities. Harry's nightmares about whether he has been put in the right house, and so on the right side in the fight between good and evil, is a reminder of how the two seem to be wedded at a number of levels. The line between good and evil is a fine one, and those who are most adept at fighting evil are also those who have had the closest brush with it. Dumbledore and Harry are both examples of this, and so is Hagrid, by dint of his genealogy.

# Who Ties the Realms Together:
# Hagrid the Hybrid

To ask who ties the realms of Harry's world together, is to ask who pulls the strings, which is a question of power. Power in Harry's world is to do with respect and magic, with who is authorized by the community to do what. For guidance on such questions, some international relations scholars turn to German sociologist Max Weber's studies of legitimacy, others turn to French philosopher Michel Foucault's studies of discipline and governmentality. Since Harry's world is saturated with references to other realms, however, we may be better served by people who have generalized about power from studies of traditional societies, where magic and religion remain aspects of most if not all other social institutions. One place to start would be a generalization made by French historian of religion Georges Dumézil. Dumézil (1977) notes how, in Indo-European conceptions, rule was a question of *celeritas* and *gravitas* both. *Gravitas* we know: it is to do with the wisdom, prudence, and so on of the well-established king. In Harry's world, Dumbledore stands out as an incarnation of *gravitas*. He is the one who holds the power to separate the good from the bad, so is the linchpin of politics. Dumbledore is also, however, the lover of lemon sherbets and pranks, and this is where *celeritas* comes in. To say it with anthropologist Marshall Sahlins, *celeritas* is a question of "youthful, active, disorderly, magical, and creative violence of conquering princes."[12] Sahlins goes on to comment that "The combination of two terms produces a third, a sovereign power, itself a dual combination of the war function and the peace function, king and priest, will and law." As head of the Order of the Phoenix, the key fighting force of good, Dumbledore is warlord, and as headmaster of Hogwarts and pillar of magical society in sundry respects, Albus Dumbledore is the lord of peace. He is the white lord (*albus*: Lat. white). But he is also flanked by two other powerful protagonists, Harry and Hagrid.

If we look at the symbolic geography of Harry's world through Dumézil's lens, it is immediately clear why Harry is so important. He has the power of celerity in abundance, and he uses it in order to deal with the general fight between good and evil. Danger, however, is not only to be found at this all-encompassing level. It resides not only on the boundary between good and evil, but also at the boundary of the different realms of the world. Harry has a foot in two of these realms. He is Dumbledore's key mediator between the realm of magic folks ("home") and the realm of muggles. There also exists another key mediator in this world, however, one who mans (or rather half-mans) the boundary between the magic realm and the monster realm. This is Hagrid, Keeper of the Keys and Grounds of Hogwarts. Like Harry, he is the offspring of a liaison between beings from different realms. Like Harry, he has celerity. And like Harry, Albus Dumbledore trusts him with his life. To Dumbledore, an alliance with the giants is key to winning the imminent battle with evil, and Hagrid is key to forging this alliance. Hagrid is also a key with which to unlock the symbolic geography of the world of Harry Potter.

Hagrid is a being of the boundary, a messenger, a mediator between species and realms, even between culture and nature. He is introduced as follows: "He simply looked too big to be allowed, and so *wild*" (PS, 16). At the end of book one, "Hagrid sidled through the door as he spoke. As usual when he was indoors, Hagrid looked too big to be allowed" (PS, 219). In book three, he is described as "gigantic," "twice as tall as a normal man" (PA, 97; PA, 198) and in book four, we learn that he is indeed half giant. In book four, we also meet Olymp Maxime, who is introduced as being as large as Hagrid (GF, 268), and who also turns out to be half-giant. In book five, Hagrid pays a visit to a giant refuge, and brings back a full-blooded if somewhat impish giant, his half-brother Grawp. With unfailing geographical logic, Grawp is placed in the Forbidden Forest, part and symbol of the realm of giants and monsters from which he hails. In book six, Grawp has embarked on his domestication, appearing at Hogwarts wearing clothes, but he still resides in the Forbidden Forest, and so bears out how giants are perched on the boundary between the monster and the magic realms, between East and West.

Hagrid's very name bears the traces of his hybrid heritage. Hag (Middle English *hagge*) comes from Anglo-Saxon *hægtesse*, probably from the Anglo-Saxon *haga* meaning hedge, a place where witches were said to have their abode (Skeat 1993, 191).[13] Hedges are boundaries of sorts, and witches belong along boundaries. In Norwegian and other Scandinavian languages, the standard word for the concept of witch remains *heks* (cf. the American expression to hex someone for casting a spell on him), and Rowling's "witches and wizards" are translated as *hekser og trollmenn*. *Troll* are to be found in the realm of giants and monsters. Troll are distinct from giants, as they were in the Old Norse world. The Old Norse giants were called *jotunn*. The home world of the *jotunn*, *Utgård*, was said to be located east of the human world. They are present in *Beowolf* as *eotenas*. The Old Norse and Old English *jotunn/eoten* (two variants of the same word) were supposed to be living in mountains and caves. During the Middle Ages, they were represented ever more interchangeably with the Roman giants (lat. *gigantes*), to the extent that the standard Norwegian dictionary defines the latter in terms of the former.[14] This confluence of Roman and Norse mythologies may be seen already in *Beowolf,* where the giants were said to hail from Cain.[15] One notes a similar confluence where the half-giants of Harry Potter's world are concerned. Hagrid's name is Norse, whereas Olymp Maxime's is Graeco-Roman. There are striking similarities between the realms of magic folks, muggles, and giants in Harry Potter's world and the realms of gods, humans, and giants/*eotenas* in Old Norse religion.[16]

The similarities between the life world of Viking (ca. 700–1050) and medieval (c. 1050–1550) Scandinavia and Britain on the one hand, and the world of Harry Potter on the other, do not stop here, however. In 1555, the Swedish archbishop Olaus Magnus, who had been exiled to Rome as a result of the Reformation, wrote no less than twenty-two books about life in his native north. The full title of the work serves notice that Magnus intends to give a full description of "almost all the living creatures that dwell in the North and their characteristics." Being true to his word, Magnus gives detailed descriptions of the giants that once lived in the North, and the monsters that still live there. A number of these monsters pop up in the world of Harry Potter as well: werewolves, mermen, trolls, no less than six different kinds of mountain trolls, etc.[17] Magnus was widely read by the learned scholars of his day. It is not an overstatement that his presentation of the north lingered for centuries, not least through his influence on other widely read scholars such as Montesquieu and even Rousseau. When, in European tradition, the north is still marked as somewhat more originary, less complicated, and wilder that the south, it is among other things because of Magnus's books. The symbolic geography of the Harry Potter universe perpetuates this marking, and so contributes to uphold it as "normal."

The reason why we talk about two historical periods around the North Sea, Viking and Middle Age, and divide them around 1050, is to do with the coming of Christianity and the social changes that Christianity brought to this life world. The confluence between Norse *eotenas* and biblical and Roman giants was part and parcel of this shift (and is, to repeat, echoed in the names of Hagrid and Olymp Maxime). Hags and giants were firmly ensconced in the life world. Consider an example from Denmark of how Hags were listed on a par with foreigners: In 1524, the head of the Jutland *landsting* gave as one reason for a rebellion against King Christian II that he had neglected the council of his peers, preferring instead those of "Scots,

Dutch, Germans, Charlatans, Tyrants and Hags [*Troldqvinder*, literally troll women]."[18] Where giants are concerned, Kendrick reports how a man called John Rous

> wrote a [now lost] book on giants, and had much to say about them also in his *Histora* [*Regum Angliae* from c. 1460]: no one doubted the former existence of these creatures; there was abundant Biblical proof, and Sir John Mandeville had actually seen the forty feet long rib of one of them at Jaffa; giants' bones had also been found in England, and Rous knew of life-size hill-figures of Gogmagog and Corinius that were kept scoured even in his own time.[19]

So, who are the giants? Unfortunately, giant studies have fallen somewhat in disrepute since the days of John Rous and are no longer a well-established academic discipline. There seem to exist only two recent monographs on the topic. Furthermore, they seem to be at loggerheads. On the one hand, Stephens argues the orthodox view. To him, as giants appeared to humankind from the time of the Old Testament to Rabelais, they were wholly *other* to humans.[20] Against this, Cohen, who is particularly interested in Augustine's and Isidore of Seville's views on the matter but who also sifts the evidence presented by Stephens, arrives at the heterodox and in my view more fruitful view that the giant is "a morally and physically deformed creature arriving to demarcate the boundary beyond which lies the unintelligible, the inhuman."[21] The giant is a hybrid, half-manning the boundary of humanity. To ask about the nature of giants is to ask about the nature of the relationship between realms, between the realms of humans, gods, and giants, or muggles, magic folks, and giants, for that matter. Cohen notes how

> The northern giants married freely with gods and men, as often representing a middle step between the human and the divine as an inferior genus between man and animal. The Aesir, the most powerful gods of the Norse pantheon, were descended from giants. An elemental, perhaps autochthonous being, giants were inextricable from the earth and stone they worked, so they gained an explanatory function as creators of landscape, ancient ruins, and mysterious architecture. . . . Even after the Vanir and Aesir had been replaced by Christian monotheism, traditions of giants lingered. As erudite culture replaced the more indigenous, heathen tradition, this old order of giants became conflated with the vanished gods whom they had aided and battled so that both could then be denigrated as deceivers and impersonators, validating the superiority of *Christianitatis* as a homogeneous, erudite, right-thinking culture.[22]

Even after this disenfranchisement, then, in British and Scandinavian folk traditions there were and are a number of tales about friendly relations between gods and giants. Male gods and female giants carry on affairs, and these affairs are frequently fruitful. There are also stories of how giants, usually the fathers of daughters who have fallen in love with gods, pay the gods valuable assistance. Gods and giants, that seems to be the ticket. By contrast, there seem to be no tales of interaction between giants and humans. The twenty-two-volume *Encyclopedia of the Nordic Middle Ages* states that "according to the legends, giants [*jotner*] do not interlock with human life as do trolls . . . , who are experienced as a presence in the human environment. In distinction to these, giants appear as a people of the earliest times, who have disappeared long since."[23] In the Middle Ages, giants were located in a netherworld, in the midst of or east of our world. There was an easy passage between their world and our own. Beings with the special knowledge required could hence move freely between the two realms. One notes that these beings tended to be gods. One also notes that, in Harry's world, wizards may move into the realm where giants are to be found and vice versa, but few if any muggles who run into giants live to tell the tale (we are even told that tourists who stumble upon them by accident tend to be killed). There is a parallel between the Norse world and Harry's world in this regard.

Yet another parallel between the Norse world and Harry's world is to be found in the domination of wizards/humans over giants. As noted by Cohen, "Giants represent the unassimilated remnant of the past that, although it eludes the complete historical memory of the recorder, is integrally bound to the process of giving that history an identity."[24] As applied to Harry's world, we note that there, too, giants are placed in a peripheral setting geographically, but that, in former times, they took center stage (they used to live all over Britain). Giants were forced off the land. Giants must be seen as what social scientists call a constitutive other to wizards in Harry's world, and to humans in the Norse world. What they mean by that is that a self, be that an individual or a group, forms itself in relations to other individuals and groups, and that their formation is among other things constituted by these relationships. The relationship between magic folks and giants is one of domination. The symbolic geography of Harry Potter, where much is made of how giants have been marginalized, is therefore a geography of domination. Hagrid's genealogy suggests that, as a giant, he stands in a long line of aboriginal beings who have been forced off the land. In the next part of this chapter, I want to tease out the relevance of this insight to contemporary politics. My argument is that the modern North-European state is built on the bones of giants. The corpses of giants are, as it were, parts of the foundation.

## Giants and the State

In the world of Harry Potter, Hagrid reminds us of how giants were once living all over Britain, and how they have been driven out. A similar story is well known where medieval Britain is concerned. Geoffrey of Monmouth's *Historia Regnum Britanniae* (History of the Kings of Britain) corroborates a myth of origin that ties the Norman aristocracy to their new land, a land they had only possessed for about four generations when Geoffrey wrote his tale. According to Geoffrey, the Normans that invaded Britain hailed from Brutus of Troy. Again, Cohen is most enlightening. He points out how

> in creating a past, Geoffrey also shaped a future. The power of this "onceness and futurity" is embodied in Arthur.[25] Brutus became through Geoffrey's account the founding father of Britain, but he and the giants that he conquers are described only to provide the heroic base on which the glory of King Arthur could be erected. The *Historia* culminates in the conflicted, ambiguous, but ultimately resplendent portrait of Britain's greatest king. Geoffrey's achievement was to bestow on the Middle Ages a monarchical body through which England dreamed its own prehistory and inhabited it as if it had always been home. . . . Conveniently, the same king whom Geoffrey exalted as British could be admired by the reigning Anglo-Norman monarchy, who likewise claimed Trojan descent.[26]

In 1415, Henry II famously had two giants, Gogmagog and Corineus, erected on London Bridge. The king trooped his colors at the giants' expense on a regular basis: "The giants were regularly featured in mayoral processions. Records indicate that they greeted Philip and Mary at their public entry into London on 1554 and hailed Elizabeth four years later as part of a ceremony preliminary to her coronation. Such occasions served as political theater in which to repeat the legendary history of Britain, a performance that aimed to materialize royal power in the present through the invocation of a long and therefore authoritative genealogy" (Cohen 1999: 29). To political entities that define and legitimate themselves in terms of their history, their origin is of the essence, for history is the chronological aspect of their identity. If we turn to the origins of modern states in the late Middle Ages, we find that it was a common trait that kings drew up genealogies for themselves going back to a progenitor who is said to have taken over the country in a violent confrontation with an aboriginal population. The above-mentioned history by Geoffrey of Monmouth is, after all, the key source on royal British mythical genealogy. Written around 1135, it

> contained information that the author regarded as his own very special contribution to antiquarian studies. It was, Geoffrey claimed, a scoop, the triumphant publication of a most important discovery, a complete account of the British kings between Brutus the Trojan and Cadwallader, the last of the ancient rulers and a known historical personage. . . . He maintained that his good fortune was due to a *vetustissimus liber,* a book in the British tongue brought from Brittany by a learned and important friend.[27]

Geoffrey recounts that the ancient Britons were the descendants of Brutus, who was himself the grandson of Aenaeas of Troy. Brutus established himself on the throne around 1170 B.C. by conquering a number of giants, among whom we find Gogmagog, and founded London in celebration.[28] Subsequently, he divided his realm for his three sons to share. His descendant Arthur (head of the Round Table) famously rebuffed a Saxon invasion, but the Saxons eventually triumphed over Arthur's descendant Cadwallader. Before he died, however, Cadwallader saw an angel who told him that the sons of Arthur would once again rule in Britain. Both Edward IV and Henry VIII had genealogies drawn up for them which proved that they were the rightful descendants of Cadwallader, and so rightful rulers of Britain. Henry VII even named his eldest son Arthur, having seen to it that he was born in Winchester, sometime home of Arthur's Round Table. When the union was made between Scotland and England in 1707, the country was renamed Great Britain, the reason given being that this was what it had been called before Brutus divided it into England, Wales, and Scotland.[29] Here we have an example of how, in Europe, these genealogies were key political assets well into the modern period.

Indeed, making such use of history was the European rule at the time. Robert Filmer was right when he stated that "most of the civilised nations of earth labour to fetch their original from some one of the sons or nephews of Noah."[30] In the case of Scandinavian kings, they were said to have taken over land that had once belonged to the giants after the Old Norse gods had victoriously conquered them. In 1544, the Swedish nobleman and former archbishop Johannes Magnus wrote a work that went on to become one of the key texts for Europe's understanding of the North.[31] He drew up a genealogy for the Swedish Vasa kings that stretched back to none other than the giant Magog.[32] The numbering that he introduced for the kings is still in use, despite there being no referents for half a dozen Charleses and a sprinkling of Eriks outside that numbering system itself. Again, these practices stretch well into the modern period. In the early Norwegian stages of nation building in the late eighteenth and early nineteenth centuries, authors referred to Norway as a "home of giants" on a regular basis. Like the Norse gods before them, and like the wizards of Harry Potter's world, Swedes and Norwegians were said to have conquered their land from the giants.

To sum up so far, giants are written into the foundation of modern states by dint of their place in the mythologies of how rule was established. This may be read directly out of the listing of kings. As we have seen, in the case of Sweden, the numbering of kings that is still in daily use is dependent on giants to hold up. There is, however, yet another way in which giants remain relevant to contemporary international relations. As noted above, giants may be said to represent an autochthonous being, a people of the earliest times and the *unassimilated* remnant of the past. Why unassimilated? Because there remain traces and memories of giants that have not been fully erased, but that surface in social settings such as the Harry Potter books. If the story just told is Hagrid's genealogy, it stands to reason that Hagrid is the genealogy's trace. There do, however, exist not only traces and memories, but peoples—even nations—that are being categorized in contemporary debates in the light of this genealogy. I am referring to a number of aboriginal peoples.

As we have seen, in the self-presentation of the victors of early North European state building, the taking of the land from autochthonous giants played a key role. As also noted, in the North European life world, there were no hard and fast boundaries made between humans—particularly foreigners—and giants. Indeed, as demonstrated by Viking historian Gro Steinsland, Vikings drew on the category of giants to make sense of the existence of autochthonous groups to their north and northeast. These were referred to as *finnar,* meaning Finns and Saamis. They were said to have strong magical powers and to live in *Finnmork*. The word *mork* meant forest or borderland. When Christianity came, laws were passed that forebade Christians to seek Saami guidance.[33] The realm of the Finns— *Finnmork*—literally became the Forbidden Forest. The Finns and Saamis may be said to have been relegated to a magical realm east of the lands of humans proper. The use of giant categories for Saami aboriginals does not stop there, however. In a direct parallel to how human kings were said to have married giant women, stories began to appear about how Norwegian heroes begat offspring by or even married Saami women. For example, in one saga, "The hero, Ketill, has an affair with the daughter of a giant, Brúni, and has a son by her. . . . in this text there is no sharp distinction between giants and Saamis, the brother of Brúni is said to be Saami."[34] Viking Historian Else Mundal suggests that we read such stories as legitimating stories of rule by a state-building people, Norwegians, over an autochthonous people, the Saami. Such a reading sounds eminently plausible to a social scientist, not least for comparative reasons. It is a fact that a number of aboriginal groups all over the world are being read into similar categorization schemes as the ones that were used in Viking and Middle Age Northern Europe to make sense of giants. To note but one example from the anthropological literature, the Korekore Shona of Zimbabwe tell a similarly structured story of how their people conquered and intermarried the autochthons.[35]

To sum up, the relationship between wizards, muggles, and giants seems to be structurally similar to the one between Old Norse gods, humans, and giants. In both cases, the three realms involved seem to be progressively more ancient, more northeasternly located, and closer to nature relative to one another. In both cases, there is acknowledgment of the key role played by a founding victory over giants, and an uneasiness about what this victory tells us about the political project. The giants are the unassimilated trace of the political order. Hagrid is not only a boundary figure between realms and a link back to a past now (almost) lost. He is also the last and tamed remnant of once-rightful owners of the land. Like the last of the Mohicans, he may stand as a symbol for all aboriginal nations that have been forced off their land. To stretch the point, when Hagrid repeatedly points out that Dumbledore, being the real leader of the magic folks, is "a great man," it may be read as an aboriginal acknowledgment of the inevitability of defeat.

## Conclusion: The Return of the Sacred

The structural parallels between Harry's world(s) and the world(s) around the North Sea in the Viking Age and the Middle Ages are not only a matter of the belief system surrounding witches and astrology, then, but also extend to the political world of the time. Giants have been absent from certain Western life-worlds for centuries now. Anthropologist Kirsten Hastrup reports from fieldwork in Iceland, however, that there, they never left.[36] In Scandinavian peasant society, they were a key presence. With the advent of Harry Potter, giants have returned to a number of other life worlds as well, and so has the symbolic geography of realms. These realms, and the beings that populate them, are geographically marked in at least two ways. First, what happens in the realm of magic folks is more important overall than what happens in the two other realms. Second, within each realm, north and east are marked as at least unusual, and probably as morally inferior.

To conclude, Harry's world is able to spellbind us among other things because it recirculates historical (and, for most readers, partially subconscious) energies. In this chapter, I have tried to tease out how this works in the case of geography. One effect of this spellbinding is to naturalize a certain symbolic geography, where giants stand in for all aboriginal peoples who lie buried in the foundations of modern states. If, to complement such an analysis, we turn to the question of the author's intentionality, what is striking is how an author from whom Rowling seems to have learned a lot and to whose books she alludes in her work, J. R. R. Tolkien, always insisted that the fantasy world he created was *our* world, albeit in a previous version. He was also quite explicit in characterizing his activity as mythmaking. He gave as his motivation a wish to forge ties for what he saw as increasingly rootless Englishmen back to "their own" history. J. K. Rowling may be said to do the same. As may be seen by the phenomenal reception of the project, the demand is certainly there. I argue elsewhere that the success of the entire undertaking may be seen as one among a number of signs that religion and magic, that is, the sacred, is back in vogue.[37] The layering of realms that is to be found in Harry Potter's world and the sundry kinds of slippage between them signal a return of a sacred and mythical symbolic geography that was pervasive in Europe well into modernity, but that has been hibernating as of late.

# Notes

A previous version of this chapter was read to a conference, Europe's Symbolic Geographies, Central European University, Budapest, 27–29 May 2004. I should like to thank Sorin Antoni and Larry Wolff for comments on that occasion, and Halvard Leira and Gro Steinsland for comments on a subsequent draft.

1. Tunander 2001.
2. Ó Tuathail, Dalby, and Routledge 1998.
3. See, for example, Ó Tuathail 1996 and references cited therein.
4. See Wolff 2003.
5. Neumann 1998.
6. See Harle 2000, 29.
7. Cohn 1995, 226.

8. Chydenius 1985.

9. The house elf Dobby is introduced as the bearer of a warning to Harry: "Harry Potter must not put himself in peril. He is too important, sir!" (CS, 18). Dobby leans toward the messianic when he elaborates on why this should be so: "If he knew what he means to us, to the lowly, the enslaved, us dregs of the magical world! Dobby remembers how it was when He Who Must Not Be Named was at the height of his powers, sir! We house-elves were treated like vermin, sir! . . . life has improved for my kind since you triumphed over . . . the Dark Lord" (CS, 134). Hermione spells out what this looks like in a social democratic optic: "But they get paid?" she said. "They get holidays, don't they? And—and sick leave, and pensions and everything?" (GF, 201).

10. Another group that seems to be internally split is ghosts.

11. There seems to be a difference between mountain trolls and trolls, however, with the former being wilder and more stupid, for we learn that at least at one point, a group of them is employed at Hogwarts: "A bunch of surly security trolls had been hired to guard her. They paced the corridor in a menacing group, talking in grunts and comparing the size of their clubs" (PA 292). Sundry snakes are a key asset for the dark side, with one type of snake even being described as "a sort of monster Voldemort" (CS, 208).

12. Sahlins 1987, 90.

13. Hagrid's mother is thus a very special kind of hag. The perfect Norwegian translation of Hagrid's name is Gygrid—a *gyger* was a female *jotun* or giant.

14. *Riksmålsordboken* 1937.

15. See Kendrick 1950.

16. This kind of division is of course well known from *The Lord of the Rings,* and indeed, J. R. R. Tolkien, whose academic work centered on the Viking age in what we now call Northern Europe, definitely drew up his mythological world out of this historical material. In light of what has just been said about the fight between good and evil in Harry Potter's world, it is worth noting that to the Vikings, gods and giants did *not* embody good and evil in this way, but were rather seen as embodying two different kinds of will.

17. Magnus 1996–1998 [1555]. Of course, the Harry Potter world also harbors a number of monsters who were not parts of this life world.

18. Gustafsson 2000, 77.

19. Kendrick 1950, 24.

20. See Stephens 1989. The Book of Wisdom (Wisd. 14:15–21) underscores how giants predate the flood. Genesis (Gen. 6:4) states how giants lived on earth, as children of sons of Gods (angels? devils?) and daughters of men.

21. Cohen 1999, xiv.

22. Cohen 1999, 6, 19.

23. Halvorsen and Rooth 1963, 697.

24. Cohen 1999, 9–10.

25. Arthur wanted to secure world domination for Britain by conquering the Holy Roman Emperor, who was named Lucius. One notes how there is an Arthur

and a Lucius in the Harry Potter saga, and wonders whether the relationship between Arthur Weasley and Lucius Malfoy will develop anything like the one between Arthur and Lucius. The hunt for a historical Arthur goes on, cf., e.g., Ashe
1985. In the eighteenth century, furthermore, a standard historical reading saw
Odin/Othwen as an historical person. Following a Roman battle, Odin was said
to have travelled north, and to have died in the Swedish town of Sigtuna.

26. Cohen 1999, 36, 40.

27. Kendrick 1950, 5.

28. See Kendrick 1950, 7. Throughout the Middle Ages, Gog and Magog appeared as the henchmen of Anticrist; see Cohn 1970. There is a riddle here, for
before Brutus came, there were only giants, and the place was called Albion. Myth,
from the Anonymous Riming Chronicle, in the Auchinleck manuscript: Albina, a
Greek princess and her sisters cast out by their father for disobedience to their hus-
bands, were shipwrecked on the island, where they began lusting. The devil
popped up, and the offspring was the giants. This is a nice reworking of the same
theme (see Cohen 1999, 47–50).

29. Thomas 1971, 416–17. One notes that Polydor Vergil's scholarship, which
proved decisively that these genealogies were mythical, was published before the
forging of the union, but that neither this nor the widespread scepticism surrounding these stories barred them from being considered of use by the kings involved. An interesting reaction to Vergil was Bishop John Bale's, when he raised
the ante by drawing up an even more elaborate genealogy stretching back via King
Albion, the Amphitrite King Neptunus, and Osiris, to Ham and Noah (Kendrick
1950, 34, 69–70).

30. Quoted in Kendrick 1950, 76. Filmer was a key philosopher of his day, and
remains perhaps the most eloquent apologist for patriarchy.

31. See Neumann 2002. Johannes was Olaus's brother.

32. In this scheme, Magog is presented as the son of Jafeth. In the Old Testament, Magog appear as a people and Gog among other things as its king, whereas
in the New Testament they are a *pars pro toto* for God's enemies. Magnus's use of
Gog as a forefather probably mirrors his problems in defending the northernness
of his subject in a Roman world where barbarians of the north such as Teodoric
and indeed himself (the frontispiece has him down as "Olaus Magnus the Goth")
traditionally had invaded the city and its countryside. The marking of the north as
the abode of barbarians crops up in his scheme, but in an apologetic form. In Potter's world, the giant spider (lat. *arachnida*) raised by Hagrid (CS, chap. 15) is called
Aragog—Gog the spider.

33. Steinsland 1991.

34. Mundal 1996, 105, 107.

35. See Lan 1985, chap. 5.

36. Hastrup 1985, 1998.

37. Neumann 2006.

**8**

# The Fantasy of Realism, or Mythology as Methodology

MARTIN HALL

A FTER HAVING DEFEATED THE EVIL WIZARD VOLDEMORT, Harry Potter asks his teacher, protector, and, indeed, headmaster Dumbledore if this evil wizard has gone?

> "No Harry, he has not. He is still out there somewhere, perhaps looking for another body to share . . . not being truly alive, he cannot be killed. He left Quirrell to die; he shows just as little mercy to his followers as his enemies. Nevertheless, Harry, while you may only have delayed his return to power, it will merely take someone else who is prepared to fight what seems a losing battle next time—and if he is delayed again, and again, why, he may never return to power."[1]

Dumbledore's pithy speech, in the last pages of J. K. Rowling's first book about Harry Potter, is more than the end of a first-rate fantasy book. It also expresses, wittingly or not, the essence of both Western civilization and the theory of international relations called Realism. This chapter explains how this is so.

Fantasy—a popular literary genre—is basically a set of books that deals with the struggle between Good and Evil. So, in its way, does Realism—a theory long dominant in the academic study of international relations. Given that these two very different bodies of work engage with the same problem, are there any similarities in how they relate to this problem? In this chapter I show that there is an essential connection between fantasy and Realism. In few words, I show that both fantasy—here exemplified by the Harry Potter books—and the theory of international relations called Realism are derived from the Christian myth of Satan, which is central to

Western civilization. The purpose of the chapter is to provide tools for reflection on the theoretical assumptions of international relations theory.[2] In the chapter I show that Realism and other social theories must be understood as civilizational or cultural creations, and not as disembedded constructs of rational and disinterested minds. Using fantasy as a mirror for Realism helps me make this argument. Using the social scientific study of myths as a springboard, the following section of this chapter seeks to develop mythology as a methodology for theoretical criticisms of international relations theory.[3] The centerpiece of this methodology is to read social scientific theories as if they were myths. Drawing on work on mythology in sociologically inclined religious studies and anthropology, the chapter shows that social theories can be read as myths and that this way of approaching social theory opens up for a wide spectrum of critical stances.

The third and fourth sections of the chapter illustrate the mythology as methodology form. I argue that the genealogy of the fantasy literature relies on a distinct myth, and that the Harry Potter books exemplify this myth in an interesting way. I then juxtapose the Realist story of the nonexistence of history to the myth the Harry Potter books rely on, and suggest that both the Realist and the Harry Potter texts are fundamentally tragic and powered by fear.[4] Realism can thereby be seen as a particular cultural response to fear as a defining characteristic of society rather than as an accurate or, alternatively, politically incorrect account of recent world history.

## Mythology as Methodology

We commonly use the word *myth* to refer to stories that many people believe to be true but are actually false. Many scholars of religion and anthropology, however, write about myths in a more technical sense. For these scholars, a myth is a story believed to be true by a group of people and that in general terms provides building blocks for this group's efforts in defining meaning, a purpose, and a collective identity. Myths, then, serve as the frame into which other phenomena are fitted and then interpreted. This is the sense in which "myth" and "mythology" are used in this chapter.

Two major strands of thought have dealt with mythology as methodology in history and politics. First, stories are central to postmodernism. Postmodernists by and large concentrate on the ideological dimensions of stories. Roland Barthes, for instance, investigated how ideology is translated into myth and is thereby depoliticized.[5] He argued that anything that becomes part of a myth becomes natural, and anything that is natural is not political. Second, sociology scholars in the poststructuralist tradition have emphasized the extent to which power is always central to the construction of myths and stories. Those who produce a myth or a story also have the power to make it "true," to enforce a particular reading of an event according to which people and groups are defined. To this we can add those sociologically inclined religious scholars and religiously interested anthropologists, among others, who have directed their endeavors toward a similar goal.[6] Particularly relevant are the efforts of understanding myth and scholarship on myth as ideology in the form of stories.[7]

In her exceptionally stimulating introductory textbook on international relations, Cynthia Weber draws on Barthes in developing a critical stance from which to study international relations theories.[8] The centerpiece of Weber's analysis is the "transformation of what is particular, cultural, and ideological (like a story told by an international relations tradition) into what appears to be universal, natural, and purely empirical."[9] This is what Weber calls the "myth function" of international relations. For instance, an important concept in Realism is "anarchy." With anarchy Realism means that there is no international authority, and that each state therefore must take care of its own security. According to Weber the concept of "anarchy" has attained mythological status in Realism and is seen as something natural and self-evident. In Weber's view, Realism suggests that there is no need to explain anarchy, since it is natural. Recognizing that the mechanisms of mythologization vary from context to context, Weber's general argument is that international relations restricts critical self-examination through this naturalization of what is actually political. What is natural is not strange, and what is not strange does not make for a puzzle, and therefore it does not get studied.

Inspired by Weber's analysis, in this chapter I develop a similar argument with a slightly different target. Weber goes to work on demythologizing international relations theories by reading them through popular films. The argument is that certain films and certain international relations theories produce and circulate the same myths and thereby support each other's naturalness. My argument is not about the direct relationship between fantasy and international relations theory—and more particularly Realism; nor is it about the alleged nonpolitical status of Realism. My argument is instead that fantasy and Realism both can be read as particular expressions of a myth that is a crucial source for Western civilization.

**Table 8.1.    Stories Classified in Terms of Claims and Reception**

|          | Truth-Claims | Credibility | Authority |
|----------|:------------:|:-----------:|:---------:|
| Fable    | −            | −           | −         |
| Legend   | +            | −           | −         |
| History  | +            | +           | −         |
| Myth     | +            | +           | +         |

We can classify stories by the claims of the storytellers and the ways in which audiences receive these claims.[10] Classifying stories in terms of claims and reception, Bruce Lincoln comes up with table 8.1.

The interesting distinction, for this chapter, is the one between credibility and authority. A story with authority is one "for which successful claims are made not only to the status of truth, but what is more, to the status of paradigmatic truth."[11] Lincoln's approach is thus sociological. Unlike many social scientists with philosophical interests, Lincoln is not pursuing the "true truth"; what is important in his studies is what is believed to be true by groups of people, and believed so firmly that the belief has some control over how they live their lives. This is the first step in transcribing stories into myth in this chapter. Truth and its characteristics are nonissues. In other words, in this chapter I study paradigmatic truth as myth, and this has no implications for history—or the empirical stuff of international relations. Now we need a theory of where authority comes from.

Hayden White's *Metahistory* is conceptually and imaginatively rich and detailed.[12] In this chapter I use one component of White's theory of historiography: the theory of emplotment.[13] White's basic argument is that a historical narrative is a text, much like any prose text, and that it can be submitted to textual analysis. Historical events or facts may be compiled to form a chronology, but the formation of a story requires a poetic act as well. The story does not lie hidden in the facts, there to be discovered by the historian. Instead, the historian transforms a chronology into a meaningful story by connecting the events of the chronology with one another. For instance, a chronology can have the following form: X took place before Y which in turn took place before Z. A story, instead, has the following form: Y happened because X had previously happened, and this later led to Z. In other words, for there to be a story, there has to be both a chronology and a plot, and it is the historian, not the facts, that contributes the plot. White calls this process "emplotment." To emplot a chronology, then, is to give it a plot and thus to

make it a story. White argues that there are four standard forms of emplotment that historians are restricted to. These are romance, comedy,
tragedy, and satire. White argues that these four modes of emplotment,
and no others, are legitimate "ways of endowing human processes with
meaning" by the "myths of the Western literary tradition." In other
words, according to White, a historian must emplot her chronology in
a standard and therefore culturally resonant mode in order to achieve an
explanatory effect. A given culture or civilization is thus seen as, among
other things, a fund of myths upon which the historian can draw in
making sense of a chronology. And this is the second step in transcribing international relations stories into mythologies in this chapter: The
myths of Western civilization are, or at least contain, the designs, or the
molds, of international relations stories.[14] Authority—the status of paradigmatic truth—is anchored in these myths: we are thus dealing with
authority by recognition, authority by "common sense," or authority by
compatibility with the greater world.

What does White mean by tragedy, satire, comedy, and romance? A romance is a story of "the ultimate transcendence of man over the world in
which he was imprisoned by the Fall."[15] Romance thus contains a struggle
and a happy, and even triumphant, end. Satire, being the opposite of romance, instead emphasizes that "man is ultimately a captive of the world
rather than its master,"[16] fated to suffer without redemption. Between romance and satire White positions comedy and tragedy, the first of which
emphasizes reconciliation and the second, resignation. In comedy, thus,
there is hope. Man can, temporarily, triumph over his world since those social and natural forces, which at first sight seem inalterably in conflict with
one another, in fact can harmonize. In tragedy, instead, forces are fixed.
Mankind can work within them and need not suffer endlessly, but they are
eternal. Put simply, then, the four modes of emplotment are about mastery
and captivity, and about what mankind can do about it. Expressed thus,
White's four modes of emplotment form an intuitively appealing whole:
these are two either-or questions, which together address the basic existential concern of humankind.

So far I have argued that myths constitute paradigmatic truth. By
emplotting international relations stories in the modes of the myths that
help define a civilization, scholars define what kind of story they are
telling and acquire both recognition and sense, and authority, on behalf
of their stories. By studying the myths it is possible to critically discuss
international relations stories without having to discuss their validity or
truth-content. Just because an international relations story is cast in a

mythologically derived emplotment, in other words, it is not therefore invalid. Which are the myths that define the Western civilization, and that provide the emplotments for international relations stories? There are many, of course, but some of the most interesting ones deal with fear.

According to the Hungarian sociologist Elemér Hankiss, "fear and anxiety have played a major role in the generation of human civilizations."[17] Furthermore, fear:

> may have been a more important factor than the Kantian or Herderian forces of human betterment, the Durkheimian necessities of social coexistence, the Freudian mechanisms of sublimation, the Foucauldian strategies of domination, or any of the other motive forces so often alluded to in mainstream theories of culture.[18]

Fear, in other words, may be the most important driving force of history. But why do we fear, and what do we do about our fear? The answers lie in the myth of the titans Prometheus and his brother Epimetheus. Epimetheus had been given the task of giving all the creatures of earth their various qualities, such as cunning, fur, strength, and so on. By the time Epimetheus got to man he had run out of qualities. Alone and afraid man wondered how he got into this world in which he did not fit. Prometheus, who hated injustice, took pity on him and gave him fire and handicraft. And so "Human beings began to build their own world within the alien world. A world of protecting walls, houses and cities, tools and weapons, myths, religions, and compromises."[19] We fear, then, because we are incompatible with the world, and we try to deal with fear by building civilizations.

Humans employ two strategies when they deal with fear, or the construction of civilization. Hankiss call these the Promethean strategy and the Apollonian strategy, where the former is technological and scientific, and the latter symbolic. With the Promethean strategy we build houses, develop drugs, design political systems, all in order to protect ourselves from the alien world. Obviously, the popularity of Star Trek can be understood as the promise of the ultimate triumph of the Promethean strategy—here, we have finally created our own world. The history of the Promethean strategy has been written, and is being written, in a great many different ways. The other strategy—the Apollonian—is less well known.[20] And yet, the Promethean strategy does not suffice; it does not address "death, our existential anxieties, the monsters in our souls, the basic uncertainties of our lives. It could not answer the ultimate questions of the human condition."[21] And so humans surrounded themselves with a sphere of symbols, or a culture, as well. This is the Apollonian strategy. Hankiss suggests that culture "does us the favour of leading us by our noses."[22] Culture, a symbolic system, defines roles and meaningfulness, and so helps battle fear.

Among the number of myths important for a discussion of Realism and fantasy, I have chosen the Christian myth of evil. The Christian myth of evil directly addresses fear and has played a very significant part in the development of Western civilization. The French historian Robert Muchembled argues that

> Satan became the driving force of the Western world: he embodied that part of mankind that has to be continuously fought. For the sake of God, as the contemporaries would have said. To create ties of identity through the civilizing myths and to generate a dynamic tension that urges mankind to conquer itself and the world, as the historians say.[23]

Hankiss, similarly, argues that the invention of Satan "was one of the most ingenious feats of humankind—or at least of those cultures which developed this myth."[24] The reason is that he was turned, and "became one of the most powerful weapons against evil in the world."[25] This happened in three steps. First, evil was personified. By identifying evil, and giving it a name, people gained a degree of control over it. They could then bind it by magic, persuade it by prayers, and rid themselves of it by exorcism. The second step, and the more historically rare, was to condense the myriad of little devils and demons to one super-devil: Satan. It is with this second step—the condensation—that we arrive at the most crucial component in the Christian myth of evil. For surely Hankiss is correct in arguing that in "mono-demonism" the fight against evil became "more dramatic and apocalyptic but, at the same time, it became much more simple and promising."[26] The foe is fearful and defeat is final, but victory is possible. And both defeat and victory are possible precisely because evil has been personified and condensed.

With the third step an ambiguity enters. Christianity is allegedly a monotheistic religion. Where then does Satan fit in? Without pretending to do more than peek at the issue it seems fairly clear that Christianity, as opposed to Islam, takes an ambivalent standpoint. Satan of the Old Testament, the few times he is ever mentioned, is clearly a creature of God—even his minion.[27] Also in antiquity Satan was a servant of God. For instance, the important theologian St. Augustine (354–430 A.D.) had argued that Satan was a tool for God. God allowed Satan, and evil, to exist as part of His plans for the world. Later, in the Middle Ages Satan was no longer thought of as the obedient servant of God, however. Instead, he had now become the condensation of old heathen polytheism and an independent force.[28] The relationship between God and Satan was now that of two forces—one good and one evil—forever linked in battle. This view was influenced by the ancient religion of Zoroastrianism and by the third century A.D. attempt at synthesizing a range of religions into one—Manichaeism. Again later on, however, Luther claimed that "The Devil, is God's Devil."[29] Evil, in Christianity, can thus be both an independent force, a negation of God, and, at the same time, a necessary tool for good.

Obviously, the myth of Satan is not the only Western myth. No known culture is so simple as to be entirely dominated by any one myth. Civilizations are always, in some sense, a field of negotiations among myths. Two myths, or more generally cosmological stories, as important for Western civilization as the Satan myth are "time's arrow" and "time's cycle."[30] These are very general stories about the nature of time but are powerfully connected to both the myth of Satan and to how Western civilization deals with fear.[31] Time's arrow and time's cycle are two different and competing approaches, and therefore two different emplotments, of the myth of evil. Time's arrow is romantic. In this type of story good defeats evil in the end. And the very idea that there is an end is important. History is going from one place, the origin, to another, the end. The time's arrow emplotment of the myth of Satan is the Christian theory of how the world will end, or eschatology. Evil is necessary but will ultimately be transcended, and good will triumph. This is also, of course, liberalism's story epitomized naively in the ideology of globalization and more thoughtfully in Fukuyama's *The End of History and the Last Man.*[32] Time's cycle instead is tragic. Evil is eternal and the terrors of history intolerable since there is no meaning to them, such as there is if they are tools for good. God and Satan are forever locked in battle, and there is no end. What can be done is to be a good Christian and hope for salvation.

Western civilization, and as a part of it Christianity, express both a time's arrow and a time's cycle understanding of evil. One understanding or the other may be more dominant at a given time or in a specific group, but both are always present. In fantasy literature, the time's cycle understanding is supreme, whereas science fiction typically makes use of the time's arrow emplotment. Realism, too, is based on a time's cycle understanding of evil. Still, time's arrow is not entirely absent from fantasy. There is sometimes mention of an End, although that end is not included in the story at hand.

Where are we, and what has any of this to do with international relations? I have tried to outline a civilization-defining myth and have argued that it can be emplotted either in a romantic mode, or in a tragic mode. I have given no support to the implied suggestion that this myth constitutes paradigmatic truth in Western civilization.[33] For international relations theory the relevance of my discussion lies in its capacity to generate some new knowledge about international relations theories, and in its capacity to generate a critical, but not necessarily unsympathetic, discussion of Realism as a cultural expression. The remainder of this chapter deals with this.

## Fantasy and Harry Potter

The authoritative *Encyclopedia of Fantasy* refrains from offering a clearcut definition of fantasy but notes that it has something to do with that which is impossible, while retaining self-coherence.[34] In other words, the story and world in which it takes place must be logical on its own premises, even if those premises are not valid for the real world.

Brian Atterbery has best expressed a crucial aspect of the history of fantasy:

> The history of the fantasy genre may be viewed as the story of the imposition of one particular set of restrictions on the mode of the fantastic. . . . George MacDonald helped to popularize a certain type of hero. William Morris introduced a distinctive vocabulary and style. Lord Dunsany set a fashion in naming places and characters. Tolkien showed that a particular structure worked well. Paradoxically, the more restricted the genre has become, the more productive it is of new texts. As the rules grow more definitive, the game becomes easier for the novice, and, at the same time, more challenging for the expert, the artist who wishes to redefine the game even as she plays it.[35]

It is the structural restrictions imposed since Tolkien that are most interesting. What are these structural restrictions in fantasy, and which sort of emplotment do they represent? Although there are obviously a great many kinds of fantasy, and jailbreaks and "cross-disciplinary" books are numerous, there is still a basic core structure to fantasy. Fundamentally a fantasy begins with a wrongness, or a thinning. Something in the world has gone askew, and the story cannot go on as one would have expected or wished it to. For instance, Gandalf and Aragorn have long been concerned with the growing presence of Sauron, even before the One Ring of Power is discovered. When this state of affairs is recognized—and recognition is absolutely central and usually occupies a good portion of any fantasy book—the wrongness can be named (i.e., personified) and, in most fantasy, condensed into one force. For instance, although understated in Peter Jackson's movie, the importance of the Council of Elrond in *The Lord of the Rings* can hardly be overstated—this is where the threat is recognized and identified, and this is where it is decided what to do about it.

Much fantasy written after *The Lord of the Rings* follows this core structure —and Harry Potter is no exception. Recognition of a certain state of affairs—that Harry is a wizard, that Harry's parents were killed by an evil wizard rather than in an accident, the very existence of a wizarding world, and so on—takes up nearly half of the first book. In the same book, as well as in each of the next five books to date, the recognition of the wrongness constitutes much of the story. In each book, the return of Voldemort needs to be discovered—it is never transparent to start with. While almost all wizards in the Harry Potter books refuse to mention the name—Voldemort— of the personified evil, it is Harry's and Professor Dumbledore's recognition of his return, and their subsequent naming of him, that allows them to combat evil. Each time, then, Harry identifies a wrongness, names it, and is able to condense it into one force—Voldemort. This corresponds to the Christian myth of Satan. It is by identifying, naming, and finally condensing evil that a measure of control can be gained. If evil was unnameable— if we understood it as the absence of good, for instance—there would be much less that could actively be done about it. The absence of an antagonist would render the protagonist slightly bizarre—not entirely unlike Don Quixote. The dramatic point, as well as the function, of the recognition, in both the myth of Satan and in Harry Potter, is that the recognition generates fear. The world turns out to be different from what it was thought to be, and the protagonist feels at a loss. In Hankiss's terms, the recognition is a recognition that one is incompatible with the world, and this incompatibility is what generates fear. Of course, that the protagonist in fantasy— and this is not least true of Harry Potter as well as his friends—tends to stand up bravely against evil only supports this argument.

Two important features of fantasy are the cyclical repetition of events and the absence of endings. In the typical fairy tale or children's story, by contrast, the protagonist goes out in the world, meets many different foes and obstacles, which he or she overcomes, and lives happily ever after. The story of that particular individual ends. Harry Potter and other fantasy protagonists, instead, are caught in a cyclical struggle against one singular foe. Every summer Harry returns to the Dursleys, abides his time there, returns to Hogwarts, begins to recognize the return of Voldemort, makes battle with him, and returns to the Dursleys again. The Harry Potter books—for obvious reasons—have so far not *ended*. Equally obvious, the last Harry Potter book has not yet been published so there is no way of knowing whether Harry will live happily ever after or not. But a brief look at two other popular fantasy series—*The Lord of the Rings* and Philip Pullman's *His Dark Materials*—support my point. In *The Lord of the Rings* the story does not end. Frodo, Gandalf, and Bilbo sail into the West (which *is* an end) but on Middle Earth the age of man has come and nothing in the victory over Sauron suggests that this will be an age without History. In Pullman's *His Dark Materials*, while the story apparently ends, the end implies that History will go on. While the attempt at creating a kingdom in heaven has been thwarted, it is now time to create a Republic of Heaven. It is difficult, then, not to understand fantasy as tragedy, as an example of a time's cycle-understanding of the myth of Satan. It is important, as well, however, to note that fantasy is not satire. Forces are fixed, but mankind can work within these forces and achieve temporary relief. Each time when Voldemort has been defeated, there is a time for a normal wizarding life—a respite. There is also a certain form of meaning to this recurrent battle. Random violence and evil perpetrated by one mad wizard after another, rather than a thought-out strategy by Voldemort, would have denied higher meaning to Harry's efforts since they would not have formed parts of a comprehensible whole. Harry would still have been a hero, perhaps, but then more of the type of hero one encounters in fairy tales, of a more fleeting quality and without those almost sacral overtones Harry's heroism does have. Harry's victories over this hypothetical myriad of mad wizards would likewise have been banal or, at best, eventually tedious. It is by the strength and superiority of Voldemort that Harry's victories achieve their qualities. Harry becomes the personification of good exactly because Voldemort is the personification of evil, and their struggle is a materialization of the constant struggle between good and evil. Still, as in Christianity, time's arrow lurks in the background:

> "So," said Harry, dredging up the words from what felt like a deep well of despair inside him, "so does that mean that one of us has got to kill the other one . . . in the end?"
> "Yes," said Dumbledore.[36]

The third step in transforming Satan into a powerful tool for Western civilization, as discussed above, was not to take a firm stance on the issue of whether Satan is God's tool or an independent force. Fantasy books, and certainly the Harry Potter books, tend also to replicate this step. Simply put, Harry's wizard world is emptied of religion, and the issue of whether Voldemort is his own wizard or whether he serves some unknown and unknowable greater good cannot be directly addressed in the books. What we do know is that Voldemort does not seem to be aware of a purpose higher than his own return to corporeal existence, and that Dumbledore—the figure most easily imagined as the equivalent of a religious functionary with deep insights—makes no allusions to higher powers. These two facts suggest that Voldemort is an independent force. On the other hand, it is the very existence of Voldemort, or more generally of fear and evil, that generate much of what is excellent in the wizarding world, such as the standards Dumbledore maintains at Hogwarts and the moral caliber of Harry and his friends. In contrast, those wizards who remain agnostic about Voldemort's return, such as the politicians and the media people, are quite ridiculous and lack any qualities that might earn them our respect. In this sense, Voldemort *is* a tool for goodness. He strengthens his own opposition.

In the following few paragraphs, I show also that Realism can be read as a version of the Christian myth of Satan, employed in the tragic, or time's cycle, mode. I repeat the basic feature of this myth: Satan was turned and as a target became a driving force of the Western world and one of the most powerful weapons against evil. This happened in three steps. First, evil was *personified*. Second, evil was *condensed* into one force. Now Satan has been created. Third, Satan was *ambiguously* construed as either an independent force, or as a tool of God. In either case, the belief in his existence generates a driving force, or a higher motive, for action. The existence of Satan generated a creative anxiety and an imperative for betterment. This, in the Western and Christian mythology, explains the European miracle.

## Realism

Realism is not a single theory of international relations. Realism is rather a group of theories that share some important characteristics. Here I focus on those shared characteristics, and ignore the sometimes significant variations within the Realist tradition.

The Realist personification of evil, or rather threat, ultimately lies in the concept of sovereignty, which by all accounts is the singularly most important concept in Realism. During the Middle Ages Western European politics was nonsovereign. The Catholic Church and the Holy Roman Empire held dominant positions and, more importantly, legitimacy was premised on religion, not politics. Christendom, it was argued, was *one* political entity over which the Pope had final authority, although kings, princes, city-states, and so on had varying degrees of independence. With time, as the popes became weaker and individual polities stronger, a new political theory developed. Kings, too, could have their mandate directly from God. Therefore, the Pope did not have final political authority. Individual polities became independent states, and the phenomenon of sovereignty began to take shape. This is absolutely crucial for Realism in at least two ways. Freed from the dominance of the Church and theology, the now sovereign states discovered that they had interests of their own. The primary interest was survival, and survival was ensured by power. For Realism, this created political strangers where before there had been fellow Christians. There had of course always been strangers but they had been defined in terms of identity or religion (the strange types living next valley, eating cheese made of cows' milk instead of goats' milk like us normal folks, or Muslims, for instance). What laid the foundation for Realism was that identity and religion could be taken out of the equation. The only thing that matters is the survival of your own state. And the threat to your own state comes from other states. Thus, states, in the Realist account, had to recognize that their own sovereignty implied that there were also other survival-seeking sovereign states. And this observation leads to another crucial Realist concept: anarchy.

Second, and following on the first point, we can here understand Realism as being firmly rooted in the struggle against universalism, or hegemony, or imperialism. If the means to ensure survival is power, then the power of the other states must be checked. From this insight comes the important Realist principle of the balance of power: whenever a new Napoleon, for instance, is on the rise, alliances must be made to balance against this threat. Far from being a handy justification in the hands of the powers that be, then, Realism *as a theory* is designed for anti-imperialist purposes.

In brief, then, Realism recognizes the loss of sovereignty as the overriding threat. The "wrongness" in fantasy literature here becomes the potential rise of new empires. The personification of evil (read threat) as other sovereign states affords the Realist a measure of control, and a means to fight against evil: strengthen yourself and make alliances without regard to identity or religion whenever it is called for. Your enemy's enemy is your friend. Or as Dumbledore says toward the end of *Harry Potter and the Goblet of Fire*, "If You are against him [Voldemort], then we remain, Cornelius, on the same side."[37]

If the recognition of the political stranger—or sovereignty—constitutes the first correspondence between Realism and the Christian myth of Satan, and fantasy, then the security dilemma stands for the second set piece of this archetypal story. The security dilemma is the "active ingredient" of Realism. The logic of the security dilemma is that you cannot know whether your neighbors' armament is a defensive or offensive stance. Therefore, your only reasonable reply to the armament of your neighbors is to increase your own military strength. And the same is true for your neighbors. In the end, it turns out that everybody needs to continuously build military strength, because you *might* always be threatened from your neighbors, whose motives you cannot know. And so here we have the condensation of evil, or fear. Realism reduces the multitude of political strangers to one single security dilemma. It does so not only in space—that, for instance, contemporary India and Syria both have the same fundamental strategic reality (read security dilemma) to contend with. It does so also in time. This is how, in Realist textbooks of international relations, the Peloponnesian war, the Warring States period in China, the Italian Renaissance, and Westphalian Europe, for instance, can be—in structure and logic—the same sort of international relations. Never mind differing cultural and economic fundamentals, and never mind that we have now moved to nonsovereign politics. Once the security dilemma was identified as an important principle governing relations among sovereign states, it was soon discovered to have also ruled nonsovereign relations.

It is here, with the identification of the security dilemma as a perennial characteristic of international relations, that Realism makes explicit its grounding in tragedy. In suggesting that there is no way in which to defeat the security dilemma—that this is one of the fixed forces mankind can work within but not triumph over—Realism has canceled out History (with a meaning and direction), or time's arrow. Time is instead cyclical, and history (without meaning and direction) does not end. The beginning of modern Realism as a critique of what was understood as the naiveté of Liberalism should be understood in these terms. Liberalism had authored a History where industrialization and capitalism led to democratization and international cooperation. Together these processes would lead to what Kant had called "perpetual peace" a century previously, and what contemporary liberals call the democratic peace. Against this romantic view, Realism set a tragic history, where the ever-recurring security dilemma led to an emphasis on national interests and to the primacy of politics.

This condensation of all threat into one prima facie security dilemma does afford a mode of consolation. It is certainly not the consolation of the democratic peace of liberalism. Rather, it is the religious-like consolation of normalization and naturalization. In other words, the security dilemma provides consolation by normalizing insecurity. That which is normal we can study, learn, and master, and therefore we need to fear it less. That is, since we know the threat we also know what to do about it—strengthen our military capacity. And here Realism also takes the third step—that of entering an ambiguity. The recognition of the political stranger, of other survival-seeking states, generated fear. This fear could be dealt with by condensing the source of it to one principle—the security dilemma—and to prepare for the implications of this principle. Machiavelli—an important Realist thinker in the Renaissance—formulated it in terms of necessity. In the words of David Boucher, "Fear of the enemy and the desire for security," or the security dilemma in other words, constituted a necessity to do things they would not otherwise have done.[38] In the view of Machiavelli, "Men never do good unless necessity drives them to it; but when they are too free to choose and can do just as they please, confusion and disorder become everywhere rampant."[39]

Just as the existence of Satan/Voldemort compels humanity/Harry to self-improvement, then, the security dilemma inspires states or state leaders to greatness. Humans, suggests Machiavelli, would not "have attained such perfection in their work or have carried man's works to the height which one can see they have reached, if they had not been driven to it by necessity."[40]

## Conclusion

What does it all mean, and what is the point? My argument in the chapter has been that myth constitutes paradigmatic truth. By emplotting their stories along the lines of civilization-defining myths, scholars and authors acquire recognition and sense, and thereby authority, on behalf of these stories. The Christian Satan myth thus provides recognition, sense, and authority to both the Realist narrative and the Harry Potter books. The main similarities of the three stories are summarized in table 8.2.

In the introduction to this chapter I claim that Realism can be seen as a civilizational response to fear, and that this has no bearing on the theory's validity. The primary fear Realism is a response to is the fear of imperialism. Having found themselves freed from the dominion of church and empire, states—or rather their theoreticians—discovered their own interests and reasons for being and realized that their own interests might not be compatible with the wider world.

I am not suggesting that the Realist tradition of international relations is consciously steeped in the mold of the Christian myth of Satan. The Christian myth of Satan did not determine that Realism was to be developed.

**Table 8.2.  Similarities between the Christian Satan Myth, the Realist Narrative, and the Harry Potter Books**

|  | Christianity | Harry Potter | Realism |
|---|---|---|---|
| Recognition | Evil Personified | Wrongness | Political stranger, imperialism |
| Condensation | Satan | Voldemort | Security Dilemma |
| Ambiguity | Satan is the driving force of the Western world | Evil, but strengthens forces for good | Necessity leads to glory |
| Emplotment | Ambivalent: tragic (continuous struggle) *and* romantic (final redemption) | Tragic (time does not end) | Tragic (History is cancelled) |

The tradition of thought that was to become Realism could have been given another form or just never developed. But I am suggesting that the Christian myth of Satan, ambiguous as it is, constitutes paradigmatic truth in Western civilization. The Christian myth of Satan provided recognition and sense to Realism, and thereby, first, made it possible and, second, gave it authority.[41]

Fantasy—as opposed to science fiction—makes the same tragic interpretation of the Christian myth of Satan as Realism does. I am empathetically not suggesting that students of international relations substitute *Harry Potter and the Philosopher's Stone* for the classical studies of international relations. Neither has the point of juxtaposing Harry Potter with Realism been to ridicule this theoretical tradition. Rather, the popularity of the Harry Potter books and the preponderance of Realism as approach to international relations have a source in common. In other words, one cannot learn anything about international relations by reading Harry Potter. But I have shown that social theories are civilizational or cultural creations, rather than free-floating constructs of rational and objective minds, by tracing both fantasy and Realism to a civilization-defining myth. Again, however, this in itself does not invalidate social theory.

# Notes

1. PS, 216.
2. See the introduction to this volume.
3. Cf. Cynthia Weber 2001.
4. Weber 2001 emphasizes the role of fear in Realism, and Barry Buzan leaves one in no doubt about the role of fear in his *People, States and Fear* 1991—which stands in a nice juxtaposition to Waltz's *Man, the State and War* 1954.

5. Roland Barthes 1972.

6. E.g., Lincoln 1989.

7. See Lincoln 1999. Here I obviously simplify mythology and politics as a field of study. Any such survey would obviously have to begin with Ernst Cassirer and Eric Voegelin from the politics half of the field, and Claude Levi-Strauss and Mircae Eliade from the anthropological and theological sides, respectively. See Flood 2002 for an overview and discussion of some approaches to politics and myth. I therefore reiterate that the interest here is mythology as methodology.

8. Weber 2001.

9. Weber 2001, 7, box 1.5.

10. Lincoln 1989, 24.

11. Lincoln 1989, 25.

12. White 1973.

13. See Puchala 2003, 76, for a similar procedure.

14. I uncritically assume that international relations is a Western social science. Obviously much international relations research is taking place in various non-Western contexts. A comparative study of international relations in different civilizations would be extremely interesting: should the hypothesis be that non-Western international relations is derivative of Western international relations and that we shouldn't expect to find significant variation; should it be that international relations theory has nothing to do with civilization and that we therefore shouldn't expect to find significant variation for that reason; or should it be that there will be variation and that this can be accounted for in terms of civilization?

15. White 1973, 9.

16. White 1973, 9.

17. Hankiss 2001, 1.

18. Hankiss 2001, 1.

19. Hankiss 2001, 70.

20. Hankiss 2001, 48.

21. Hankiss 2001, 49.

22. Hankiss 2001, 59.

23. Muchembled 2002, 163. I am referring to Muchembled's *Une histoire du diable*, which was published in 2000 and translated into Swedish in 2002. I am here using the Swedish text, and any quotation is my own translation and from the Swedish translation.

24. Hankiss 2001, 146.

25. Hankiss 2001, 147.

26. Hankiss 2001, 147.

27. Sharma 1987.

28. Muchembled 2002, chap. 1.

29. Quoted in Sharma 1987, 82.

30. Gould 1987.

31. Eliade 1965.

32. Fukuyama 1993.

33. It is difficult to determine what would constitute such support, except a demonstration that the myth stands as a model for a range of different scientific and aesthetic narratives. This is what I do in the next two sections.

34. Clute and Grant, *The Encyclopedia of Fantasy* 1997.

35. Atterbery 1992, 10.

36. OP, 744.

37. GF, 615.

38. Boucher 1998, 133.

39. Machiavelli 1970, 112.

40. Machiavelli 1970, 440.

41. It should be noted that also Liberalism and Marxism are conversant with the Christian myth of Satan—both employing a Romantic emplotment of it.

# PEDAGOGY

IV

# Dumbledore's Pedagogy
## Knowledge and Virtue at Hogwarts

TORBJØRN L. KNUTSEN

## On Knowledge and Virtue

The Harry Potter books are about life at a boarding school and draw on conventions from a literary tradition that describes life at such schools—such as Thomas Hughes's books about Tom Brown.[1] In most respects, Harry Potter's Hogwarts is quite similar to Tom Brown's Rugby. Both schools are divided into houses, both schools have a wise and Solomonlike headmaster (Rugby had Thomas Arnold and Hogwarts has Albus Dumbledore), both schools are rent with competition and rivalries among students and between students and staff. Sports play a major role in these books as an outlet for competitive energies (Rugby in one case and Quidditch in the other).

The books about Tom Brown do not focus on the school curriculum. The books about Harry Potter do. They put more emphasis on going to school and taking classes because Hogwarts is not just any run-of-the mill school; it is a school of wizardry and witchcraft. The subjects taught are not the traditional arithmetic, history, and Latin; they include arithmancy, astronomy, and charms and spells. These magical subjects are an intrinsic part of the Potter books. They are strange and new and add information and ambience to the magical world that the characters inhabit. They fuel the action and they lend intricacies to the unfolding of the plot. Finally, these subjects provide connections to contemporary international relations scholarship. For Hogwarts is in many respects eerily similar to the world that international relations scholars study and whose properties they try to impart to their own students.

This chapter discusses magic and some of the subjects that are taught at Hogwarts. It also discusses the values and virtues that are imparted through this teaching. The books about Tom Brown, Harry Potter, and international relations are, each in their own ways, books about knowledge and virtue.

## The Magic Touch

On the face of it, Harry Potter is an ordinary boy. (His family name, Potter, emphasizes his ordinariness.) But he lives in extraordinary circumstances. For at least three-quarters of the year, Harry attends an extraordinary school. Here he is a hero. The rest of the time he spends in an ordinary neighborhood in an ordinary suburb outside of London. Here he is not a hero—in fact, in this trivial world of muggles he behaves very unheroically most of the time. This raises an obvious question in the minds of the contemporary international relations scholar: What is the relationship between these two worlds in which Harry exists? This question is begged throughout the Harry Potter books. We might as well tackle this question first.

### Parallel Worlds

Traditional scholarship of international relations (IR) is preoccupied with relations among territorial states. Geography is the quiet setting for this kind of traditional IR; territories, resources, and contested boundaries are very much the life blood of traditional international relations. Geography plays some role in the Harry Potter books as well—the division of the muggle world into territorial states is apparently replicated in the wizarding world. Yet, geography is not that important for wizards. They conquer space with brooms, floo-powder, portkeys, and—if they are over seventeen—with apparating devices.

If geographical boundaries play a smaller role in the wizarding world, social boundaries play a bigger one. The wizarding world consists of liminal societies of great complexity. Outside is the muggle world. Witches and wizards inhabit the same geographical space as ordinary people, or "muggles." Yet, the wizards live in a hidden, parallel world. They occupy an alternative society with its own social infrastructure: It has its own means of communications (brooms, portkeys, and other devices, as noted above, for travel; the Hogwart's Express and the Knight Bus for collective transport; and owls and the Floo System for messages); its own media structure—complete with publishing houses and newspapers (where *The Daily Prophet* plays an authoritative role whereas *The Quibbler* caters to the boulevard tastes); its own economy; and its own government. The boundaries between the wizarding world and the muggle world are unclear and, at times, contested. It is evident that the two worlds interact; but it is not clear how they do so.

The social relations between the two worlds are complicated. Many wizards can exist equally well in both worlds—indeed, many of Hogwarts' students come from ordinary British cities and neighborhoods.[2] Others cannot—Harry's friend, Ron Weasley, was raised in a wizard family whose members neither master the social norms nor comprehend the technology of the muggle world; their minds are boggled by items like telephones and dishwashers. Indeed, so many of Hogwarts' students are ignorant about the muggle world that the school offers special classes in "Muggle Studies."[3]

Economically the two worlds are not integrated. The wizarding world has its own currency and financial system (with the wizards' bank, Gringotts, guaranteeing the stability of the galleon). Trade between the two worlds is minimal and unsystematic.

Politically, the relationship is equally unsystematic. The wizarding world is a sovereign political entity with its own government. Its interaction with the muggle world is not firmly structured. Interaction is slight, intermittent, and dependent on the wizards' Minister of Magic. All in all, the two worlds do not really interact politically.[4]

The two worlds relate in an uneasy and lopsided coexistence. The inhabitants of the wizarding world are aware of the muggle world; but the opposite is not the case. Regular relations do not exist; the closest there is to a diplomatic institution is a small oil painting in 10 Downing Street, fastened to the wall with a permanent sticking charm. It gives the Minister of Magic a possibility to enter the office of the British prime minister if extraordinary circumstances should require it.[5] As a matter of daily interaction, however, the basic wizarding policy is one of concealment: The Ministry of Magic actively seeks to conceal the wizarding world and keep the muggles in blissful ignorance of its existence. This policy is implemented, for example, by the Departments of Magical Law Enforcement and of Magical Accidents and Catastrophes.[6] The main reason for this policy of concealment is connected to the nature of magic.

## Magic and Science

There is no accepted definition of *magic*. As an approximation to a definition, *magic* can be seen as a general term for the practice and power of wonder-working. Beyond this, many different definitions exist. These can be grouped into two different schools of thought. On the one hand is the subjective school; it considers as magic all phenomena that practicing wizards and witches qualify with the name *magic*. This is not a good definition. It reduces magic to a function of the tastes and whims of self-proclaimed individuals. By this definition, there is no inherent quality that makes a phenomenon magical.

On the other hand is the objective school; it regards magic as a system of knowledge. This system is based on general claims supposed to operate with the regularity ascribed to the natural laws by the sciences of today. By this definition, magic is a thing by itself. But what kind of thing is it?

First, magic is a system of knowledge that is essentially traditional. Hubert and Mauss argue that one distinguishing feature of traditional societies is that they are unchanging—in marked contrast to the modern material muggle world.[7] Here they must surely be mistaken. It is quite obvious that magic is not an unchanging form of knowledge, but that magic, too, changes and evolves just like science does. This is obvious by some of the introductory texts studied at Hogwarts, such as *A Study of Recent Developments in Wizardry* and *Important Modern Magical Discoveries*. These titles testify to progress and cumulation of magical knowledge.[8] Magic knowledge can be said to be traditional not because it is static or stagnant, but because it represents an unbroken tradition of knowledge.[9]

Second, magic operates in an environment that is different from the ordinary muggle world. The wizarding world has a parallel existence to the world of muggles. However, physical laws of necessity reign in the wizarding world, just as they do in the world of muggles. David Hume notes, in his famous and authoritative contribution to the philosophy of science, that necessary relations operate along the three channels of contiguity, similarity, and contrast. Hubert and Mauss build on Hume to account for the performance of magical operations. And by doing so they raise the question: What are the main differences between scientific and magical forms of knowledge?

The short answer is that wizard and muggle scholars rely on different ontological assumptions. Both of them agree that a Real World exists. However, muggle scientists define this Real World more narrowly than wizards.[10] For whereas wizards acknowledge the existence of beings and objects that exist in both the muggle world and the wizarding world, muggle scientists acknowledge the *noumena* in the muggle world alone.

Magic knowledge, then, is not that different from science. However, it is not possible to explain magic in terms of the regularities of the natural world alone. It is necessary to add a dynamic principle. Hubert and Mauss (2001) refer to this principle as *mona*. This *mona* is rejected by muggle scientists, but wizards exploit it. Wizards seize upon and harness the *mona*. And to do this, they employ an individualized wand. The wand is the distinguishing tool of the wizard and it serves to differentiate the wizard from the muggle scientist. Through the wand, the wizard can gain access to the *mona* of the world. Distance is no obstacle to contact,[11] and time can be compressed or expanded or even circumvented.[12]

## How Does Magic Work?

Magic is a specialized field of knowledge. It has wider boundaries than science. Also, it is more complex and subdivided than often assumed. Much like the field of contemporary international relations, magic is a system of knowledge, the contents of which can be taught by teachers and learned by students. There are institutions of education dedicated to its maintenance, development, and diffusion—of which Hogwarts is a famous instance.[13] From Hogwarts' curricula, it is apparent that *magic* is subdivided into several specialized subjects. Among them are "Arithmancy," "Astronomy," "Charms and Spells," "Divination," "Herbology," "Potions," and "Transfigurations." There are also classes taught in "Muggle Studies," "Care of Magical Creatures," "History of Magic," and "Defence Against Dark Arts," but these are hardly fields of science per se.

When Harry Potter and his wizarding friends are taught to make objects levitate, cast spells, or turn themselves into animals, they do not do this by making contact with a supernatural world.[14] They are taught to exploit and harness the *mona*, but they do this in ways that are mechanical rather than occult.[15]

Both science and magic are equally instrumental, or technocratic. But magic can be said to be the historically more original and traditional system of knowledge of the two. At one point in human history, science branched off from the common trunk of knowledge. The scientists rejected the *mona* of traditional knowledge and reconstituted knowledge on a narrower basis. It would be worthwhile exploring this break at greater length, in order to identify the locus at which the two branches of knowledge parted ways. Chances are that the separation occurred later than is often assumed, for some of the most celebrated scientists of the seventeenth century—Newton, Kepler, and Galileo among them—leaned on both branches, magic as well as science.[16]

What is magical practice? How is magic actually performed? The Potter books do not discuss this in any depth. However, the texts suggest that the ability to practice magic involves three things: First, it involves knowledge about the world. Magic involves concrete knowledge about the objects and the creatures of the world, and about how to handle them properly. However, it does not involve particularly deep insights into the natural sciences or technology. These are explicitly portrayed as fields that lie outside of the wizard's curricula.

Second, magic depends on sincerity of execution. On the face of it, the gestures performed by the magician are strictly prescribed—no less strictly than those of the muggle scientist or craftsman. Yet, in magic the results of the gesture are not of the same order as the results of the craftsman's movements. The wizard employs a personalized magic wand to harness the *mona* of the world. He must be determined, deliberate, and pay great attention to correct diction.

Speech, then, is the third thing that is involved in the ability to practice magic: Magic acts are always attended by linguistic enunciation or command. Only when a command is flawlessly enunciated—preferably in Latin[17]—is the intended effect produced.[18] It must be noted, however, that whereas most wizards speak the command loudly, advanced wizards can replace the spoken command with a mental deliberation, thus executing the command silently.

## The Educational Message

On a superficial level, the books about Harry Potter are about going to school, taking classes, and acquiring knowledge about the world. Like muggle students of international relations, the young wizards at Hogwarts acquire knowledge about subjects that are important for the world they live in. On a deeper level, the books are about learning social norms and political values.

The stories about Tom Brown have a crystal clear moral message. Tom Brown wears his moral principles on his sleeve, and the edifying subtext of the Tom Brown books may sometimes appear thick and Victorian for the modern reader.[19] The stories about Harry Potter carry a similar message. The norms and values that are instilled in Harry and his Hogwarts friends are anchored in the wizarding world that they live in. And because this world is different from the muggle world—it is a more varied and more dangerous world—one would expect the norms and values to be different. But they are really very similar.

Tom Brown's muggle world was clearly divided into good and bad. The political message of the Tom Brown stories is most apparent when Tom faces a choice of sides; he always chooses the good, of course. The books about Harry Potter are not very different. Here, too, the story carries a normative message. Again, the message is most apparent when Harry must make choices. But it is even more evident in the comments the school's wise headmaster, Albus Dumbledore, gives in his year-end public speech or in his concluding conversations with Harry Potter toward the end of the school year.

What norms and values does Dumbledore express? They are not that different from the norms expressed by Thomas Arnold, headmaster of Tom Brown's Rugby. Arnold modernized the curricula at Rugby—he introduced mathematics, modern history, and modern languages. He introduced a new system to keep discipline. He directed students' attention to literary and moral questions. He made it clear to his students that they were not expected to automatically accept the attitudes and views of others, but to examine the evidence and to think for themselves. So does Albus Dumbledore.

Arnold appreciated Kiplingesque virtues like courage, cooperation, honesty, diligence, and decency. So does Dumbledore. However, whereas Arnold expressed the civic virtues of an individualist and liberal society whose order harmonizes with the primness and the democratic limitations of its Victorian times, Dumbledore expresses the virtues of a society that is violent, dangerous, heterogeneous, and hardly democratic. In this sense, the Harry Potter books communicate a world view that is akin to that depicted in the contemporary curriculum of realist international relations scholarship.

Hogwarts, like Rugby, imposes stern rules upon its students. In theory, the school rules are strictly enforced—for example, by a singular incentive system, where students are given points if they behave in exemplary ways, and points are taken away if they break the rules. In practice the rules are elastic. They are even disregarded at times. Hermione Granger was a stickler for school rules during her first year at Hogwarts; in her second year she learns to become more "relaxed about breaking the rules"—she disobeys the teachers, walks into a troll-infested area, and finds herself in danger.[20] Harry Potter disobeys the same rule, saves Hermione, and earns five points for bravery. Harry in fact violates school rules with distressing frequency and regularly ends up in dangerous situations because of it.[21] Nevertheless, he somehow ends up earning points because he behaves valiantly in the face of danger.

"I seem to remember telling you that I would have to expel you if you broke any more school rules," says Dumbledore at the end of *The Chamber of Secrets,* after Harry committed a heroic deed and defeated Dumbledore's evil opponent (Who-Must-Not-Be-Named). Before Harry can protest, Dumbledore adds: "Which goes to show that the best of us sometimes must eat our words." This makes one wonder, what kind of school does Dumbledore think he is running? What kind of headmaster would reward his students for violating school rules?

The answer is that he is a liberal realist—a teacher who entertains a deep conviction about the value of traditional liberal virtues but who recognizes that some conflicts are irreconcilable and that power—and alliances of power—are important when push comes to shove.

Dumbledore apparently assumes that Harry Potter and his fellow students are endowed with the qualities of reason and freedom. On the face of it, Dumbledore is a pedagogue whose attitudes may bear more resemblance to the progressive ideas of Rogers and Neill at Summerhill,[22] than to the prim theories of Thomas Arnold at Rugby. Arnold and Dumbledore both agree that students must be taught not to automatically accept the views and arguments of others, but to think for themselves. But Dumbledore puts a greater emphasis on the importance of individual choice. Arnold and Dumbledore both appreciate virtues like courage, cooperation, honesty, diligence, and decency; but only Dumbledore stresses emphatically that such virtues are taught through students' wrestling with real choices.

As a consequence, Dumbledore encourages (at least some of) his students to cultivate their practical reason by facing real choices. He allows them to use their liberties to make decisions and grapple with their consequences. He does not cultivate the rules as much as the values that inform the rules. He cultivates in each student the spirit of the law, even if this means that the letter of the law sometimes must be broken. As a result, he has earned a reputation of being idealistic, even naïve.

## The Romantic Message

What kind of headmaster is Dumbledore? The answer is suggested by the rules that Harry violates, the circumstances under which he violates them, and the reasons why he regularly earns points after violations. Dumbledore seeks to inculcate in his students the public-school virtues of classic liberalism: individual bravery, decency, dependability, diligence, honesty, kindness, and solidarity.

Dumbledore, then, seems to represent pretty much the same basic social values as Arnold.[23] However, if he inculcates fairly traditional values and liberal ideals in his students, the violent nature of the outside world forces him to adopt some original methods to achieve his purpose.

Dumbledore applies some singular pedagogical methods. But, then, the wizarding world is a singular place. It is first and foremost a dangerous world. Hogwarts is a dangerous school. It houses dark and deep secrets. It is haunted by the constant threat of Voldemort's return. It is surrounded by a dark forest filled with menacing creatures. In Harry's first night at Hogwarts, headmaster Dumbledore announced to the students, "This year, the third floor corridor on the right-hand side is out of bounds to everyone who does not wish to die a very painful death." Many parents have wanted to withdraw their child from the school once the dangers of its grounds have dawned upon them.

Death is very much present in the books about Harry Potter. Friends of Harry die in *The Goblet of Fire*, in *The Order of the Phoenix*, and in *The Half-Blood Prince*. In *The Prisoner of Azkaban*, Harry encounters the frightening, un-dead guardians of the Azkaban prison: the dementors—hauntingly enigmatic ghouls, described with lingering fear and considerable literary power. These books trespass upon the grounds of gothic horror stories and romantic novels.

The romantic qualities of the books are apparent in their structures. First, their plots are built around a clear distinction between good and bad—each with a typical representative character.[24] Second, the plots progress, like most adventure stories, along an essentially romantic structure.[25] These romantic properties are worth dwelling on, because they help define their moral message.

The imminence of danger of death lends a certain urgency to Dumbledore's task of instilling high moral ideals in his students by the means of progressive methods of education. But it also lends weight to Dumbledore's critics, who may well argue that given the dangers that mark the school, Dumbledore's permissive ways will expose innocent children to unnecessary dangers. This is the argument with which Lucius Malfoy and Cornelius Fudge sought to remove Dumbledore and replace him with a more authoritative headmaster whom they could trust would call on dementor guards from Azkaban to protect the children from danger. They did not succeed. Dumbledore remained free to pursue his educational project.

## The Liberal Hero

Dumbledore's project is to instill in his students a moral backbone, strong enough to muster integrity and will to withstand the wickedness of the world. He sees in Harry Potter a natural ally. Harry is the hero of the books because he is the exemplar of Dumbledore's project.

The Harry Potter books are romantic adventure stories, and such stories have a hero. But heroes come in many shapes and colors. What kind of hero is Harry Potter? He is not a hero of the Greek type—godlike and strong but with a fatal flaw, like Achilles in *The Iliad*. He is not a Nietzschean *übermensch*, head and shoulders above all the others. Rather, he is a hero of modest origins. He is ordinary—he is not big, and he wears glasses.[26] He is uncertain about fame and timid about public approval. His ego is not swollen by fortune and fame. Harry is also an accidental hero. His heroic situation is a function of someone else's flawed decision—it is a result of Voldemort singling him out as a victim but, by somehow failing to destroy him, instead imparting some of himself in Harry. He is, in short, very much a hero particularly suited for exemplifying Dumbledore's high virtues in a dangerous and undemocratic society.

And in this lies one of the messages of the Harry Potter books: They display liberal values in a complex and tumultuous society. They show that the world is a dangerous place, and that freedom is risky. Therefore risk must be attended by responsibility. Children must grow up quickly. And they must turn out as engaged citizens informed by civic virtues, rather than as passive consumers. The way to do that is to make them practice civic virtues by making choices.

Dumbledore's pedagogic insight is simple: Virtue is a function of choice, and if people have no choice, they can have no moral qualities. In a predetermined world ethics is emptied of meaning. But in a world where individuals can make choices, practical reason will evolve and people may develop a real sense of right and wrong. Dumbledore's project is to teach his students to choose wisely, because only then can they be free.

Dumbledore explains his position to Harry at the end of the second book. Reconvalescing after a nasty bout with Voldemort, Harry realizes that he has exceptional powers. But he also begins to fear that he will be corrupted by them—that he will be tempted, like Tom Marvolo Riddle, to use his powers for egotistical or evil purposes. His fear is deepened when he recalls his first encounter with Hogwarts: The magic Sorting Hat was initially uncertain about which house Harry should be assigned to. The hat mumbled for a moment whether Harry perhaps would fit well in Slytherin House where the villains inevitably go. When Harry heard this, he concentrated all his energies into a mental protest: "Not Slytherin," he begged, "Not Slytherin." The hat acquiesced and assigned him to Gryffindor, house of the brave.

Harry blurts out his fears to Dumbledore:

"Professor, the Sorting Hat told me I . . . should be in Slytherin," Harry
said, looking desperately into Dumbledore's face. "The Sorting Hat could
see Slytherin . . . in me, and it—"
　　"Put you in Gryffindor," said Dumbledore calmly.
　　"It only put me in Gryffindor," said Harry in a defeated voice, "because
I asked not to go in Slytherin . . ."
　　"Exactly," said Dumbledore, beaming once more. " . . . It is our choices,
Harry, that show what we truly are, far more than our abilities."

This is Dumbledore's position. It is not a particularly original position;
it draws on a long romantic tradition. It is not a radical position either;
rather, it has been famously elaborated upon by Edmund Burke, for example, in his long letter to "a gentleman in Paris"—in the view of many observers, the founding text of modern conservatism. Finally, it is hard to
defend it as an idealistic position. Dumbledore's critics may well be mistaken when they fault him for his utopian permissiveness. Cornelius Fudge,
the weaselly Minister of Magic, argues at one point that Dumbledore risks
sending his students into the wicked world like innocent sheep into a
world of wolves. Dumbledore is, however, very much aware of the dangers and the wicked ways of the wizarding world. If he appears utopian in
his rhetoric, he is a realist at heart.

In the end, Dumbledore is less likely to side with headmaster Arnold
and more likely to agree with Arnold's contemporaries, Methodist minister James Buckley and anti-vice crusader Anthony Comstock: "Each generation of youth is sent out into the world as sheep in the midst of wolves.
The danger, however, is not that they will be devoured . . . but that they
will be transformed into wolves."[27]

# Conclusion

The Harry Potter books are about life at a boarding school. But only at the
surface. The first book clearly drew on conventions from the literary tradition of boarding school life. The more recent books move the series toward other literary genres—from the genres of the boarding school and the
exceptional child, toward the genres of adventure and fantasy. However, all
the Potter books have a couple of things in common. First, they are ro-
mances. They are well-crafted tales about mysteries that must be solved and
about the dangers involved in solving them. Each book contains a mystery
that gets its proper denouement in the final chapters; at the same time, the

series of books represents a larger mystery—a "meta-mystery"—which slowly deepens with the publication of each new volume.[28]

Second, because the books are about school, they are also about learning and knowledge. "Knowledge" must here be understood broadly: Books about boarding schools do not really focus much on the academic aspects of education. They discuss school rules more than they do academic subjects. They are really books about social rules and social skills. Also, they are edifying novels. They do more than tell stories about school life; they use life at a boarding school as a simple simile of life itself. It is tempting to say that they are *Bildungsromane*. They relate tales about young people coming of age, and they seek to convey to young readers lessons about virtuous behavior in the world where they live.

Finally, the books about Harry Potter import lessons about life in the wizarding world. This world is violent, dangerous and multicultural. It is essentially liberal although not particularly democratic. It is a world in which it is hard to distinguish between friend and enemy—so hard that the Ministry of Magic has institutionalized a system in which the most potent forms of magic are certified and monitored (not unlike the contemporary muggle world in which suspicious individuals are monitored and all prospective passengers are screened by magnetic and chemical detectors upon entering airports and boarding planes). It is a world in which friends and enemies inhabit the same land, and where it has become so difficult to distinguish between the two that entire ministries have been established and staffed by aurors to observe society, enhance public security, and protect the homeland. Those who practice Dark Arts without a license may, in extreme cases and through murky mechanisms, be removed from society and incarcerated at some Azkaban-like camp or prison.

One of the most influential contributors to modern international relations scholarship was Reinhold Niebuhr. He defined his world very broadly. He refused to limit his definition to the *noumena* of the muggle world alone. He did not want to understand IR in terms of laws of logic, but approached it in terms of principles of grammar. He made the same point as Dumbledore: that although geography provides a quiet framework for international action, geography alone cannot explain why the world is such a violent place. Territorial relationships are not contested unless there are social actors that contest them—often liminal actors, individuals, networks, or alliances who slip into the margins of society, who give voice to ambivalence and claim to speak for the marginalized or unjustly treated and fire up moods of powerful resentment.[29]

For Niebuhr, the task of the international relations pedagogue was to spread concrete knowledge about the diverse objects and creatures of the world, about the power of sincerity and of language when serenely crafted and flawlessly enunciated. It was also about teaching people to make choices (and on the basis of a solid knowledge about right and wrong). All of this was reflected in a small prayer Niebuhr wrote during the darkest days of World War II: "God, give us the grace to accept with serenity the things that cannot be changed, courage to change the things that should be changed, and the wisdom to distinguish one from the other."[30]

## Notes

1. Thomas Hughes (1823–1896) wrote his famous *Tom Brown's School Days* in 1857; it was followed by a less successful sequel, *Tom Brown at Oxford,* in 1861. Other famous contributors to this genre are Rudyard Kipling (with his book about *Stalkey & Co.* [1899]) and Anthony Buckeridge (who wrote several *Jennings* and *Rex Milligan* in the 1950s and 1960s).

2. Harry Potter is one of them; when he grew up in the muggle world, he was entirely unaware of the wizarding world.

3. Given the course descriptions at Hogwarts, "Muggle Studies" appears to be what muggle academics simply refer to as "Sociology."

4. A quick comparison of the histories of the two worlds suggests that there is little causal connection between them: Is there some connection in 1945 between Albus Dumbledore defeating the Dark Wizard Grindelwald and the death of Adolf Hitler in his muggle bunker in Berlin? Is there some relationship between the opening of Hogwarts' Chamber of Secrets in 1952 and the muggle war in Korea? Lord Voldemort made his bid for power over the wizarding world in the late 1970s: did this have any repercussions in the muggle world—is there a link to the Soviet support for radical revolutions in many Third World countries and the rise of militant Islamism? In a final showdown, on 31 July 1980, Voldemort killed several people, among them Harry's parents, James and Lily Potter; did this have any repercussions in the muggle world—e.g., in the neoliberalism that began to sweep the muggle West at the time? Harry Potter first came to Hogwarts on 1 September 1991, according to the muggle calendar; is it purely by chance that this occurred in the immediate wake of the Cold War?

5. It is not known whether other wizarding leaders have comparable channels of communications to reach muggle heads of government in the Kremlin or the White House.

6. In 1932 a rogue dragon swooped down on a beach of sunbathing muggles in Ilfracombe. Fatalities were avoided due to the quick thinking of a family of vacationing wizards. The incident still makes members of this agency sweat bullets. Incidentally, the muggle ignorance of the wizarding world is discussed in a classic book by Professor Mordicus Egg: *The Philosophy of the Mundane: Why Muggles Prefer Not to Know* [1963].

7. Hubert and Mauss 2001.

8. Also, it is apparent from the Hogwarts curriculum that some books are "classics" in the field of magic. This can only mean that their publication represented some new level of insight or knowledge.

9. During the long history of Western knowledge, magic was tightly intertwined with science. However, magic remained when science broke away in a so-called "scientific revolution." This point is strengthened by the fact that magic still relies significantly on the traditional language of Western scholarship, namely Latin.

10. It is useful to add, here, that wizard scholars hardly differ from muggles in their *epistemological* assumptions; both assume that scholars have access to a Real World and that they can obtain knowledge about it. Also, they hardly differ on *methodological* grounds, for not only do they agree that scholars have access to the Real World, they also agree on the ways in which they have access to it: On the one hand, they have access *directly*—i.e., through systematic observation through the human senses; on the other, they have access *indirectly*—i.e., through the descriptions other observers have made of it through the medium of language—be it speech, writing, drawings, or mathematical representations.

11. As demonstrated, e.g., by the use of floo powder.

12. As demonstrated, e.g., by the use of time turners.

13. There are also other schools of magic—such as the Gallic Beaux Baton and the Teutonic Durmstrang. They are not discussed here. As a scholarly pursuit, "magic" appears to be as thoroughly an Anglified field of knowledge as, e.g., "international relations."

14. Professional wizards do not acknowledge the existence of a "sixth sense" or some "extra-sensory" access to the world. Professor Trelawney, who teaches divination at Hogwarts, seems to be universally derided by her colleagues. In the *Goblet of Fire* the professor herself concedes that "divination is not an exact science."

15. In this connection it is useful to recall that magic and science are still divided by a gray line. During the long history of Western knowledge, the two have been tightly intertwined, and the main difference between wizards and muggles is that they follow different ways in seeking control over their environment. Wizards rely on magic where muggles rely on science and technology. Science and technology is viewed, at Hogwarts, as some kind of compensatory device for nonwizards—it is what muggles rely on to compensate for their deficient skills in magical abilities.

16. It is common knowledge today that Isaac Newton devoted as much time to alchemy as to optics, that Johannes Kepler intended his orbital equations to capture the music of the spheres, that mystical neo-Platonism encouraged Galileo to reduce natural phenomena to an ideal world of numbers, that an element of solar worship drove Copernicus into heliocentrism.

17. Either the Harry Potter books give an incomplete picture of the classes taught at Hogwarts, or there exists a yawning gap in the school's curriculum: Even the lowliest wizard seem to use Latin for the most elementary of tasks, yet Hog-

warts has apparently no Latin teachers, and the students get no systematic introduction to the Latin language.

18. That the command must be perfectly enunciated is stressed, e.g., by Hermione Granger admonishing Ron Weasley for his imperfect pronunciation of *winigardium leviosa*—a command that makes objects levitate.

19. It is apparent from Hughes's account that Harry Flashman, the school bully, lacked the civic virtues, which Thomas Hughes sought to impart to British officers and gentlemen. Hughes may have been wrong on the first count, for Flashman seems to have possessed the right qualifications for a bright career in the colonial service. Indeed, as George MacDonald Fraser (1986) reveals, Flashman ended up as a highly decorated brigadier general and a Knight of the Empire in the end.

20. And, Rowling comments, "she was much nicer for it."

21. In his third year, the teachers warn Harry not to leave the school grounds, yet he locates a secret passage that leads straight into the magical candy store, Honeydukes. To find his way, he employs a magical map—a devise which his much-admired father helped design. His father, James Potter, was apparently just as much a rule-breaker as his son.

22. Rogers 1969; Neill 1995.

23. One reviewer argues that this set of traditional values helps account for the books' popularity in an age of studied indolence. "The paradox of Harry's success, is that much of his appeal lies in his old-fashionedness, the slightly starchy whiff of brisk English traditionalism that the books give off. The values of Hogwarts stand proudly athwart the tide of mass culture" (Scott 2000).

24. Thus Harry Potter as the representative of "the good" is contrasted with Draco Malfoy who represents "the bad"—or "the other" or "the politically incorrect."

25. As a narrative form, the romantic plot structure often begins with an established state of order. This state is soon revealed to be unstable; it is rocked by some crisis, which triggers the unfolding of dramatic events. The romantic plot is typically propelled by deep, titanic forces, which, through conflict and struggle, ultimately produce a happy ending—a new order, often marked by a higher state of harmony or bliss (Frye 1968 [1957]).

26. When Harry's glasses crack, Hermione fixed them by a simple spell. The fact that Harry's eyesight apparently cannot be similarly fixed is a conundrum perhaps suggesting the limits of magic.

27. Comstock's 1883 book is appropriately entitled *Traps for the Young*. The quote is from the introduction by Minister James Monroe Buckley. Comstock, his concerns, and his times have received a fine biography in Beisel (1998).

28. This evolutionary element makes the Potter books a unique series. Not only because the students at Hogwarts age in ways that the students at other boarding schools rarely do—Jennings, Darbishire, and their friends at Linbury Court School remain essentially the same from one volume to the next. But also because

millions of *readers* have matured and changed together with the students at Hog-warts. If a reader became acquainted with the first Harry Potter book in 1997 at the age of ten, she is likely to be a grown-up woman of twenty by the time she finishes the last volume.

29. This is explored sympathetically in Niebuhr (1932, esp. chap. 7), and from a not-so-sympathetic, Christian-conservative vantage point in Niebuhr (1941).

30. Sifton (2003).

# Bibliography

✶

Abanes, Richard. 2001. *Harry Potter and the Bible: The Menace behind the Magick.* Camp Hill, Penn.: Christian Publications, Inc.

ABC Nightly News Report on AOL–Time Warner Merger. 2004. abcnews.go.com/sections/wnt/WorldNewsTonight/harrypotter011113.html (September).

Allison, Lincoln, and Terry Monnington. 2002. "Sport, Prestige and International Relations." *Government and Opposition* 37, no. 1 (January): 106–34.

Anatol, Giselle Liza, ed. 2003. *Reading Harry Potter: Critical Essays, Contributions to the Study of Popular Culture.* Westport, Conn.: Praeger.

Anderson, Bennedict. 1991. *Imagined Communities: Reflections on the Origins and the Spread of Nationalism.* New York: Verso.

Ang, Ien. 1985. *Watching Dallas: Soap Opera and the Melodramatic Imagination.* New York: Methuen.

———. 1996. *Living Room Wars: Rethinking Media Audiences for a Postmodern World.* London: Routledge.

Anonymous. n.d. "Harry Potter . . . 'Fantasy' or the Face of Evil Subtly Disguised." InPlainSite.org. www.inplainsite.org/html/harry_potter_and_the_occult.html (accessed 14 March 2004).

Ashe, Geoffrey. 1985. *The Discovery of King Arthur.* London: Guild.

Ashley, Richard K. 1988. "Untying the Sovereign State: A Double Reading of the Anarchy Problematique." *Millennium Journal of International Studies* 17 (2): 227–62.

Associated Press. 2005a. *Media Blitz Underway for Potter VI* [Website]. CBS News, May 7. www.cbsnews.com/stories/2005/03/30/print/main684089.shtml (accessed 7 May 2005).

———. 2005b. "New Potter Book Topples U.S. Sales Records." MSNBC.com, July 18. www.msnbc.msn.com/id/8608578/ (accessed 27 July 2005).

Atterbery, Brian. 1992. *Strategies of Fantasy*. Bloomington: Indiana University Press.

Audisio, Gabriel. 1999. *The Waldensian Dissent: Persecution and Survival, c1170–1570*. Cambridge: Cambridge University Press.

Auletta, Ken. 2001. "Leviathan: How Much Bigger Can AOL Time Warner Get?" *The New Yorker*, October 29, 2001. www.kenauletta.com/leviathan.html (accessed 12 September 2004).

Axelrod, Robert. 1984. *The Evolution of Cooperation*. New York: Basic Books.

Baehr, Peter. 2001. "The 'Iron Cage' and the 'Shell Hard as Steel': Parsons, Weber, and the *Stahlhartes Gehäuse* Metaphor in *the Protestant Ethic and the Spirit of Capitalism*." *History and Theory* 40: 153–69.

Baig, Khalid. 2003. "Harry Potter: Facts About Fiction." *Albalagh*. albalagh.net/current_affairs/harry_potter.shtml (accessed 14 January 2005).

Barber, Malcolm. 1978. *The Trial of the Templars*. Cambridge: Cambridge University Press.

Barbieri, Katherine, and Gerald Schneider. 1999. "Globalization and Peace: Assessing New Directions in the Study of Trade and Conflict." *Journal of Peace Research* 36 (4): 387–404.

Barnier, Alan. 2001. *Sport, Nationalism and Globalization*. Albany: State University of New York Press.

Barstow, Anne Llewellyn. 1994. *Witchcraze: A New History of the European Witch Hunts*. New York: HarperCollins.

Bartelson, Jens. 1995. *A Genealogy of Sovereignty*. Cambridge: Cambridge University Press.

Barthes, Roland. 1972. *Mythologies*. Trans. Annette Lavers. New York: Hill and Wang.

———. 1977. "Rhetoric of the Image." Pp. 32–52 in *Image, Music, Text*, ed. Roland Barthes. London: Fontana.

Bates, William. n.d. "Magic, Christianity and Harry Potter." Anglican Diocese of Durham. www.durham.anglican.org/force_reference.htm (accessed 5 March 2004).

BBC News. 2002a. "Emirates Ban Potter Book." *BBC News Online*. news.bbc.co.uk/1/hi/entertainment/arts/1816012.stm (accessed 13 December 2004).

———. 2002b. "Harry Potter Casts Spell on China." *BBC News Online*. news.bbc.co.uk/2/hi/entertainment/1785871.stm (accessed 21 January 2005).

———. 2003a. "'Potter in Calcutta' Banned." *BBC News Online*. news.bbc.co.uk/1/hi/world/south_asia/2988673.stm (accessed 13 December 2004).

———. 2003b. "The Potter Phenomenon." news.bbc.co.uk/1/hi/entertainment/820885.stm (accessed 7 March 2003).

Beisel, Nicola. 1998. *Anthony Comstock and Family Reproduction in Victorian America*. Princeton, N.J.: Princeton University Press.

Benghozi, Pierre-Jean. 2003. "Economy and Culture: Looking for Public Regulation Issues." *Planetagora*. July. www.globalpolicy.org/globaliz/cultural/2003/07regulation.htm (accessed 15 November 2004).

Berg, Aase. 2000. "Smygauktoritärt under trollkarlskappan" [Veiled Authoritarianism Behind the Wizard's Cloak]. *Göteborgs-posten,* January 11, 40.

Berger, Peter L., and Thomas Luckmann. 1966. *The Social Construction of Reality:
A Treatise in the Sociology of Knowledge.* New York: Anchor Books.

Beskow, Per. 2000."Fenomenet Harry Potter" [The Harry Potter Phenomenon].
*Signum* 9: 36–39.

Beyer, Peter. 1994. *Religion and Globalization.* London: Sage Publications.

Bhushan, Nyay. 2003. India Falls under Harry Potter's Spell. *BBC News Online.*
news.bbc.co.uk/1/hi/world/south_asia/3065389.stm (accessed 6 January
2005).

Biersteker, Thomas J., and Cynthia Weber, eds. 1996. *State Sovereignty as Social
Construct.* Cambridge: Cambridge University Press.

Blake, Andrew. 2002. *The Irresistible Rise of Harry Potter.* New York: Verso.

Blake, Kathleen. 1974. *Play, Games, and Sport: The Literary Works of Lewis Carroll.*
Ithaca, N.Y.: Cornell University Press.

"Blockbusters Boost UK DVD Sales." 2004. *BBC Online, Entertainment News.*
January 8. news.bbc.co.uk/1/hi/entertainment/film/3380247.stm (accessed
September 2004).

Blyton, Enid. 1995. *In the Fifth at Mallory Towers.* London: Mammoth [1950].

Bolce, Louis, and Gerald De Maio. 1999. "Religious Outlook, Culture War Politics, and Antipathy Toward Christian Fundamentalists." *The Public Opinion
Quarterly* 63 (1): 29–61.

Bolle, Koes W. 1970. "Secularization as a Problem for the History of Religions."
*Comparative Studies in Society and History* 12 (3): 242–59.

Bond, Ernie, and Nancy Michelson. 2003. "Writing Harry's World: Children
Coauthoring Hogwarts." Pp. 109–22 in *Harry Potter's World: Multidisciplinary
Critical Perspectives,* ed. Elizabeth E. Heilman. New York: RoutledgeFalmer.

Boucher, David. 1998. *Political Theories of International Relations: From Thucydides to
the Present.* Oxford: Oxford University Press.

Briggs, Robin. 1996. *Witches & Neighbors: The Social and Cultural Context of European Witchcraft.* New York: Penguin Books.

Brooks, Stephen. 1999. "The Globalization of Production and the Changing Benefits of Conquest." *Journal of Conflict Resolution* 43 (5): 646–70.

Bruck, Maggie, Stephen J. Ceci, et al. 1997. "External and Internal Sources of
Variation in the Creation of False Reports in Children." *Learning & Individual
Differences* 9 (4): 289–317.

Buckeridge, Anthony. 1950. *Jennings Goes to School.* London and Glasgow: Collins.

———. 1956. *Rex Milligan's Busy Term.* London: Transworld Publishers.

Bueno de Mesquita, Bruce D. 1981. *The War Trap.* New Haven, Conn.: Yale University Press.

Burr, Ty. 2005. "Tale from the Darth Side Review: Remarkable 'Sith' Brings 'Star
Wars' to an Epic Conclusion." *Boston Globe,* May 18, C1.

Buruma, Ian, and Avishai Margalit. 2004. *Occidentalism: The West in the Eyes of Its
Enemies.* New York: Penguin.

Buzan, Barry. 1991. *People, States, and Fear.* 2d ed. London: Harvester Wheatsheaf.

Buzan, Barry, Charles Jones, and Richard Little. 1993. *The Logic of Anarchy: Neo-realism to Structural Realism.* New York: Columbia University Press.

Caldwell, Chistopher. 2003. "Censoring 'The Reagans' Is Dangerous Nonsense." *Financial Times,* November 8, 15.

Campbell, David. 1992. *Writing Security.* Minneapolis: University of Minnesota Press.

———. 1993. *Politics Without Principle: Sovereignty, Ethics, and the Narratives of the Gulf War.* Boulder, Colo.: Lynne Rienner.

———. 1998. "Why Fight: Humanitarianism, Principles and Post-structuralism." *Millennium* 27 (3): 497–521.

Carrington, Ben. 2004. "Introduction: Race/Nation/Sport." *Leisure Studies* 23 (1): 1–3.

Carroll, Terrance G. 1984. "Secularization and States of Modernity." *World Politics* 36 (3): 362–82.

Carter, John Marshall. 1992. *Medieval Games: Sports and Recreation in Feudal Society.* New York: Greenwood Press.

Casson, Andrew. 1999. "Det väsentliga är hur frågorna ställs" [Importance Lies in How the Questions Are Posed]. *Svenska Dagbladet,* December 13, 13.

Cavanaugh, Michael A. 1986. "Secularization and the Politics of Traditionalism: The Case of the Right-to-Life Movement." *Sociological Forum* 1 (2): 251–83.

"Çevirmen Sevin Okyay ile Söyleşi" [Interview with the Translator Sevin Okyay]. 2003. *Milliyet,* 23 June.

Cha, Victor D. 2000. "Globalization and the Study of International Security." *Journal of Peace Research* 37 (3): 391–403.

Chambers, Joseph. 2004. "Harry Potter and the Antichrist." Pawcreek Ministries. www.pawcreek.org/articles/endtimes/HarryPotterAndTheAntichrist.htm (accessed 10 March 2004).

Chase-Dunn, Christopher, and Thomas Hall. 1997. *Rise and Demise.* Boulder, Colo.: Westview, 1997.

Chaves, Mark. 1994. "Secularization as Declining Religious Authority." *Social Forces* 72 (3): 749–74.

Christensen, Thomas J., and Jack Snyder. 1990. "Chain Gangs and Passed Bucks: Predicting Alliance Patterns in Multipolarity." *International Organization* 44 (Spring): 137–68.

Chydenius, J. 1985. *Humanism in Medieval Concepts of Man and Society.* Helsinki: Societas Scientiarum Fennica.

Clark, Lynn Schofield. 2003. *From Aliens to Angels: Teenagers, the Media, and the Supernatural.* Oxford: Oxford University Press.

Clute, John, and John Grant. 1997. *The Encyclopedia of Fantasy.* New York: Palgrave Macmillan.

Cohen, Jeffrey Jerome. 1999. *Of Giants: Sex, Monsters, and the Middle Ages.* Minneapolis: University of Minnesota Press.

Cohn, Norman. 1970. *The Pursuit of the Millennium: Revolutionary Millenarians and Mystical Anarchists of the Middle Ages*. London: Temple Smith.

——. 1973. *Europe's Inner Demons: The Demonization of Christians in Medieval Christendom*. London: Pimlico.

——. 1993. *Cosmos, Chaos, and the World to Come*. New Haven, Conn.: Yale University Press.

Comstock, Anthony. 1883. *Traps for the Young*. New York: Funk and Wagnalls.

Coşkun, Zeki. 2002. "Şenlikli Cenaze" [The Joyful Funeral]. *Radikal*, 8 February.

——. 2003. "Madonna, Pınar, Harry Potter . . . Markalardan Marka Beğen" [Take Your Pick among the Brands]. *Radikal*, 27 June.

Cowen, Tyler. 2002. *Creative Destruction*. Princeton, N.J.: Princeton University Press.

Crews, Frederick. 2004. "The Trauma Trap." *New York Review of Books*, March 11, 37–40.

Darby, Philip, and A. J. Paolini. 1994. "Bridging International Relations and Postcolonialism." *Alternatives* 19: 371–97.

Dargis, Manohla. 2004. "The 21st-Century Cinephile." *New York Times Magazine*, November 14.

DeFrancia, Cristian. 2002. "Ownership Controls in the New Entertainment Economy: A Search for Direction." *Virginia Journal of Law and Technology* (Spring). Web-based journal. www.vjolt.net/vol7/issue1/v7i1_a01-DeFrancia .PDF (accessed 10 December 2005).

Desch, Michael C. 1996. "War and Strong States, Peace and Weak States?" *International Organization* 50 (Spring): 237–68.

Desira, Joanna. 2004. "No Spells in Our School Library Harry." *Evening Gazette*, February 13, 1.

Diller, Barry. 2003. "Keynote Speech to the National Association of Broadcasters." Las Vegas, April 7. www.wga.org/pr/0403/diller.html (accessed 5 September 2004).

Dougherty, James E., and Robert L. Pfaltzgraff, Jr. 1997. *Contending Theories of International Relations: A Comprehensive Survey*. 4th ed. New York: Addison-Wesley Longman.

Drezner, Daniel W. 2003. Harry Potter and the Threat of Lashkar-E-Taiba. www.danieldrezner.com/archives/000720.html (accessed 14 January 2005).

Dumézil, Georges. 1977. *Les Dieux Soverains des Indo-Européens*. Paris: Gallimard.

Dunn, Kevin C. 2003. *Imagining the Congo: The International Relations of Identity*. New York: Palgrave.

Dunning, Eric. 1996. "On Problems of the Emotions in Sport and Leisure: Critical and Counter-Critical Comments on the Conventional and Figurational Sociologies of Sport." *Leisure Studies* 15: 185–207.

Dunning, Eric, and Kenneth Sheard. 1979. *Barbarians, Gentlemen and Players: A Sociological Study of the Development of Rugby Football*. Oxford: Martin Robertson.

Durkheim, Emile. 1965. *The Elementary Forms of Religious Life*. Translated by Joseph Ward Swain. New York: Free Press.

Ehn, Billy. 1993. "Kamouflerad försvenskning" [Camouflaged Swedenization]. Pp. 234–67 in *Försvenskningen av Sverige: det nationellas förvandlingar* [The Swedenization of Sweden: The Transformations of the National], ed. Billy Ehn et al. Stockholm: Natur and Kultur.

Eliade, Mircea. 1965. *The Myth of Eternal Return: Or, Cosmos and History.* Princeton, N.J.: Princeton University Press [1954].

Elias, Norbert. 1978. *The Civilizing Process.* New York: Urizen Books.

Ellis, Bill. 1993. "The Highgate Cemetery Vampire Hunt: The Anglo-American Connection in Satanic Cult Lore." *Folklore* 104: 13–39.

Enloe, Cynthia. 1996. "Margins, Silences and Bottom Rungs: How to Overcome the Underestimation of Power in the Study of International Relations." Pp. 186–202 in *International Theory: Postivism and Beyond*, ed. Steve Smith. Cambridge: Cambridge University Press.

Evans, Peter. 2000. "Fighting Marginalization with Transnational Networks: Counter-Hegemonic Globalization." *Contemporary Sociology* 29 (1): 230–41.

Falconer, Bruce. 2003. "Murder by the State." *Atlantic Monthly.* November, p. 5.

Fearon, James D., and David D. Laitin. 2003. "Ethnicity, Insurgency, and Civil War." *American Political Science Review* 97 (February): 75–90.

Ferguson, Yale H., and Richard W. Mansbach. 1996. *Polities: Authority, Identities, and Change.* Columbia: University of South Carolina Press.

Flood, Christopher G. 2002. *Political Myth.* London: Routledge.

Foucault, Michel. 1994. "'Réponse à une question' item 58." Pp. 673–95 in *Dits et écrits 1954–1988.* Paris: Gallimard [1968].

Frankfurter, David. 2001. "Ritual as Accusation and Atrocity: Satanic Ritual Abuse, Gnostic Libertinism, and Primal Murders." *History of Religions* 40 (4): 352–80.

Fraser, George MacDonald. 1986. *Flashman: From the Flashman Papers, 1839–1842.* London: Plume, 1986.

Free Press Staff. 2004. "Online Book Sites Enchanted by 'Potter' Sales." *Detroit Free Press Online.* www.freep.com/money/business/potter22e_20041222.htm (accessed 10 January 2005).

Frye, Northrop. 1968. *Anatomy of Criticism.* Harmondsworth: Penguin [1957].

Fukuyama, Francis. 1993. *The End of History and the Last Man.* New York: Avon Books.

Garnham, Nicholas. 1986. "The Media and the Public Sphere." In *Communicating Politics*, ed. Peter Golding, Graham Murdock, and Philip Schlesinger. New York: Holmes and Meier.

Geertz, Clifford. 1983. "Deep Play: Notes on the Balinese Cockfight." In *Play, Games, and Sports in Cultural Contexts*, ed. Janet C. Harris and Roberta J. Park. Champaign, Ill.: Human Kinetics Publishers [1972].

Gellner, Ernst. 1973. *Legitimation of Belief.* Cambridge: Cambridge University Press.

Gertner, Jon. 2004. "Box Office in a Box." *New York Times Magazine*, November 14, 104.

Giles, Darrell. 2001. "Protesters Hope to Break Harry's Spell." *Herald Sun*, November 14, 38.

Gilpin, Robert. 1981. *War and Change in World Politics*. Cambridge: Cambridge University Press.

Ginzburg, Carlo. 1966. *The Night Battles: Witchcraft and Agrarian Cults in the Sixteenth and Seventeenth Centuries*. Baltimore, Md.: Johns Hopkins University Press.

———. 1991. *Ecstacies: Deciphering the Witches' Sabbath*. New York: Pantheon Books.

Given, James B. 1997. *Inquisition and Medieval Society: Power, Discipline, and Resistance in Languedoc*. Ithaca, N.Y.: Cornell University Press.

Gmelch, George. 1999. "Baseball Magic." In *Anthropology, Sport, and Culture*, ed. Robert R. Sands. Westport, Conn.: Bergin and Garvey.

Godwin, Mike. 2003. "Harry Potter and the Prisoners of the DTV Transition." *Public Knowledge Online*. December 18. www.publicknowledge.org/news/analysis/harrypotter (September 2004).

Goff, Patricia M. 2000. "Invisible Borders: Economic Liberalization and National Identity." *International Studies Quarterly* 44, no. 4 (December): 533–62.

———. 2002. "Trading Culture: Identity and Culture Industry Trade Policy in the U.S., Canada, and the EU." Pp. 194–229 in *Constructivism and Comparative Politics: Theoretical Issues and Case Studies*, ed. Daniel Green. Armonk, N.Y.: M. E. Sharpe.

Goffman, Erving. 1990. *The Presentation of Self in Everyday Life*. New York: Doubleday [1959].

Goldstein, Steven. 2005. "Translating Harry." *Byte Level Research*. bytelevel .com/global/translating_harry_potter.html (accessed 21 January 2005).

Gonzalez-Servin, Mariana, and Oscar Torres-Reyna. 1999. "Trends: Religion and Politics." *The Public Opinion Survey Quarterly* 63 (4): 592–621.

Goodman, Robin Truth. 2004. "Harry Potter's Magic and the Market: What Are Youth Learning About Gender, Race, and Class?" *Workplace: A Journal for Academic Labor* 6.1 (February).

Gould, Steven Jay. 1987. *Time's Arrow, Time's Cycle: Myth and Metaphor in the Discovery of Geological Time*. London: Penguin Books.

Grant, Peter, and Chris Wood. 2004. *Blockbusters and Trade Wars*. Toronto: Douglas and McIntyre, 2004.

Greenblatt, Stephen. 1988. *Shakespearean Negotiations: The Circulation of Social Energy in Renaissance England*. Oxford: Clarendon.

———. 1992. *Marvelous Possessions: The Wonder of the New World*. Oxford: Clarendon.

Grimes, M. Katherine. 2003. "Harry Potter: Fairy Tale Prince, Real Boy, and Archetypal Hero." Pp. 89–124 in *The Ivory Tower and Harry Potter: Perspectives on a Literary Phenomenon*, ed. Lana A. Whited. Columbia: University of Missouri Press.

*The Guardian*. 2000. "School Puts a Hex on Harry." March 29, 10.

Guidry, John A., Michael D. Kennedy, et al. 2000. "Globalization and Social Movements." Pp. 1–32 in *Globalization and Social Movements: Culture, Power, and the Transnational Sphere*, ed. J. A. Guidry, M. D. Kennedy, and M. N. Zald. Ann Arbor: University of Michigan Press.

Guilbert, Sébastien. 2004. "Sport and Violence: A Typological Analysis." *International Review for the Sociology of Sport* 39 (1): 45–55.

Gustafsson, Harald. 2000. *Gamla riken, nya stater. Statsbildning, politisk kultur och identiteter under Kalmarunionens upplösningsskede 1512–1541.* Stockholm: Atlantis.

Guttmann, Allen. 1978. *From Ritual to Record: The Nature of Modern Sports.* New York: Columbia University Press.

Hagedorn, Roger. 1995. "Doubtless to Be Continued: A Brief History of Serial Narration." Pp. 27–48 in *To Be Continued . . . : Soap Operas around the World,* ed. Robert C. Allen. London: Routledge.

Hall, Rodney B. 1999. *National Collective Identity: Social Constructs and International Systems.* New York: Columbia University Press.

Hall, Susan. 2003. "Harry Potter and the Rule of Law: The Central Weakness of Legal Concepts in the Wizarding World." Pp. 147–62 in *Reading Harry Potter: Critical Essays,* ed. Giselle Liza Anatol. Westport, Conn.: Praeger.

Hallberg, Kristin. 2001. "Potter—dragplåster mellan jul och rea" [Potter—Attraction between Christmas and the Sales], *Svenska Dagbladet,* January 24, 54.

Halvorsen, Eyvind Fjeld, and Anna Birgitta Rooth. 1963. "Jotner." Pp. 694–700 in *Kulturhistorisk leksikon for nordisk middelalder fra vikingtid til reformasjonstid,* vol. 7. Oslo: Gyldendal.

Hankiss, Elemér. 2001. *Fears and Symbols: An Introduction to the Study of Western Civilization.* Budapest: Central European University Press.

Hardt, Michael, and Antonio Negri. 2000. *Empire.* Cambridge, Mass.: Harvard University Press.

Harle, Vilho. 2000. *The Enemy with a Thousand Faces: The Tradition of the Other in Western Political Thought and History.* Westport, Conn.: Praeger.

"Harry Potter and the Synergy Test." 2001. *The Economist.* November 10. pages .stern.nyu.edu/~mgittelm/bps/aol_synergies.doc (accessed 5 September 2004).

Hastrup, Kirsten. 1985. *Culture and History in Medieval Iceland: An Anthropological Analysis of Structure and Change.* Oxford: Clarendon.

———. 1998. *A Place Apart: An Anthropological Study of the Icelandic World.* Oxford: Clarendon.

Hauser, Christine, and Katharine Q. Seelye. 2005. "Newsweek Retracts Account of Koran Abuse by U.S. Military." *New York Times,* May 16, 3.

Hechter, Michael. 2000. *Containing Nationalism.* New York: Oxford University Press.

Heilman, Elizabeth E., ed. 2003. *Harry Potter's World: Mutidisciplinary Critical Perspectives.* New York: RoutledgeFarmer.

Held, David. 1996. "The Decline of the Nation State." In *Becoming National: A Reader,* ed. G. Eley and R. G. Suny. New York: Oxford University Press.

Held, David, Anthony McGrew, David Goldblatt, and Jonathan Perraton. 1999. *Global Transformations.* Palo Alto, Calif.: Stanford University Press.

Hirschberg, Lynn. 2004. "What Is an American Movie Now?" *New York Times Magazine,* November 14, p. 89.

Hobsbawm, Eric, and Terence Ranger, eds. 1992. *The Invention of Tradition.* Cambridge: Cambridge University Press.

Hoenisch, Steve. 1996. "French Social Thought for Media Criticism." (updated 10 July 2004) www.criticism.com/md/media-criticism-with-french-social thought .html (accessed 12 May 2005).

Holsti, Kal J. 1992. "Governance Without Government: Polyarchy in Nineteenth-Century European International Politics." In *Governance Without Government: Order and Change in World Politics,* ed. James N. Rosenau and Erst-Otto Czempiel. Cambridge: Cambridge University Press.

Hopf, Ted. 2002. *Social Construction of International Politics: Identities and Foreign Policies, Moscow 1955 and 1999.* Ithaca, N.Y.: Cornell University Press.

Horowitz, Donald. 1985. *Ethnic Groups in Conflict.* Berkeley: University of California Press.

Hubert, Henri, and Marcel Mauss. 2001. *Outline of a General Theory of Magic.* London: Routledge [1904].

Hughes, Thomas. 1994. *Tom Brown's School Days.* Harmondsworth: Penguin [1857].

———. 1861. *Tom Brown at Oxford.* New York: Lovell, Coryell and Co.

Huss, Pia. 2001. "Rowling uppfinner sagan på nytt" [Rowling Reinvents the Fairytale]. *Dagens Nyheter,* January 22, B03.

Hutton, Ronald. 1999. *The Triumph of the Moon: A History of Modern Pagan Witchcraft.* Oxford: Oxford University Press.

Ikenberry, G. John, ed. 2002. *America Unrivaled: The Future of the Balance-of-Power.* Ithaca, N.Y.: Cornell University Press.

Ingram, Mike. 2001. "AOL-Time Warner Threatens Children Running Harry Potter Fan Sites." *World Socialist Web Site.* February 28. www.wsws.org/articles/ 2001/feb2001/pott-f28.shtml (September 2004).

IOL Staff. 2003. "Malaysia Bans Tales of the Supernatural." *The Independent Online* .www.iol.co.za/index.php?click_id=126&art_id=qw1068094442235B241&set_ id=1 (accessed 21 January 2005).

İşigüzel, Sebnem. 1998. "Ambalaj ve Algılama Bozuklukları" [Packaging and Perception Defects], *Radikal,* 11 May 1998.

Jackson, Patrick, and Daniel Nexon. 2003. "Representation Is Futile? American Anti-Collectivism and the Borg." Pp. 143–68 in *To Seek Out New Worlds: Science Fiction and World Politics,* ed. Jutta Weldes. New York: Palgrave Macmillan.

Jackson, Robert, ed. 1999. *Sovereignty at the Millennium: Getting Beyond Westphalia.* Oxford: Blackwell.

Jacobs, Alan. 2000. "Harry Potter's Magic." *First Things, the Journal of Religion in Public Life* 99: 35–38.

James, Ken. 2001. "Is 'Harry Potter' Harmless?" ChristianAnswers.net. www .christiananswers.net/q-eden/harrypotter.html (accessed 14 March 2004).

Jenkins, Henry. 1992. *Textual Poachers: Television Fans and Participatory Culture.* New York: Routledge.

Jentsch, Nancy K. 2003. "Harry Potter and the Tower of Babel: Translating the Magic." Pp. 285–304 in *The Ivory Tower and Harry Potter,* ed. Lana Whited. Columbia: University of Missouri Press.

Jervis, Robert. 2002. "Theories of War in an Era of Leading Power Peace." *American Political Science Review* 96 (March): 1–14.

Jindra, Michael. 1994. "Star Trek Fandom as a Religious Phenomenon." *Sociology of Religion* 55 (1): 27–51.

Johnson, Tom. 2000. "That's AOL Folks . . ." *CNN Money.* January 10. money.cnn.com/2000/01/10/deals/aol_warner/ (accessed 5 November 2004).

Juergensmeyer, Mark. 1993. *The New Cold War? Religious Nationalism Confronts the Secular State.* Berkeley: University of California Press.

Kapur, Jyotsna. 2003. "Free Market, Branded Imagination: Harry Potter and the Commercialization of Children's Culture." *Jump Cut.* Summer. www.ejumpcut .org/currentissue/kapur.potter/index.html (accessed 12 December 2004).

Karr, Rick. 2003. "Rick Karr Interviews FCC Chairman Michael Powell." *NOW, with Bill Moyers.* April 4, 2003. www.pbs.org/now/transcript/transcript_powell .html (accessed 15 September 2004).

Kaufman, Stuart. 2001. *Modern Hatreds: The Symbolic Politics of Ethnic War.* Ithaca, N.Y.: Cornell University Press, 2003.

Kegley, Charles W., Jr., ed. 1995. *Controversies in International Relations Theory: Realism and the Neoliberal Challenge.* New York: St. Martin's Press.

Kendall, Blanchard. 1995. *The Anthropology of Sport: An Introduction.* Rev. ed. Westport, Conn.: Bergin and Garvey.

Kendrick, T. D. 1950. *British Antiquity.* London: Methuen.

Keohane, Robert O. 1984. *After Hegemony: Cooperation and Discord in the World Political Economy.* Princeton, N.J.: Princeton University Press.

———. 1990. "International Liberalism Reconsidered." In *The Economic Limits to Modern Politics,* ed. John Dunn. Cambridge: Cambridge University Press.

Keohane, Robert O., and Joseph S. Nye. 1977. *Power and Interdependence: World Politics in Transition.* Glenview, Ill.: Scott, Foresman and Company.

Kidd, C. 1999. *British Identities Before Nationalism: Ethnicity and Nationhood in the Atlantic World, 1600–1800.* Cambridge: Cambridge University Press.

Killinger, John. 2002. *God, the Devil, and Harry Potter.* New York: St. Martin's Press.

Kingdon, John. 1995. *Agendas, Alternatives, and Public Policies.* 2d ed. New York: Harper Collins.

Kipling, Rudyard. 1999. *Stalkey & Co.* Oxford: Oxford World's Classics [1899].

Kirby, Andrew. 2000. "The Construction of Geopolitical Images. The World According to Biggles (and Other Fictional Characters)." Pp. 52–73 in *Geopolitical Traditions: A Century of Geopolitical Thought,* ed. Klaus Dodds and David Atkinson. London: Routledge.

Kjos, Berit. n.d. "Harry Potter Lures Kids to Witchcraft with Praise from Christian Leaders." www.crossroad.to/text/articles/Harry&Witchcraft.htm (accessed 10 March 2004).

Kleder, Martha. 2001. "Harry Potter: Seduction of the Occult." Concerned Women for Amercia. www.cwfa.org/familyvoice/2001-11/06-12.asp (accessed 5 March 2004).

Kors, Alan Charles, and Edward Peters, eds. 1972. *Witchcraft in Europe, 1100–1700: A Documentary History*. Philadelphia: University of Pennsylvania Press, 1972.

Kottak, Conrad. 1990. *Prime Time Society*. Belmont, Calif.: Wadsworth.

"Kraliçe Bile, Harry Potter." 2004. In "Yazarından Fakir Çıktı" [Even the Queen Is Poorer than Harry Potter Author], *Sabah*, 19 April.

Krasner, Stephen D. 1999. *Sovereignty: Organized Hypocrisy*. Princeton, N.J.: Princeton University Press.

Kubalkova, Vendulka, Nicholas G. Onuf, and Paul Kowert, eds. 1998. *International Relations in a Constructed World*. Armonk, N.Y.: M. E. Sharpe.

Kugler, Jacek, and Donald Lemke. 1996. *Parity and War*. Ann Arbor: University of Michigan Press.

LaBarbera, Peter. 2003. "Proud of America, and a Bit Ashamed, Too: Yearning for Bush's Moral Clarity in Our Cultural Exports." Concerned Women for Amercia.www.cultureandfamily.org/articledisplay.asp?id=3578&department=CFI&categoryid=cfreport, 2003 (accessed 24 April 2005).

Lambert, Michael. 1977. *Medieval Heresy: Popular Movements from the Gregorian Reform to the Reformation*. London: Blackwell.

Lan, David. 1985. *Guns & Rain: Guerrillas & Spirit Mediums in Zimbabwe*. London: James Currey.

Lancaster, Kurt. 1994. "Do Role-Playing Games Promote Crime, Satanism, and Suicide Among Players as Critics Claim?" *Journal of Popular Culture* 28 (2): 67–79.

Laustsen, Carsten Bagge, and Ole Wæver. 2000. "In Defence of Religion: Sacred Referent Objects for Securitization." *Millennium* 29 (3): 705–39.

Lawrence, Elissa. 2001. "The Man Who Says Harry Potter's Evil." *Sunday Mail*, January 28, 17.

Le Roy Ladurie, Emmanuel. 1975. *Montaillou: The Promised Land of Error*. New York: George Braziller, Inc.

Leege, David C. 1992. "Coalitions, Cues, Strategic Politics, and the Staying Power of the Religious Right, or Why Political Scientists Ought to Pay Attention to Cultural Politics." *PS: Political Science and Politics* 25 (2): 198–204.

Lerner, Daniel. 1958. *The Passing of Traditional Society: Modernizing the Middle East*. Glencoe, Ill.: Free Press.

Levy, Jack S. 1998. "The Causes of War and the Conditions of Peace." *Annual Review of Political Science* 1: 139–66.

Lincoln, Bruce. 1989. *Discourse and the Construction of Society: Comparative Studies of Myth, Ritual, and Classification*. Oxford: Oxford University Press.

———. 1999. *Theorizing Myth: Narrative, Ideology, and Scholarship*. Chicago: University of Chicago Press.

Lindau, Jesper. 2004. "Ny Harry Potterbok—samma story för femte gången" [New Harry Potter Book—Same Story for the Fifth Time]. *Sveriges Radio— Nyhetssidan*, January 4.

Lipschutz, Ronnie. 2001. *Cold War Fantasies: Film, Fiction, and Foreign Policy*. Lanham, Md.: Rowman & Littlefield.

Luhmann, Niklas. 2000. *The Reality of Mass Media*. Cambridge: Polity.

Lurie, Alison. 1990. *Not in Front of the Grown-Ups*. Pewamo, Mich.: Cardinal Books.

Lundgren, Maja. 2001. "Hatet mot de vanliga" [Hatred of the Common People]. *Aftonbladet*, March 26.

MacCarthy, Clare. 2004. "Deputy Chief Sacked as Lego Tries to Rebuild Christmas Sales." *Financial Times*, January 9, 25.

MacCormack, Helena. 2000. "'Harry Potter' Author Recounts Tale of Best Seller." *Japan Economic Newswire*, April 10.

MacGregor, Roy. 2001. *Power Play in Washington*. McClelland and Stewart.

Machiavelli, Niccolo. 1970. *The Prince*. London: Penguin Books [1513].

Mackintosh, Donald, and Michael Hawes. 1994. *Sport and Canadian Diplomacy*. Montreal: McGill-Queen's University Press.

Magnus, Olaus. 1996–1998 [1555]. *Description of the Northern Peoples [Historia de gentibus septentrionalibus]*. Ed. Peter Foote. London: Hakluyt Society.

Malcolm, Dominic. 2002. "Cricket and Civilizing Processes: A Response to Stokvis." *International Review for the Sociology of Sport* 37 (1): 37–57.

Mangan, J. A. 1986. *The Games Ethic and Imperialism: Aspects of the Diffusion of an Ideal*. Harmondsworth: Viking.

———, ed. 1998. *Pleasure, Profit, Proselytism: British Culture and Sport at Home and Abroad 1700–1914*. London: Frank Cass.

———. 2001. "Emulation, Adaptation and Serendipity." *International Journal of the History of Sport* 18 (3): 1–8.

Manning, Charles Anthony. 1962. *The Nature of International Society*. New York: Wiley.

March, James G., and Johan P. Olsen. 1989. *Rediscovering Institutions: The Organizational Basis of Politics*. New York: Free Press, 1989.

Martin, David. 1978. *A General Theory of Secularization*. Oxford: Blackwell.

———. 1991. "The Secularization Issues: Prospect and Retrospect." *British Journal of Sociology* 42 (3): 465–74.

McAlister, Melani. 2001. *Epic Encounters: Culture, Media, and U.S. Interests in the Middle East, 1945–2000*. Berkeley: University of California Press.

McChesney, Robert W. 1993. *Telecommunications, Mass Media, and Democracy: The Battle for the Control of U.S. Broadcasting, 1928–1935*. New York: Oxford University Press.

McInnes, Colin. 2002. *Spectator-Sport War: The West and Contemporary Conflict*. Boulder, Colo.: Lynne Rienner.

McLemee, Scott. 2003. "The Devil and Bill Ellis." *Chronicle of Higher Education*, December 19.

McNamee, Mike. 1997. "Review Essay: Philosophy Meets the Social Theory of Sport." *Leisure Studies* 16 (1): 27–35.

Mendelsohn, Farah. 2003. "Crowning the King: Harry Potter and the Construction of Authority." Pp. 159–81 in *The Ivory Tower and Harry Potter: Perspectives on a Literary Phenomenon*, ed. Lana A. Whited. Columbia: University of Missouri Press.

Messenger, Christian K. 1990. *Sport and the Spirit of Play in Contemporary American Fiction*. New York: Columbia University Press.

Midlarsky, Manus I. 2000. *Handbook of War Studies II*. Ann Arbor: University of Michigan Press.

Miller, Daniel. 1995. "The Consumption of Soap Opera. *The Young and the Restless* and Mass Consumption in Trinidad." Pp. 213–33 in *To Be Continued . . . : Soap Operas around the World*, ed. Robert C. Allen. London: Routledge.

Mills, C. Wright. 1959. *The Sociological Imagination*. New York: Oxford University Press.

*The Mirror*. 2003. "Harry's Still Just Wizard," January 1, 17.

Moen, Matthew C. 1996. "The Evolving Politics of the Christian Right." *PS: Political Science and Politics* 29 (3): 461–64.

Morrison, James. 2002. "Potter Tops US Books Blacklist." *Independent*, October 6, 11.

Muchembled, Robert. 2002. *Djävulens Historia*. Stockholm: Norsteds Förlag.

Mundal, Else. 1996. "The Perception of the Saamis and Their Religion in Old Norse Sources." Pp. 97–116 in *Shamanism and Northern Ecology*, ed. Juha Pentikäinen. Berlin: Mouton de Gruyter.

Murray, John Andrews. 2000. "The Trouble with Harry." Focus on the Family. www.family.org/cforum/citizenmag/coverstory/a0019032.cfm (accessed 5 March 2004).

Murray, Simone. 2002. "Harry Potter, Inc." *M/C: A Journal of Media and Culture*. August. www.mediaculture.org.au/mc/0208/recycling.php (accessed 7 December 2004).

Nandy, Ashis. 1987. *Traditions, Tyranny and Utopias: Essays in the Politics of Awareness*. Delhi, N.Y.: Oxford University Press.

Nathan, Ian. 2003. "Vladimir Putin and Dobby." *Times*, London, February 3, 14.

*The Nation* (Thailand). 2000. "Asian Readers under Harry Potter's Spell." October 11.

Neal, Connie. 2001. *What's a Christian to Do with Harry Potter?* Colorado Springs: Waterbrook Press.

———. 2002. *The Gospel According to Harry Potter*. Louisville, Ky.: Westminster John Knox Press.

Neill, Alexander S. 1995. *Summerhill*. New York: St. Martin's Press [1960].

Nel, Philip. 2002. "You Say Jelly, I Say Jell-O? Harry Potter and the Transfiguration of Language." Pp. 261–84 in *The Ivory Tower and Harry Potter: Perspectives on a Literary Phenomenon*, ed. Lana A. Whited. Columbia: University of Missouri Press.

Neumann, Iver B. 1998. *Uses of the Other: 'The East' in International Relations*. Minneapolis: University of Minnesota Press.

———. 2002. "This Little Piggy Stayed at Home: Why Norway Is Not a Member of the EU." Pp. 88–129 in *European Integration and National Identity: The Challenge of the Nordic States*, ed. Lene Hansen and Ole Wæver. London: Routledge.

———. 2006. "Pop Goes Religion: Harry Potter Meets Clifford Geertz." *European Journal of Cultural Studies* 9 (1): 81–101.

Niebuhr, Reinhold. 1932. *Moral Man and Immoral Society*. New York: Charles Scribner's Sons.

———. 1941. *The Nature and Destiny of Man*. New York: Charles Scribner's Sons.

Nikolajeva, Maria. 2002. "*Harry Potter*: A Return to the Romantic Hero." Pp. 125–40 in *The Ivory Tower and Harry Potter: Perspectives on a Literary Phenomenon*, ed. Lana A. Whited. Columbia: University of Missouri Press.

On the Media. 2002. "China's Harry Potter." *On the Media*. www.onthemedia .org/transcripts/transcripts_071902_china.html (accessed 8 January 2005).

Onuf, Nicholas G. 1989. *World of Our Making: Rules and Rule in Social Theory and International Relations*. Columbia: University of South Carolina Press.

Osnos, Evan. 2003. "Not Everyone Is Enchanted with Potter." *Gazette*, Montreal, June 21, A3.

Ostling, Michael. 2003. "Harry Potter and the Disenchantment of the World." *Journal of Contemporary Religion* 18 (1): 2–23.

Ostry, Elaine. 2003. "Accepting Mudbloods: The Ambivalent Social Vision of J. K. Rowling's Fairy Tales." Pp. 89–102 in *Reading Harry Potter: Critical Essays*, ed. Giselle Liza Anatol. Westport, Conn.: Praeger.

*Ottawa Citizen*. 2005. "U.S. Army Faces Wrath of Harry Potter Creator," 7 February.

Ó Tuathail, Gearóid. 1996. *Critical Geopolitics: The Politics of Writing Global Space*. Minneapolis: University of Minnesota Press.

Ó Tuathail, Gearóid, Simon Dalby, and Paul Routledge. 1998. *The Geopolitics Reader*. London: Routledge.

Oye, Kenneth A., ed. 1986. *Cooperation under Anarchy*. Princeton, N.J.: Princeton University Press.

Özgüven, Fatih. 2002. "Sınıf İçinde Sınıf" [Class Within Class], *Radikal*, February 6.

Park, Julia. 2003. "Class and Socioeconomic Identity in Harry Potter's England." Pp. 170–90 in *Reading Harry Potter: Critical Essays*, ed. Giselle Liza Anatol. Westport, Conn.: Praeger Publishers.

Peace, Richard. 2002. "Harry and the Evangelicals." Leonard E. Greenberg Center for the Study of Religion in Public Life. www.trincoll.edu/depts/csrpl/ RINVol5No1/Harry%20Potter.htm (accessed 5 March 2004).

Penley, Constance. 1997. *NASA/Trek: Popular Science and Sex in American London*. London: Verso.

Petersen, Roger D. 2002. *Understanding Ethnic Violence: Fear, Hatred, and Resentment in Twentieth-Century Eastern Europe.* Cambridge: Cambridge University Press.

Philpott, Daniel. 2002. "The Challenges of September 11 to Secularism in International Relations." *World Politics* 55: 66–95.

Pieterse, Jan Nederveen. 2004. *Globalization and Culture: Global Mélange.* New York: Rowman & Littlefield.

Pike, Robert, and Dwayne Winseck. 2004. "The Politics of Global Media Reform, 1907–1923." *Media, Culture & Society* 26 (5): 643–75.

*Pittsburgh Post-Gazette.* 1999. "On the Side of Right: Vatican Says Harry Potter Casts a Good Spell," November 2, A22.

*Pravda.* 2003. "The People vs. Harry Potter," english.pravda.ru/main/18/90/359/10765_potter.html (accessed 5 March 2004).

Press, Viva Sarah. 2003. "The Trouble with 'Harry.'" *Jerusalem Post,* August 21, 10.

Pringle, Greg. 2004. "Mistranslations: Sybill's Second-Rate Prophecies?" *CJVLang.com.* www.cjvlang.com/Hpotter/mistranslations/trelawney2.html (accessed 10 January 2005).

Puchala, Donald. 2003. *Theory and History in International Relations.* London: Routledge.

Rapoport, Anatol. 1960. *Fights, Games and Debates.* Ann Arbor: University of Michigan Press.

Rasler, Karen A. 1989. *War and State Making: The Shaping of the Global Powers.* Boston: Unwin Hyman.

Remí, Cornelia. 2004. Harry Potter International Duolingo. www.eulenfeder.de/int/gbframes.html (accessed 10 January 2005).

Reus-Smit, Christian. 1999. *The Moral Purpose of the State: Culture, Social Identity, and Institutional Rationality in International Relations.* Princeton: Princeton University Press.

Reuters. 2005. "Belgium Apology for 'Potter Jibe.'" June 6. edition.cnn.com/2005/WORLD/europe/06/06/belgium.potter.reut/ (accessed 14 June 2005).

Reynolds, Susan. 1983. "Medieval 'Origines Gentium' and the Community of the Realm." *History* 68: 375–90.

*Riksmålsordboken* [Dictionary of the Norwegian Language]. 1937. Oslo: Aschehoug.

Robertson, Roland. 1992. *Globalization: Social Theory and Global Culture.* London: Sage.

Rodrik, Dani. 1998. "Symposium on Globalization in Perspective: An Introduction." *Journal of Economic Perspectives* 12 (4): 3–8.

Rogers, Carl. 1969. *Freedom to Learn.* New York: Charles E. Merrill.

Rosecrance, Richard. 1986. *The Rise of the Trading State: Commerce and Conquest in the Modern World.* New York: Basic Books.

Rosen, Joel Nathan. 2004. "Self-concept and the Discussion of Youth Sport: A Critique." *Journal of Mundane Behaviour* 5 (1). mundanebehavior.org/issues/v5n1/rosen.htm (accessed 20 December 2005).

Rosenau, James N. 1992. "Citizenship in a Changing Global Order." In *Governance without Government: Order and Change in World Politics*, ed. James N. Rosenau and Erst-Otto Czempiel. Cambridge: Cambridge University Press.

———. 2003. *Distant Proximities: Dynamics Beyond Globalization*. Princeton, N.J.: Princeton University Press.

Rowling, Joanne Kathleen. 1997. *Harry Potter and the Philosopher's Stone*. London: Bloomsbury.

———. 1998. *Harry Potter and the Chamber of Secrets*. London: Bloomsbury.

———. 1999. *Harry Potter and the Prisoner of Azkaban*. London: Bloomsbury.

———. 2000. *Harry Potter and the Goblet of Fire*. London: Bloomsbury.

———. 2001. *Conversations with J. K. Rowling*. Ed. Lindsey Fraser. New York: Scholastic.

———. 2003. *Harry Potter and the Order of the Phoenix*. London: Bloomsbury.

———. 2005. *Harry Potter and the Half-Blood Prince*. London: Bloomsbury.

Ruggie, John G. 1998. *Constructing the World Polity: Essays on International Institutionalization*. New York: Routledge.

Rumelili, Bahar. 2002. "Producing Collective Identity and Interacting with Difference: The Security Implications of Community-Building in Europe and Southeast Asia." PhD dissertation, University of Minnesota.

———. 2004. "Constructing Identity and Relating to Difference: Understanding the EU's Mode of Differentiation." *Review of International Studies* 30, no. 1 (January): 27–47.

Rummel, Rudolph J. 1994. *Death by Government*. New Brunswick, N.J.: Transaction Publishers.

———. 1997. *Statistics of Democide: Genocide and Mass Murder since 1900*. Piscataway, N.J.: Transaction Publishers.

Sagan, Carl. 1996. *The Demon-Haunted World: Science as a Candle in the Dark*. New York: Random House.

Sahlins, Marshall. 1987. *Islands of History*. London: Tavistock.

Scamander, Newt [J. K. Rowling]. 2001. *Fantastic Beasts and Where to Find Them*, Special Muggle Edition. London: Raincoast/Obscurus Books [1927].

Schnoebelen, William J. n.d. "Straight Talk on Harry Potter." *With One Accord*. www.withoneaccord.org/store/potter.html (accessed 12 March 2004).

Schofield, James. 2002. Russian "Potter" Author Defends Book. *BBC News Online*. news.bbc.co.uk/2/hi/entertainment/2261752.stm (accessed 14 January 2005).

Schweller, Randall L. 1998. *Deadly Imbalances: Tripolarity and Hitler's Strategy of World Conquest*. New York: Columbia University Press.

Scott, A. O. 2000. "The End of Innocence." *The New York Times Magazine*, July 2.

Shablool, Ahmed Fadl. 2003. "The Eastern Influence in Harry Potter." *Middle East Online*. www.middle-east-online.com/english/?id=6856 (accessed 13 December 2004).

Shapiro, Michael. 1989. "Representing World Politics: The Sport/War Intertext." In *International/Intertextual Relations: Postmodern Readings of World Politics*, ed. James Derin and Michael Shapiro. Lexington, Mass.: Lexington Books.

———. 1992a. *The Politics of Representation: Writing Practices in Biography, Photography, and Policy Analysis.* Madison: University of Wisconsin Press.

———. 1992b. *Reading the Postmodern Polity.* Minneapolis: University of Minnesota Press.

Shapiro, Michael, and Hayward Alker, eds. 1996. *Challenging Boundaries: Global Flows, Territorial Identities.* Minneapolis: University of Minnesota Press.

Sharma, Arvind. 1987. "Satan." In *The Encyclopedia of Religion, Vol. 13*, ed. Mircea Eliade. New York: Macmillan.

Shister, Neil. 2003. *Media Convergence, Diversity, and Democracy: A Report of the Aspen Institute Forum on Communications and Society.* www.aspeninstitute.org/ AspenInstitute/files/CCLIBRARYFILES/FILENAME/0000000300/ mediaconvergfocus.p (November 2004).

Sifton, Elisabeth. 2003. *The Serenity Prayer.* New York: W. W. Norton.

Silj, Alessandro, et al. 1988. *East of Dallas: The European Challenge to American Television.* London: British Film Institute.

Sipes, Richard. 1973. "War, Sports and Aggression: An Empirical Test of Two Rival Theories." *American Anthropologist* 75 (1): 64–86.

Skeat, Walter W. 1993. *The Concise Dictionary of English Etymology.* London: Wordsworth.

Smith, J., J. Collins, Terrance K. Hopkins, and A. Muhammad, eds. 1988. *Racism, Sexism, and the World System.* New York: Greenwood Press.

Snidal, Duncan. 1986. "The Game *Theory* of International Politics." Pp. 25–27 in Kenneth A. Oye, ed. *Cooperation under Anarchy,* ed. Kenneth A. Oye. Princeton, N.J.: Princeton University Press.

Sørensen, George. 1999. "Sovereignty: Change and Continuity in a Fundamental Institution." *Political Studies* 47: 590–604.

Spruyt, Hendrik. 1994. *The Sovereign State and Its Competitors: An Analysis of Systems Change.* Princeton, N.J.: Princeton University Press.

Sreekumaran, P. 2004. "Harry Potter in Malayalam." *India Express Online.* www .indiaexpress.com/news/entertainment/20041227-0.html (accessed 10 January 2005).

Srinivasan, S. 2005. "Spider-Man Spins a Magical Web in India." *Washington Post,* January 3, C3.

Steger, Manfred B. 2002. *Globalism: The New Market Ideology.* New York: Rowman & Littlefield.

Steinsland, Gro. 1991. *Det hellige bryllup og norrøn kongeideologi: En undersøkelse av hierogamimyten i Skírnismál, Ynglingatal, Háleygjatal og Hyndluljód.* Oslo: Solum.

Stephens, Rebecca. 2003. "Harry and Hierarchy: Book Banning as a Reaction to the Subversion of Authority." Pp. 51–68 in *Reading Harry Potter: Critical Essays,* ed. G. L. Anatol. Westport, Conn.: Praeger.

Stephens, Walter. 1989. *Giants in Those Days: Folklore, Ancient History, and Nationalism.* Lincoln: University of Nebraska Press.

Sterling-Folker, Jennifer. 2005. "Realist Global Governance: Revisiting *Cave! hic dragones* and Beyond." In *Contending Perspectives on Global Governance: Coherence,*

*Contestation, and World Order,* ed. Matthew Hoffmann and Alice Ba. London: Routledge.

*Straits Times.* 2000. "Principal Tells Boys: Keep Away from Harry Potter." August 12, 3.

———. 2003. "Buzzing," June 2.

Street, John. 1997. *Politics and Popular Culture.* Philadelphia: Temple University Press.

Suarez, Ray. 2001. "Newsmaker Interview with William Kennard." *Online News Hour.* January 12. www.pbs.org/newshour/bb/business/jan-june01/kennard_1-12.html (accessed 5 September 2004).

Sundvall, Maria. 2001. "Sagolikt år för pojkar" [Dreamy Year for Boys]. *Expressen,* 29 December, 2.

Talbot, Margaret. 1999. "Against Innocence: The Truth About Child Abuse and the Truth About Children." *The New Republic,* March 15, 27–38.

Thomas, Keith. 1971. *Religion and the Decline of Magic: Studies in Popular Beliefs in Sixteenth and Seventeenth Century England.* New York: Oxford University Press.

Thompson, Kenneth, and Anita Sharma. 1998. "Secularization, Moral Regulation and the Mass Media." *British Journal of Sociology* 49 (3): 434–55.

Thomson, Janice. 1994. *Mercenaries, Pirates, and State Sovereignty.* Princeton, N.J.: Princeton University Press.

Tilly, Charles, ed. 1975. *The Formation of National States in Western Europe.* Princeton, N.J.: Princeton University Press.

———. 1990. *Coercion, Capital, and European States, AD 990–1990.* Cambridge, Mass.: Blackwell.

———. 2002. *Stories, Identities, and Political Change.* New York: Rowman & Littlefield.

Towns, Ann. 2002. "Paradoxes of (In)Equality: Something Is Rotten in the Gender Equal State of Sweden." *Cooperation & Conflict* 37 (2): 157–79.

———. 2004. "Norms and Inequality in International Society: The International Politics of Women and the State." PhD dissertation, University of Minnesota.

Tunander, Ola. 2001. "Rudolf Kjellen's 'The State as a Living Organism.'" *Review of International Studies* 27 (3): 451–63.

Tunstall, J. 1977. *The Media Are American: Anglo-American Media in the World.* London: Constable.

Turner-Vorbeck, Tammy. 2003. "Pottermania: Good, Clean Fun or Cultural Hegemony." Pp. 13–24 in *Harry Potter's Word: Multidisciplinary Critical Perspectives,* ed. Elizabeth E. Heilman. New York: RoutledgeFarmer.

University of Surrey. 2001. "Harry Potter Takes up Baseball." www.surrey.ac.uk/news/releases/01-1214potter.html (accessed 14 January 2005).

Vasquez, John A. 1993. *The War Puzzle.* Cambridge: Cambridge University Press.

———. 2000. *What Do We Know About War?* Lanham, Md.: Rowman & Littlefield.

Vasquez, John A., and Colin Elman, eds. 2003. *Realism and the Balancing of Power: A New Debate.* Upper Saddle River, N.J.: Prentice Hall.

Veblen, Thorstein. 1978. "Modern Survivals of Prowess." In *Sport and International Relations*, ed. Benjamin Lowe, David B. Kanin, and Andrew Strenk. Champaign, Ill.: Stipes Publishing.

Victor, Jeffrey S. 1995. "The Dangers of Moral Panics." *Skeptic* 3(3): 44–50.

Walby, Sylvia. 2000. "Analyzing Social Inequality in the Twenty-first Century: Globalization and Modernity Restructure Inequality." *Contemporary Sociology* 29 (6): 813–18.

Wallerstein, Immanuel. 1979. *The Capitalist World-Economy*. Cambridge: Cambridge University Press.

Walt, Stephen M. 1987. *The Origins of Alliances*. Ithaca, N.Y.: Cornell University Press.

Waltz, Kenneth. 1954. *Man, the State and War: A Theoretical Analysis*. New York: Columbia University Press.

———. 1979. *Theory of International Politics*. New York: McGraw-Hill.

Wang, Andrew. 2003. "Harry to Cast His Magic in Hindi." *The Age Online*. www.theage.com.au/articles/2003/11/08/1068243304732.html?from=storyrhs& oneclick=true (accessed 21 January 2005).

Waters, Darren. 2004. "Rowling Backs Potter Fan Fiction." *BBC News Online*. news.bbc.co.uk/1/hi/entertainment/arts/3753001.stm (accessed 21 January 2005).

Watters, Ethan. 1991. "The Devil in Mr. Ingram." *Mother Jones*, July/August: 30–36.

Weber, Cynthia. 1995. *Simulating Sovereignty Intervention, the State and Symbolic Exchange*. Cambridge: Cambridge University Press.

———. 1999. "IR: The Ressurection." *European Journal of International Relations* 5 (4): 435–50.

———. 2001. *International Relations Theory: A Critical Introduction*. London: Routledge.

Weber, Max. 1930. *The Protestant Ethic and the Spirit of Capitalism*. Translated by Talcott Parsons. London: Routledge [1992].

———. 1946. "Science as a Vocation." Pp. 77–179 in *From Max Weber: Essays in Sociology*, ed. H. H. Gerth and C. W. Mills. New York: Oxford University Press.

———. 1949. "'Objectivity' in Social Science and Social Policy." Pp. 49–112 in *The Methodology of the Social Sciences*, ed. Edward A. Shils and Henry A. Finch. New York: Free Press.

Webster, Richard. 2002. "The Childcare Libel." *Observer*, August 4, 10.

Weiss, Paul. 1969. *Sport: A Philosophic Inquiry*. Carbondale: Southern Illinois University Press.

Weldes, Jutta. 2001. "Globalization Is Science Fiction." *Millennium: Journal of International Studies* 30 (3): 647–67.

———. 2003a. "Popular Culture, Science Fiction, and World Politics: Exploring Intertextual Relations." Pp. 1–30 in *To Seek Out New Worlds: Exploring the Links Between Science Fiction and World Politics*, ed. Jutta Weldes. New York: Palgrave.

———, ed. 2003b. *To Seek Out New Worlds: Exploring the Links Between Science Fiction and World Politics*. New York: Palgrave.

Wendt, Alexander. 1992. "Anarchy Is What States Make of It: The Social Construction of Power Politics." *International Organization* 46 (Spring): 391–425.

Whisp, Kennilworth [J. K. Rowling]. 2001. *Quidditch Through the Ages.* Special Muggle Edition. London: Raincoast/Whizz Hard Books.

White, Hayden. 1973. *Metahistory: The Historical Imagination in Nineteenth-Century Europe.* London: Johns Hopkins University Press.

Whited, Lana A., ed. 2003. *The Ivory Tower and Harry Potter.* Columbia: University of Missouri Press.

Wilcox, Clyde. 2002. *Onward Christian Soldiers? The Religious Right in American Politics.* Boulder, Colo.: Westview.

Wildoren, Jodi. 1999. "Don't Give Us Little Wizards, the Anti-Potter Parents Cry." *New York Times,* November 1, 1.

Wilmer, Franke. 2002. *The Social Construction of Man, the State, and War: Identity, Conflict, and Violence in the Former Yugoslavia.* New York: Routledge.

Winch, Peter. 1988. *The Idea of a Social Science and Its Relation to Philosophy.* 2d ed. New York: Routledge.

Wines, Michael. 2003. "Putin, Dobby and the Axis of Weirdness." *New York Times,* February 2, 2.

Wohlforth, William C. 1993. *The Elusive Balance: Power and Perceptions During the Cold War.* Ithaca, N.Y.: Cornell University Press.

Wolff, Larry. 2003. "Die Erfindung Osteuropas: Von Voltaire zu Voldemort." Pp. 21–34 in *Wieser Enzyklopädiede des europäischen Ostens, Band II, Europa und die Grenzen im Kopf,* ed. Karl Kaser, Dagmar Gramshammer-Hohl, and Robert Pichler. Wieser: Klagenfurt.

Woodberry, Robert D., and Christian S. Smith. 1998. "Fundamentalism et al.: Conservative Protestants in America." *Annual Review of Sociology* 24: 25–56.

Wright, Quincy. 1942. *A Study of War.* Chicago: University of Chicago Press.

Young, Oran. 1989. *International Cooperation: Building Resources for Natural Resources and the Environment.* Ithaca, N.Y.: Cornell University Press.

Yuval-Davis, Nira. 1997. *Gender and Nation.* London: Sage.

Zacher, Mark W. 1992. "The Decaying Pillars of the Westphalian Temple: Implications for International Order and Governance." In *Governance Without Government: Order and Change in World Politics,* ed. James N. Rosenau and Ernst-Otto Czempiel. Cambridge: Cambridge University Press.

# Index

# About the Contributors

**Brian Folker** is an assistant professor of English literature at Central Connecticut State University.

**Maia A. Gemmill** is a master's candidate at the Johns Hopkins School of Advanced International Studies, where she is studying Russian and Eurasian studies. Her interests include nationalism, civil society, and the intersection of religion and politics.

**Patricia M. Goff** is assistant professor of political science at Wilfrid Laurier University and special research fellow at the Centre for International Governance Innovation (CIGI). She specializes in international political economy and international relations theory. She is coeditor, with Kevin C. Dunn, of *Identity and Global Politics: Empirical and Theoretical Elaborations,* and coeditor, with Paul Heinbecker, of *Irrelevant or Indispensable: The United Nations in the 21st Century.*

**Martin Hall** is a researcher in political science at Lund University, Sweden. His main research interests lie in the intersection of international relations theory and historical sociology. He is coauthor (with Christer Jönsson) of *Essence of Diplomacy,* and he has published articles in *International Studies Perspectives, European Journal of International Relations, Review of International Political Economy,* and *Cooperation and Conflict.*

**Patrick Thaddeus Jackson** is currently assistant professor of international relations in the School of International Service at the American University in Washington, D.C., having previously taught at Columbia University and New York University. Jackson's research interests include culture and agency, international relations theory (particularly the intersection of realism and constructivism), sociological methodology, the role of rhetoric in public life, the concept of "Western Civilization," and the political and social theory of Max Weber. He has published articles in numerous journals and is the author of *Civilizing the Enemy: German Reconstruction and the Invention of the West*, forthcoming from the University of Michigan Press.

**Torbjørn L. Knutsen** (PhD in International Studies, University of Denver, 1985) is professor of international relations in the department of sociology and political science at the Norwegian University of Science and Technology (NTNU), in Trondheim, Norway. His publications include *A History of International Relations Theory* and *The Rise and Fall of World Orders*. His interests include diplomatic history, history of ideas, and issues of war and peace.

**David Long** is professor of international affairs in the Norman Paterson School of International Affairs at Carleton University. He is the author of a study on J. A. Hobson, as well as the coeditor of books on disciplinary history and international functionalism.

**Peter Mandaville** is associate professor of government and politics and director of the Center for Global Studies at George Mason University. He is the author of *Transnational Muslim Politics: Reimagining the Umma* and has also coedited two volumes of essays, *The Zen of International Relations* and *Meaning and International Relations*. Previous teaching and research affiliations include the University of Kent at Canterbury, American University, and the Center for Strategic and International Studies.

**Iver B. Neumann** is assistant professor of Russian studies at Oslo University and research professor at the Norwegian Institute of International Affairs. He holds an M.Phil in social anthropology from Oslo University and a D.Phil in politics from Oxford University. Among his twelve books is *Uses of the Other: "The East" in European Identity Formation*, which has been published in both English and Russian editions. He recently published a piece on Harry Potter and religion in *European Journal of Cultural Studies*.

**Daniel H. Nexon** received his doctorate in political science from Columbia University. In 2001–2002, he was a MacArthur Consortium Fellow at Stanford University's Center for International Security and Cooperation. He is currently assistant professor in the Department of Government and the School of Foreign Service at Georgetown University and, during 2005–2006, was a postdoctoral fellow at the Mershon Institute at Ohio State University. He has published articles and chapters on international relations theory, globalization, and American foreign policy, including one, with Patrick Thaddeus Jackson, exploring parallels between narratives in *Star Trek* and American foreign policy.

**Bahar Rumelili** (PhD, University of Minnesota, 2002) is assistant professor in the Department of International Relations at Koc University, Istanbul, Turkey. Previously, she worked as a Research Fellow in the EU and Border Conflicts project, funded by the EU's Fifth Framework Programme. Her research has focused on security communities, self/other interaction in IR, and the EU's impact on the Greek-Turkish conflicts and domestic transformation in Turkey. Her articles have appeared in the *European Journal of International Relations* and the *Review of International Studies*.

**Jennifer Sterling-Folker** is an associate professor of political science at the University of Connecticut. She is author of *Making Sense of International Relations Theory*.

**Ann Towns** (PhD, University of Minnesota) currently holds a post-doc at the Department of Political Science, Göteborg University, in Sweden. She writes on norms and inequality in international society, with a focus on the status of women as a mechanism of international rank. Her dissertation work has received Best Paper Awards from the International Studies Association and the American Political Science Association and is currently being reworked into a book manuscript. Her current research is titled "Culture on Trial? Gender, Lethal Violence and the Maintenance of Civilizational Rank in the Swedish Legal System."